English Dialects
An Introduction

English Dialects

An Introduction

Martyn F. Wakelin

THE ATHLONE PRESS of the University of London

1972

Published by
THE ATHLONE PRESS
UNIVERSITY OF LONDON
at 4 Gower Street London WC1

Distributed by
Tiptree Book Services Ltd, Tiptree, Essex

North America, Humanities Press Inc, New York

0 485 11136 5 *cloth*

0 485 12020 8 *paperback*

Printed in Great Britain by
WILLIAM CLOWES & SONS, LIMITED
London, Beccles and Colchester

To Di

Preface

This book owes its origin in a large measure—like so many other things—to Professor Harold Orton. When I had completed my Leeds M.A. thesis—an edition of Mirk's *Festial* (*c.* 1400)—in December, 1960, Professor Orton, then head of the department of English Language at Leeds University, invited me to work in his Dialect Room in the department on what he referred to as 'starvation wages'. I accordingly entered upon a daily routine which, to be frank, can only be described as dull by a colossal understatement, checking the manuscript of the first volume of the *Survey of English Dialects* before it was sent to the printer. Up to and throughout this time I was a medievalist in interests and training, knowing nothing of and having no training in dialectological method, and remained so even when I returned to Leeds in 1961 as Editorial Assistant to the *Survey of English Dialects*, editing the recording books and later preparing the manuscript of *SED*, Vol. iv (Southern). It was not in fact until later on in my work with the *Survey* that I came to have a firm interest in dialect, and to appreciate its possibilities. Indeed, I do not think I quite understood the implications of dialect study in the wider field of linguistics, both medieval and modern, until after leaving the *Survey*, where I continued work until 1967, becoming successively Assistant Editor and then Co-Editor.

Altogether, then, I spent about seven years working with the materials of *SED* and sitting daily opposite Professor Orton, and sometime during that period I became a convinced dialectologist, without relinquishing my medieval interests in the slightest. It was not as a result of Harold's enthusiasm—although this, as his friends and colleagues know so well—is tireless and unquenchable. I can only put it down to the effect of the subject itself working on me over the whole period of time. For those years, I should like to thank Harold, and, although this book is in no way connected with *SED*, I hope that it will in some measure help to make up for the times when I must have been a great trial to him.

What I have just tried to say is not irrelevant to my purpose as a whole, since arising from it I want to make two other points. Firstly, that my interest in dialect, and in linguistics in general, was stimulated during those years by conversations with the endless callers and visitors to the Dialect Room—friends of Harold's, distinguished and undistinguished, Australians, Russians and Japanese, Irishmen, Scots and Americans (numerous), Norwegians, Swedes and Indians, French, Germans, Swiss and many others, as well as Englishmen in abundance—many of whom would descend for the summer vacation and work and talk with us for varying periods.

Secondly, from what I have said about my academic background, it will be clear why I am a linguist of the historical school. I make no apology for the fact that I feel an historical approach to linguistics to be far more interesting than a purely descriptive one. For me, at any rate, language study without an historical perspective is a sterile abstraction. This does not mean that I believe it necessary for dialectologists to start with Middle English and work their way to the present-day reflexes of Middle English linguistic forms. On the contrary, present-day linguistic evidence is what we are in possession of here and now, and it therefore seems much more sensible to start with that and work backwards to earlier stages of the language—if this is our aim. Neither does it mean that I do not appreciate the value of dialects as systems or of merely descriptive analyses of dialects, which are obviously of basic importance, since without an initial description nothing else could be done. It means rather (*a*) that I believe diachronic and synchronic studies to be complementary, each aspect having its contribution to make to the whole picture, but (*b*) that for me personally the historical aspect is the predominantly important one. I have not, I hope, prepared this book on a doctrinaire basis, or allowed my historical bias to run away with me. My aim, at any rate, has been to present the salient facts about an engrossing linguistic subject without showing prejudice one way or the other.

I have not, of course, been able to deal with every aspect of English dialect—not only for lack of space, but, quite simply, for lack of knowledge, my own and that of others. I have left out of consideration entirely Scots, Welsh and Irish dialect, together with all types of overseas English; nor have I discussed gypsy dialect, proverbial usages, the relationship between slang and dialect, or intonation. I have said little of syntax, commented only briefly upon sociolinguistic questions, and mentioned the use of dialect in literature only incidentally. But this book has no pretensions to be anything but a modest introduction to a very large subject most aspects of which are only now being investigated intensively or are still urgently requiring separate treatment. My general intention has been to introduce the study of dialect to those who are unfamiliar with it, but who have some background in linguistic studies. Assuming, therefore, some knowledge of linguistic method and the history of English, and familiarity with elementary terms such as *phonetic, phoneme, morphological*, etc. (a short glossary of linguistic terms is, however, appended), I have tried to provide firstly an outline of the place of dialectology within those studies, and then to give something of an historical background both to dialect itself and to the study of dialect in this country. The central part of the book gives examples of regional dialect, mostly taken from the *Survey of English Dialects*, on lexical, phonological and grammatical levels, and I have also tried to say something about the relations between social and regional dialect. It is my hope that the slightness of treatment of some of these matters, which has been necessary in a book on so wide a subject, will act as a stimulus to readers to follow up individual topics for themselves.

Many academic subjects admit of a popular side in addition to their more serious one, and dialectology is no exception, as the publications of the various dialect societies will testify. There is room for the Yorkshire Dialect Society 'Christmas Crack' as well as the International Congress of Dialectologists, and womens' institutes, as well as university seminars, are interested in dialect. It is, however, often the more popular and picturesque side of dialect that is stressed —the *dowly, blashy, darksome* weather words, the eighty-odd (admittedly very expressive) words for 'left-handed', and so on. Naturally, my treatment is not slanted in this particular direction, although such an element undoubtedly imparts a certain colour to dialectal speech, and should not be ignored. Nor is it really possible in a book such as this to give much idea of the 'flavour' of dialect, which only emerges in passages of connected speech. Perhaps the expression of this 'flavour' is best left to (purely synchronic!) treatments like Scott Dobson's splendid *Larn Yerself Geordie* (Frank Graham, Newcastle, 1969), which, in addition to being excruciatingly funny, displays throughout an uncanny feeling for that interesting dialect. It seems hardly necessary to say that, since there is no place in linguistic discussion for aesthetic judgements, no such opinions have been expressed in the present book.

I feel that there is a need for this book now that the *Survey of English Dialects* is in print and its information readily available. From many points of view it has not been easy to write, but at least information was at my service which was not at that of Skeat and G. L. Brook in the only other general treatments of English dialects

ix

hitherto published. The task for me must have been ten times easier than for them. I am indebted to Professor Brook's work for a great many valuable hints and much guidance.

Finally, it is a pleasant duty to acknowledge my debts to others, first among whom is Professor Harold Orton, for introducing me to dialectology, and for his constant encouragement. To others who have helped in a similar, but more indirect, way, and especially to my former colleagues in the Dialect Room at Leeds, Wilfred Halliday, Stanley Ellis, Michael Barry and Philip Tilling, I tender my grateful thanks for friendship and frequent help. I should add to these my present colleague, Mrs Kathleen Wales, who has most generously spent valuable time discussing various matters with me, and also loaned me a typewriter at a crucial point.

To the following I am indebted for information generously given on various points: Mr David Wilson, Mr John Levitt, Mr Beverley Collins, Dr Peter Trudgill, Dr R. W. Brunskill, Dr Peter Wright, Professor Barbara Strang, Mr John Pellowe, Dr J. C. Wells.

I am indebted to the Director of the Institute of Dialect and Folk Life Studies at Leeds University, Mr Stewart F. Sanderson, for permission to use unpublished material in the archives of the Institute, including the map of the *SED* network, to Mrs Helen Smith for permission to reproduce the map of Scandinavian settlements drawn by the late Professor A. H. Smith, and to Mr P. Opie and the Clarendon Press for permission to reproduce the map of truce terms from *The Lore and Language of Schoolchildren*.

Finally, I must thank my parents, without whose help in past years my early research would have been impossible, and my wife, who has had to put up with a husband always 'under pressure' and who has typed some of the final draft of this book.

Royal Holloway College,   M. F. W.
September 1971

Contents

Maps

Abbreviations

General

adj.	adjective	ODa	Old Danish
AN	Anglo-Norman	OE	Old English
cj.	conjunction	OFr	Old French
coll.	collective	ON	Old Norse
Corn.	Cornish	ONFr	Old Northern French
Da	Danish	OSw	Old Swedish
Du	Dutch	pl.	plural
Fr	French	p.p.	past participle
indic.	indicative	pr.	present
IPA	International Phonetic	prep.	preposition
	Alphabet	pres.p.	present participle
It.	Italian	pron.	pronoun
LG	Low German	p.t.	past tense
MDu	Middle Dutch	RP	Received Pronuncia-
ME	Middle English		tion
MLG	Middle Low German	sb.	substantive
n.	noun	sg.	singular
NE	New English	Sw	Swedish
Norw	Norwegian	v.	verb

Counties

Bd	Bedfordshire	Ess	Essex
Bk	Buckinghamshire	Gl	Gloucestershire
Brk	Berkshire	Ha	Hampshire
C	Cambridgeshire	He	Herefordshire
Ch	Cheshire	Hrt	Hertfordshire
Co	Cornwall	Hu	Huntingdonshire
Cu	Cumberland	K	Kent
D	Devon	L	Lincolnshire
Db	Derbyshire	La	Lancashire
Do	Dorset	Lei	Leicestershire
Du	Durham	Man	Isle of Man

Mon	Monmouthshire	St	Staffordshire
Mx	Middlesex	Sx	Sussex
MxL	Middlesex and London	W	Wiltshire
Nb	Northumberland	Wa	Warwickshire
Nf	Norfolk	We	Westmorland
Nt	Nottinghamshire	Wo	Worcestershire
Nth	Northamptonshire	Y	Yorkshire
O	Oxfordshire	YER	Yorkshire, East Riding
R	Rutland		
Sa	Salop (Shropshire)	YNR	Yorkshire, North Riding
Sf	Suffolk		
So	Somerset	YWR	Yorkshire, West Riding
Sr	Surrey		

Books, Journals, etc.

DEPN	E. Ekwall, *The Concise Oxford Dictionary of English Place-Names*. 4th rev. edn. Oxford, 1960
EDD	J. Wright, *The English Dialect Dictionary*. Oxford, 1898–1905
EDG	J. Wright, *The English Dialect Grammar*. Oxford, 1905
EDS	English Dialect Society
EEP	A. J. Ellis, *On Early English Pronunciation, Part V: The Existing Phonology of English Dialects compared with that of West Saxon Speech*. EETS, 1889
EETS (E.S.)	Early English Text Society (Extra Series)
JEGP	*Journal of English and Germanic Philology*
LSE	*Leeds Studies in English*
MED	H. Kurath and S. M. Kuhn, *Middle English Dictionary*. Ann Arbor, Michigan, 1954–
N.S.	New Series
OED	*Oxford English Dictionary*
PMLA	*Publications of the Modern Language Association of America*
SED	H. Orton et al., *Survey of English Dialects*. Leeds, 1962–71
SPE	Society for Pure English
Trans. Phil. Soc.	*Transactions of the Philological Society*
TYDS	*Transactions of the Yorkshire Dialect Society*
YDS	Yorkshire Dialect Society

Table of Phonetic and other Symbols

The phonetic symbols are those of the International Phonetic Association: a, b, d, f, g, h, k, l, m, n, p, s, t, v, w, z have approximately the values represented by English spelling. The values of the remainder are approximately as follows:

æ	mid-way between ɛ and a	ʈ	retroflex r (superior denotes r-colouring)
ɑ	as in c*a*rt, but short; Fr p*a*s	ʂ	retroflex s
β	as in Spanish B*i*lbao	ʃ	as in *sh*ort
ç	as in German ni*ch*t	ʈ	retroflex t
ɖ	retroflex d	tʃ	as in *ch*air
dʒ	as in *j*eer	θ	as in *th*in
ð	as in *th*en	u	as in b*oo*t, but short; Fr t*ou*t
e	as in Fr th*é*	ʉ	mid-way between i and u
ə	as in chin*a*	ʊ	as in b*u*sh
ɛ	as in b*e*t	ʌ	as in b*u*t
i	as in b*ea*t, but short; Fr s*i*	x	as in Scottish lo*ch*
ɪ	as in b*i*t	y	as in Fr t*u*
j	as in *y*ear	ʏ	lowered variety of y
ł	as in i*ll* (velarized l)	ɤ	unrounded equivalent of o
ɭ	retroflex l	ʐ	retroflex z
ņ	syllabic n	ʒ	as in mea*s*ure
ŋ	as in si*ng*	ʔ	glottal stop (as in Cockney *bu'er* 'butter')
o	as in Fr *eau*	ː	indicates that the preceding sound is long, e.g. ɛː
ø	as in Fr p*eu*	~	over a vowel indicates nasality, e.g. ɛ̃
œ	as in Fr f*eu*illeton	..	over a vowel indicates centralization, e.g. ɛ̈
ɒ	as in b*o*x	–	underneath a vowel indicates retraction, e.g. ɛ̱
ɔ	as in p*au*se, but short; Fr c*o*ter		
ɹ	as in *r*un (superior denotes r-colouring)		
r	rolled (Scottish, Italian) r		
ɾ	flapped r		
ʀ	uvular ɹ		

. underneath a vowel indicates closer quality, e.g. ȩ

. underneath a vowel indicates more open quality, e.g. ɛ̨

○ underneath a consonant indicates devoicing, e.g. z̦

ˈ indicates main stress, e.g. ˈmɛnι

[ ] enclose phonetic symbols

/ / enclose phonemic symbols

~ 'alternates with'

< 'descends from'

> 'becomes'

* indicates a hypothetical form

1 Introduction to Dialectology

Many grades of vernacular exist in England today. They vary from the oldest forms of regional dialect, localised in our rural communities, down through the numerous mixed dialects of our towns and cities, to the widely acceptable type of English often called Standard English: for example, that used by the B.B.C. news-reader...[1]

This extract from a paper by Professor Harold Orton on the *Survey of English Dialects* is a fitting beginning to a book on English dialects. The word *dialect* itself is used with various shades of meaning, but for present purposes dialects will be taken to be variant, but mutually intelligible, forms of one language, whereas *language* is assumed to imply a form of speech not on the whole intelligible to other languages. Thus, the vernaculars of Devon and Yorkshire are *dialects*, whereas those of France and Spain are *languages*. It is, of course, recognized that there are occasions when it is not clear whether *dialect* or *language* is relevant: Old Norwegian and Old English, probably being mutually intelligible, must, under this definition, be regarded as dialects, but modern Norwegian is not intelligible to speakers of modern English, and thus in their later stages the two dialects become two languages. The same is presumably true of the earlier stages of most other languages, and thus many linguists refer to the *Indo-European dialects*, the *Germanic dialects*. The difference between dialect and language is therefore one of degree, not one of kind, a language being only one stage of development further on from a dialect.

A customary and useful distinction is made between *dialect* and *accent*. Quite simply, *dialect* refers to all the linguistic elements in one form of a language—phonological, grammatical and lexical—while *accent* refers only to pronunciations. Accent is thus the phonetic or phonological aspect of dialect.

Dialects are the products of linguistic change, and such change—phonological, grammatical, lexical and semantic—is taking place all the time: to take examples, the word pronounced [huːs] *hūs* in Old English is in present-day Standard English [haʊs], the long vowel having been gradually diphthongized; the 3 pr. sgs. of verbs

1

such as OE *singan, lufian* were *singeþ, lufiaþ*, whereas today they are *sings* and *loves*; *donkey*, a late word of obscure origin, has replaced the very much older word *ass*, and the word *disgusting* has changed its meaning from merely 'distasteful' to that of 'loathsome, repugnant'. Further exemplification is unnecessary, and so is a discussion of the many causes of linguistic change. We may safely leave this to the numerous textbooks on language, merely noting the basic fact that such change occurs continuously, and is the significant factor behind differentiation into dialects and languages. Even in present-day English we may note, as one example, the older [æ] of *hat, match* being replaced by [a] or, sometimes in younger speakers, a sound further back in the mouth.

So the language of any community is liable to constant change, but if the community becomes in some way divided, perhaps geographically (one part, for example, emigrating to the other side of a range of mountains) or by political factors, then the language of these groups will not cease to change, but it may change in two different directions. The language on one side of the boundary may change in a different way from that on the other side, although strong initial tendencies present in the undivided language may emerge in both the divergent forms. The degree to which the two groups diverge in language is dependent upon the amount of contact between them: obviously, two adjacent communities in constant contact are less likely to become mutually unintelligible than two which become separated by a very considerable distance or by boundaries of an impenetrable kind, geographical or political.

Communities can be divided not only by geographical or political factors, but also by such social forces as education and upbringing, employment and income, which are behind the so-called *class dialects*, as distinct from the *regional dialects* produced by the other factors mentioned.

The study of dialect

The study of any living dialect, if it is to be complete, must cover patterns of sounds or the *phonology* of the language (including stress, rhythm and intonation)—i.e. the accent, patterns of *grammar*, and patterns of vocabulary or *lexis*. When the dialect studied is a regional one, this last type of dialect study is known as *word geography*.

As in other subjects, different approaches to the material are possible. As will be seen in due course, the traditional approach up to quite recently has been *diachronic* or historical. By this method, items of a dialect are compared with items in the same dialect at some earlier period, usually Middle English. Here the dialectologist is chiefly concerned with the chronological development of features, e.g. ME $\bar{\rho}$, in one dialect. He may also, however, be making a comparison with another dialect, and may again use historical material to explain differences in development between the two dialects, e.g. in one ME $\bar{\rho}$ may > [u:], in another [y:] or [ɪu]. The dialectologist of the historical school will further want to investigate the linguistic and non-linguistic causes which lie behind such differences.

More recently, emphasis has shifted to a *synchronic* approach, comprising a pure description of a dialect without reference to historical factors, but paying special attention to the interrelationship of individual features within the systems of the dialect under investigation.

Regional dialect

The present book will deal mainly with regional dialect—i.e. dialect associated with a particular geographical area—a subject known as *linguistic geography* or *dialect geography*, and the word *dialect*, when unqualified, will be understood to mean *regional dialect*.

In England, as elsewhere, linguistic geography has usually concentrated upon the speech of the older inhabitants of rural villages. Professor Harold Orton has referred to this type of dialect as 'traditional vernacular, genuine and old',[2] and one of the interests of this form of speech lies in the fact that it is the oldest type in use in England today, often embodying features of a stratum of language different from that of Standard English, in many cases the direct descendants of ME features. A few examples will suffice. In a small area of Somerset, dialectal English preserves traces of a final consonant in the 1 sg. personal pronoun *I* < OE *ic* [ɪtʃ], that is, the pronoun emerges as [ʌtʃ] or some such form, whereas the final consonant started to disappear in the early ME period, and was later completely lost in Standard English. To take a morphological example, the 3 pr. sg. of verbs, which earlier ended in -(*e*)*th*, is preserved in this older form in one or two instances in Devon and Cornwall, instead of having the -(*e*)*s* ending now universally characteristic of Standard English. In syntax, the dialects seem occasionally to prefer the use of a simple verb as opposed to an 'expanded' construction, e.g. *the kettle boils, it rains*, rather than *the kettle is boiling, it is raining*. The latter construction is rare in ME, and even in Shakespeare and the Authorized Version of the Bible, and is in fact a comparatively recent addition to the stock of English constructions, the use of a simple verb—as shown in the dialects—being older (see pp. 121–2, below). Finally, there are numerous examples of lexical items which exist in local dialect, but are replaced by other words in Standard English: such are *shippon*, replaced by Standard English *cow-house*, and the previously mentioned *ass*, now almost completely defunct, and replaced by *donkey*.

The foregoing are merely random examples which serve to demonstrate the general principle that regional dialectal English ('traditional vernacular') may preserve different or older items not present in Standard English (an account of whose origin is given in Chapter 3). These are no less a part of the historical English language, and indeed may in some instances represent a more direct line of historical development (as, for example, in cases where Standard English has replaced a word of native stock by one of foreign origin). The distributional implications of these items are the subject of the dialect geographer.

Class dialects and others

But although regional dialects are those upon which so far most research has been done, class dialects—owing their origin in the main not to geographical but to socio-economic causes—are of no less significance, and are certainly not to be neglected. Apart from the non-regional form, Standard English, class dialects are always associated in some way with regional dialect, and regional dialectal features are often to be explained as social in origin. Although the emphasis in this book will be on regional dialects, class dialects will therefore not be forgotten, and especially in so far as they relate to local speech. Finally, a certain amount of space will be devoted to the specialized dialects of fishing communities, miners and others, since, although these dialects have not yet been fully investigated, research is being actively pursued into them, and they will undoubtedly yield material of the greatest interest, especially to the lexicologist.

Standard English and the regional dialects

The most important of any present-day English class dialect is Standard English, in origin the speech of educated Londoners (see Chapter 2), to defining which much time and space has been devoted. Professor Randolph Quirk's suggestion that:

Standard English is...'normal English'...basically an ideal, a mode of expression that we seek when we wish to communicate beyond our immediate community with members of the wider community...[3]

brings out the important distinction between Standard English and dialect, namely that Standard English is the sort of language used when communicating *beyond* the family, close friends and acquaintances, whereas dialect is nowadays often kept for intimate circles. The incipient Standard English began its rise to importance as a prestige dialect in the ME period and from that time the regional dialects began to take second place—very slowly at first, no doubt, but more quickly as time went on, and more especially with the increase of educational facilities and printed books. We may thus expect to find that Standard English has had no little effect on dialects, gradually forcing dialectal forms into out-of-the-way corners of the country, making dialect speakers bilingual (i.e. able to converse in both their local dialect and in Standard English), and generally gaining ground to the disadvantage of merely local forms of speech. The dialects are thus no longer 'pure', if ever they were, but contain a large admixture of Standard English or pseudo-Standard English forms.

Received Pronunciation (RP)

A distinction must be made between Standard English, which is a *dialect* in use by educated speakers of English throughout the world, and 'Received Pronunciation', which is the *accent* of English usually associated with a higher social or educational background, with the BBC and the professions, and that most commonly taught to students learning English as a foreign language. Many people speak unimpeachable Standard English as far as words and grammar are concerned, though with regional features in their pronunciation (accent). Like Standard English, however, RP owes its origin to educated London speech, which during the Middle Ages began to acquire social prestige and eventually changed from a regional to a class dialect. In England great prestige is still attached to this standard of pronunciation, which, throughout its history, has had a marked effect on the various regional forms of pronunciation. Between RP and the dialects it is useful to distinguish the intermediate variety 'modified regional' as a type of pronunciation modified by the adoption of RP characteristics to a greater or lesser degree, e.g. the use of RP [ɑː] in *chaff, grass, path, dance*, instead of northern dialectal [a]. (In some cases it seems more convenient to speak of 'modified RP', when a speaker uses RP modified by only one or two non-RP features, e.g. the use of a diphthong such as [ɛʊ] in *out, round, town*, instead of RP [aʊ].)

Dialectal borrowing

Dialects are influenced not only by Standard English but by each other. This is the case, for example, in west Cornwall, which on the whole has a dialect in many ways approximating to Standard English itself, but which has received influence from Devon in that initial [v] and [z] occur in words like *furrow*, *see*. A further example is the spread of an [ɒ͡ʊ] pronunciation in words like *spoon* (< ME *spōne*) from the West Riding of Yorkshire (a Midland area) to the North Riding (a northern area), encroaching upon the [ʊə] type traditional to the latter.

Thus two impulses must be seen simultaneously at work—an ever-present impulse towards alignment with Standard English and at the same time a tendency to absorb forms characteristic of neighbouring dialects. Too often dialectologists are confronted with what seem to be pictures of simple *recession*, that is of features being gradually pushed to the edges of the map by Standard English, but the situation may in fact be more complex than the map sometimes shows. A case in point is that of the voicing of initial fricative consonants, already mentioned above and discussed at greater length in Chapter 5. From the available information, both in ME and the present-day dialects, it is fairly clear that initial *f*, *s*, *th*, *sh* had at one time possessed a voiced quality everywhere south of a line approximating to Watling Street, except in west Cornwall, sporadic relic-forms found in the north and east of this area marking its outer limits. But the forms with [v z ð ʒ] are now not by any means spread solidly across this area, and the usual assumption is that they have disappeared under the influence of Standard English. On the other hand, however, as we have seen, voicing occurs to a certain extent in west Cornwall (in *fellies*, *SED* I.9.9, it occurs down to the tip of the peninsula), an area in which it is not traditional, and furthermore it appears that many French words in south-west England—words reported by Ellis and early dialectologists not to have had initial voicing—now show this feature. These facts suggest that the impulse towards voicing has not been entirely moribund since the nineteenth century but has continued.

The purpose of linguistic geography

The earliest systematic study of regional dialect arose out of the controversy centring round the Neo-Grammarian principle of the inviolability of sound-laws, that is, the doctrine that a given sound-law was true for all the examples of the sound in question and any exceptions had to be explained by external causes (e.g. loans from the written language or from other forms of the language, analogy and other disturbing influences). The disputes which took place over this subject suggested a new approach to linguistic problems, namely that which L. R. Palmer has called 'the most fruitful development of twentieth-century linguistics', linguistic geography.[4] Scholars were prompted to test their theories on living, rural dialects, where they felt that speech could be studied in its natural setting, free from such influences. The first work was done in Germany and France, and the foundations of the subject—the use of a questionnaire, the recording of items in a network of localities and the plotting of these on maps—thus laid. The results seemed to refute the Neo-Grammarians, in that in some areas no two words were seen to show an identical development. An example of this from English dialects is the development of the vowel or diphthong in *ground* (*SED* IV.4.1) and *pound* (VII.8.2). In southern England and in Standard English the *reflex* or result of OE *u* in such words (from lengthening (> ū) in ME) is [aʊ] or the like, but in northern England it remains [ʊ]. Map 1 shows the *isoglosses* separating these two areas, from which it will indeed be seen that in both words [aʊ] or another diphthong is regular for southern England, and [ʊ] for northern England, but that the region where the two areas meet is slightly different for each word—i.e. the isoglosses do not quite coincide. The mapping of, say, *found* or *sound* would probably yield yet slightly different results. It is thus obvious that in these intermediate areas sound-laws can hardly be considered rigid if OE *u* appears as, say, [aʊ] in *ground* and [ʊ] in *pound*.

This sort of result led the earlier dialectologists to react strongly against the Neo-Grammarian doctrine and to regard it as sterile and artificial. However, although dialect boundaries do continually fluctuate because of social intercourse, communications and population movement, and thus there can be no clear-cut line between dialects, yet there *are* areas (in the example above, a northern and a southern area) in which the development of the sound is regular. Confusion is recorded only in the border regions between such areas. It is due to dialect intermixture and borrowing and in no way invalidates the Neo-Grammarian dogma, which had, in fact, allowed for such borrowing. Dialect research merely showed such borrowing to be more frequent than had been supposed.

The lines drawn on Map 1 are known as *isoglosses*. These are lines drawn on a map defining areas characterized by the occurrence

Map 1 *Ground* and *pound*

－－－－ Southern limit of [ǫ] in *ground* (IV.4.1)

──── Southern limit of [ǫ] in *pound* (VII.8.2)

of certain linguistic features. It was remarked above that the mapping of, say, *found* or *sound* would provide yet other isoglosses, and if this were done, or if we went on further to map, say, the reflexes of ME ǭ, ME ā and others, we should get what is known as the *bundling of isoglosses* (cf. Maps 7 and 8, below). Such bundling usually takes place along important geographical or political boundaries, which are thus shown to have been dominant factors in the separating of one dialect from another. This does not mean that the speech in one region is necessarily uniform in every characteristic or that it does not share characteristics with a dialect outside. But within the area marked off by the bundling of isoglosses there is some degree of uniformity. The dialect geographer's task is to study these bundles of isoglosses and the areas they define and to draw all the possible inferences—in Palmer's words, 'the interpretation of the distribution of speech-forms in space'.[5] The relative importance of the bundles depends upon the number of isoglosses they contain, and also upon their character, isoglosses dividing one dialect from another in terms of differences of dialectal structure obviously being more important than 'non-structural' ones.[6]

Dialect maps also show how linguistic features radiate from centres of culture and influence, and thus how the standard form of the language encroaches upon local vernacular. Although there is little or no published work so far available on the subject, future research should illuminatingly reveal the overwhelming influence of London English on the traditional speech of the Home Counties: a comparison of the present-day dialect of Kent, for example, with that of the language of the *Aʒenbite of Inwyt* (written at Canterbury in 1340) will show that many of the latter's distinctive characteristics (e.g. initial *v* [v], *z* [z] in *farmer*, *see*, etc.) have been obliterated.

Linguistic geography can shed light on many philological problems. To take one example—the traditional explanation of the development of ME *a* before *f*, *s*, *th* (as in *chaff*, *grass*, *path*) to [ɑː] via the stages [æ], [æː] has recently been contested.[7] Now, an examination of the dialects of Cornwall shows that the reflexes of ME *a* before *f*, *s*, *th* emerge as [aː] (roughly east Cornwall) and [æː] (roughly west Cornwall). Further, the county's history and other phonological features of the dialect of west Cornwall suggest that this dialect is in origin probably a version of an earlier stage of Standard English. If this is so, the presence of [æː] as the reflex of ME *a* before *f*, *s*, *th* suggests that this may have been an earlier stage of the development of the sound, borrowed into the vernacular of west Cornwall before it proceeded to present-day Standard English [ɑː].

Traditional linguistic geography has always found it necessary to concern itself with 'external' phenomena—external, that is, to purely linguistic matters—since it conceives part of the task to be the relating of dialect features to geographical, historical, social, political and other factors. The linguistic geographer is concerned to find out how and why his dialectal forms have come to be as they are. What factors will account for the present-day geographical patterns shown by ON loan-words in this country? On what social background do the east–west dialectal divisions in Cornwall depend? As far as dialectal divisions are concerned, political and administrative boundaries appear to be of greater significance than geographical ones (some of them perhaps depending on older tribal boundaries), for example the boundary between the Anglo-Saxon kingdoms of Northumbria and Mercia is marked by several dialectal features, and Watling Street emerges as an important dialect boundary. Geographical factors are perhaps not so important: the Thames, the Severn, the Tees and Tamar rivers, for example, do not seem to be important dialectal boundaries. Indeed, it is held that rivers (at least when navigable) act more often as a means of communication than as obstacles, and where they—as also other geographical features—do emerge as dialectally significant, it is because they coincide with political boundaries.

A further and related consideration is thus that of the desirability of 'correlating the borders, centers, and overall dynamics of language areas with "culture areas" in a broader sense'—to quote Uriel Weinreich.[8] The study of 'folk speech' must always be closely linked with that of 'folk life' in all its aspects—customs and festivals, artefacts, local crafts and so on. And Weinreich goes on to illustrate the point by reference to the 'Eifel Barrier' (the Eifel mountain range) between the Cologne and Trier areas, which, in addition to marking the dividing line between various linguistic features such as *helpe* and *helfe*, *haus* and *hus*, also divides short-bladed from long-bladed scythes, grey bread in oval loaves from black bread in rectangular loaves, the cult of St Quirin as the patron saint of cattle from St Quirin as the patron of horses, and so on. This is certainly something that urgently needs investigation in England. It is an exciting task which, one hopes, will not have to wait too long for attention.

2 Historical Background

The Anglo-Saxon invasion and settlement

The English we use today, whether dialectal or 'standard', is the regular descendant—with additions and subtractions—of Old and Middle English, Old English being the term now generally preferred to designate the language of our ancestors the Anglo-Saxons. There is evidence to show that the Anglo-Saxons had reached England from their continental homeland at a very early period indeed—settling under Roman auspices as early as the second century A.D.—although their invasions did not begin in earnest until much later. Germanic pirates had been a menace since the third century, but the date at which serious hostilities are traditionally said to have begun is A.D. 449 when, according to the *Anglo-Saxon Chronicle*, Hengest and Horsa landed on the shores of Kent, at first to help the Britons repulse barbarian invaders, but later fighting against the Britons themselves.

The 'Anglo-Saxons' consisted of various peoples—according to Bede in his *Historia Ecclesiastica* (completed in 731), probably drawing on sound tradition, Angles, Saxons and Jutes. The Jutes and Angles had apparently been settled in the Danish peninsula, with the Saxons to the south and west of them, while Frisians, who were also represented in the invasion of England, occupied a strip of land along the coast from the Weser to the Rhine. From the middle of the fifth century onwards, these tribes began to add their numbers to various of their members already in England, the Jutes and Saxons, according to traditional accounts, establishing themselves in the south of England, and the Angles occupying at first eastern England, and later most of the land north of the Thames. The Romans had been forced by various internal and external causes to withdraw from England in the first part of the fifth century and left behind them a population of Romanized Britons divided into small kingdoms governed by native princes; these peoples were unable to offer effective resistance to the Germanic tribes whom they had invited here in the first place to help them keep their enemies at

DALE H. GRAMLEY LIBRARY
SALEM COLLEGE
WINSTON-SALEM, N. C.

bay, and were to a large extent pushed over to the west of the island, although there is good evidence for British survival in pockets throughout the whole country for quite a long period (see pp. 15–16, below).

From the fifth century onwards, then, the first Anglo-Saxon kingdoms were established until, after a period of several centuries, the whole country was settled from east to west. Seven small kingdoms were in existence by the time of Bede and were known as the Anglo-Saxon Heptarchy—Northumbria, Mercia, East Anglia, Kent, Essex, Sussex and Wessex. The division of the country into the administrative units known as shires (which on the whole did not correspond to the old tribal divisions) did not take place until the ninth and tenth centuries in the main.

Old English and the linguistic background

The Anglo-Saxons spoke a version of the sub-branch of the Germanic parent language known as West Germanic, which included— in addition to the language we now know as Old English—Old High German, Old Frisian, Old Low German or Old Saxon, and Old Low Franconian. For practical purposes, OE begins with the first manuscript records of the language of the Anglo-Saxons, c. 700.

From the corpus of OE documents surviving it is possible to distinguish four dialects, roughly based, as it would appear, on the Anglo-Saxon tribal divisions established in this country.[1] Although in the present work we are chiefly concerned with the modern English dialects, for the sake of completeness something must also be said of those of Old and Middle English.

First, however, it may be as well to draw attention to two facts. Whereas in our own time one form of speech and writing is regarded as 'standard', a level of linguistic communication which is obligatory in writing and often regarded as desirable in speech, though there are also in existence various regional and social forms of speech, in the early Middle Ages there was no national standard for writing and speech, each person using the local tradition or standard of whatever region he came from. In writing, this tradition would be that of the monastic scriptorium, and would be perpetuated by scribes trained within the tradition. (This situation is, however, complicated by scribal copying, which might produce a likeness of the original work containing dialectal modifications from the scribe's own—possibly different—tradition. We thus have to allow for a mixture of forms which complicates our linguistic evaluation of early texts.)

Secondly, before turning to any consideration of historical dialect material, it is important to bear in mind that such material is preserved in written form, as distinct from that of modern dialect, which, apart from poems, monologues, etc., specially written to display dialect features, exists in spoken form. This means that our knowledge of spoken Old and Middle English is based on inferences drawn from a study of the written materials, combined with the study of modern English. Since there cannot be a completely systematic correspondence between a variety of spoken English and its written equivalent, inferences should be drawn from medieval texts only with the greatest care. For example, ME texts often show features which are purely graphic and have no phonetic significance, such as the double *t* in forms like *itt* (as distinct from *it*), mentioned below, and contrariwise they cannot show variants which on the basis of modern dialects we feel sure existed, such as the different forms of *r* ([ɽ], [r], etc.).[2]

The four dialects distinguishable in OE are Northumbrian, Mercian (these two together known as Anglian), Kentish and West Saxon. The following synopsis owes much to A. Campbell's valuable *Old English Grammar*, §§6 ff.

The Northumbrian dialect is represented by the glosses on the *Lindisfarne Gospels*, the *Rushworth Gospels* (except for the part of it which is Mercian) and the *Durham Ritual*, all quite lengthy texts of the tenth century; in earlier (eighth- to ninth-century) works by the two earliest manuscripts of Cædmon's *Hymn*, the earliest manuscripts of Bede's *Death-Song* and of the *Leiden Riddle*, the runic inscriptions of the Ruthwell Cross and the Franks Casket, and other names and inscriptions of an early date.

The largest single source of our knowledge of Mercian is a collection of charters of Mercian kings; the interlinear glosses on the *Vespasian Psalter* (mid-ninth century) and part of the *Rushworth Gospels* (tenth century); the *Corpus Glossary* (eighth to ninth century), the *Épinal Glossary* and the *Erfurt Glossary* (both ninth century); the eighth-century *Leiden Glossary*; the glosses on the *Blickling Psalter* (eighth century) and the *Lorica Glosses* and the *Lorica Prayer* (ninth century); the *Royal Glosses* of *c*. 1000.

The Kentish dialect is known in the eighth century only from names in Latin charters, but in the ninth century is used for the language of a series of charters themselves. The glosses on one of the manuscripts of Bede's *Historia Ecclesiastica* may contain Kentish elements (*c.* 900), and four Latin charters again have Kentish names. After 900 the OE Kentish dialect is represented only by the *Kentish Psalm*, the *Kentish Hymn* and the glosses to *Proverbs*, all preserved in British Museum MS Cotton Vespasian D VI of the late tenth century.

Although West Saxon was later to become something of a standard literary dialect, in the earlier period it is very poorly represented, existing only in the names and boundaries of two charters, some genealogies, and fragments of two early manuscripts of a martyrology, all of the ninth century. Later, however, it is richly exemplified—'early West Saxon' is based on the Parker MS of the *Anglo-Saxon Chronicle*, the two oldest manuscripts of Alfred's translation of Gregory's *Cura Pastoralis*, and the Lauderdale MS of the OE translation of Orosius, all of the end of the ninth or the early tenth century. The works of Ælfric (*c.* 1000) constitute the bulk of later West Saxon writing and to these must be especially added the gloss on the *Junius Psalter* and the *Leech-Book* (both early tenth-century manuscripts); the Abingdon MSS of the *Anglo-Saxon Chronicle* (late tenth and eleventh centuries), the West Saxon Gospels (the early manuscripts are dated *c.* 1000); the Abingdon copy of the OE Orosius (eleventh century); MS A of the Benedictine Rule (*c.* 1000); the boundaries in the charters of West Saxon kings, and the numerous royal writs.

The dialects exhibited in these works are distinguished from each other by certain linguistic features, mainly phonological. It must be pointed out here, however, that, although the West Saxon dialect is much more fully represented than the other dialects, ultimately being adopted as a standard literary dialect, it nevertheless shows forms characteristic of other dialects, even in its later stages when it had become well established as such. Such texts as the manuscripts of the *Blickling Homilies* (late tenth century) and MS D of the *Anglo-Saxon Chronicle* (post 1050) show a substantial non-West Saxon element in orthography and inflexion. A similar lack of dialectal uniformity characterizes most of the extant OE verse, which is mainly preserved in the four great codices dating from *c.* 1000, namely the Beowulf MS, the Exeter Book, the Junius MS, and the Vercelli Book. These, while predominantly late West Saxon, are very rich in dialectal forms. It has been suggested in fact that there was a 'general OE poetic dialect', mixed in vocabulary, phonology and morphology.[3]

The material available from OE sources is too slight to enable us to draw an accurate dialect map. The distinguishing dialectal characteristics of each text, although presumably reflected in the local speech of the area concerned, are more safely regarded in the first place as evidences of local scribal practice at a number of centres. So, for example, we know that the *Durham Ritual* comes from the Durham area, and this text can therefore give us a knowledge of the written (and, presumably, therefore, spoken) language in use at this point. Similarly, the *Vespasian Psalter*—which can be distinguished as a Mercian text by comparison with independent sources—affords us a knowledge of the language of one (unknown) centre in the Mercian area. But it is obviously not possible from such information to draw boundaries defining the areas in which the various dialects were spoken, and maps of OE dialects must be based in part on inferences made from the data provided by the ME and present-day dialects. The southern boundary of the Northumbrian dialects, dividing them from the Mercian dialects, is generally more or less equated with the river Humber, Kentish was spoken in the present-day counties of Kent, Surrey and Sussex, and West Saxon in the other southern counties.

Celtic survival

For a large part of the Anglo-Saxon period, groups of Britons remained, apparently undisturbed, not only in the west (where many of them were pushed by the invading Anglo-Saxons), but scattered throughout the country. In these groups they no doubt continued, for some time at least, to speak their own native language—a fact of potential significance for a consideration of the Celtic element in English dialect. The existence of such groups is evidenced not only by provisions made for their treatment under Anglo-Saxon law, but also by place-names such as those which contain as first element a form of OE *walh* 'foreigner, Welshman', very often originally in the genitive pl. *wala*, so, for example, Walbrook (Mx) 'brook of the Welsh', Walcott (Nf) 'cottage of the Welsh', Walden (Ess, Hrt, YNR) 'valley of the Welsh', Walton (Ch, Db, Ess, K, La, Sf, St, Sx, YWR) 'farmstead, village of the Welsh'.[4] Furthermore, Professor Kenneth Jackson's examination of river-names shows, as one might expect, that Celtic survival was thicker in the west of the country.[5] In eastern England Celtic river-names are comparatively rare. They become commoner in the north-east, the Midlands and central south-west England, yet more common in the western borders of the country, and in Devon, Dorset and Somerset, and are overwhelmingly in the majority in Wales and part of the Welsh border and in

15

Cornwall. These facts suggest that in eastern England Britons who remained were quickly absorbed into the life of the settlers, while, as one travels westward, the increased number of Celtic river-names perhaps indicates that here the Britons were not expelled to the same extent.

It is not clear how long Celtic speakers remained in England, but there may be evidence for their survival in central Dorset until at least the ninth century and in Exeter until the tenth.[6] In Cornwall, the west of the county was Celtic speaking until after 1500 or so and the language did not disappear completely until the eighteenth century. Nevertheless, it is probably true on the whole that the Britons quickly adopted the language of the Anglo-Saxons, through a bilingual stage, while they themselves left no discernible effect on its sound-system (there are one or two loan-words, however, which are discussed in Chapter 7).

The Scandinavian Invasion and Settlement

During the Anglo-Saxon period one other people began to have a very profound effect on the English language, although tangible evidence of this does not become common before the ME period. These were the Scandinavian races who, as observed above, themselves spoke a Germanic dialect related to OE. The Scandinavian invasions—in general part of the great Viking expansion which took its members to all quarters of the known world—were first felt by Britain in 787, according to the *Anglo-Saxon Chronicle*, and had looting and plunder as main objectives. There were two routes from Scandinavia to Britain—a northerly, from Norway to Shetland, Orkney, the Isle of Man and Ireland, and a southerly, leading from southern Jutland along the Frisian coast to the Rhine mouths and thence along the English Channel. These routes were followed in the main respectively by Norwegians and Danes, Danish invasion and settlement being on the whole earlier than Norwegian.

From 865 onwards, when the 'Great Army' landed in East Anglia, the Danish invasions became Danish settlements. Previously, the Viking forces had been wont to spend spring and summer in Britain, penetrating not more than ten to fifteen miles inland and returning home before autumn with their loot (they had wintered in Thanet in 850, however, and in Sheppey in 854). Now, in a series of more serious invasions over a period of fifteen years the Danes actually took possession of most of eastern England. By 880 they had under their control an eastern area bounded on the north by the

Tees, on the south by the Thames, and on the west by Watling Street and—further north—Derby and York; an agreement on a territorial division was eventually reached in 886 by King Alfred and Guthrum, king of the East Anglian Danes, and embodied in a treaty known as the *Treaty of Alfred and Guthrum*. This stipulated that the boundary should be marked by the Thames estuary as far upstream as the Lea. It was then to turn north and to follow the Lea to its source. From here the boundary was to run in a straight line to Bedford and thence it was to follow the Ouse upstream to the point at which it was crossed by Watling Street, i.e. Fenny Stratford. The treaty left Alfred in possession of London but gave Guthrum modern Essex, Norfolk, Suffolk and Cambridgeshire and parts of Bedfordshire and Hertfordshire. It is not certain how much further to the north Guthrum's kingdom extended, but there were now three separate Scandinavian dominions in England—Northumbria (Yorkshire and parts of the adjoining districts), East Anglia, and Scandinavian Mercia (which included the 'Five Boroughs' of Lincoln, Stamford, Leicester, Derby and Nottingham). Alfred died probably in 899 and during the next forty years the Danish-held lands east of Watling Street were reconquered by his descendants, although the kingdom of York remained independent much longer, enjoying successive periods of independence and submission until at last in 954 it submitted to Eadred.

However, there was from about 900 onwards a new penetration into the Wirral, the Lancashire coast, Westmorland, Cumberland and the north shore of the Solway Firth, this time chiefly by Norwegians from the Norse kingdom established in Dublin. They furthermore succeeded in gaining control of the Danish settlements in Yorkshire until 955.

In 918 the northern boundary of the English kingdom stretched from the Humber to the Mersey, and in 927 Athelstan occupied York and extended this kingdom as far as the river Eamont. A further decisive victory for the English was won at *Brunanburh* (a site now unknown) in 937 when Athelstan defeated the combined Scandinavian and Scottish forces. However, on his death in 939, Olaf Guðfriðson, who had fled to Ireland after his defeat at *Brunanburh*, returned to York, invaded the Midlands as far south as Northampton, and secured an agreement with Edmund, Athelstan's brother and successor, whereby he became ruler of York and its dependent territories and also of the Five Boroughs, i.e. the northeast Midlands between the Humber and Welland. But these lands were recovered within three years after Olaf's death in 941.

17

The second phase of Viking attack began two years after the accession (978) to the English throne of Æthelred the Unready, much of it conducted by highly trained professional soldiers, to whom England was in no position to offer adequate opposition. A series of campaigns in 1013 by the Dane, Swein Forkbeard, established him as king of England (Æthelred fleeing to Normandy), but he died early in the following year. There followed a series of campaigns between Æthelred, who returned from Normandy but died in 1016, and Cnut, Swein's younger son, and between Edmund (Æthelred's son) and Cnut, the final result of which was an agreement which left Wessex to Edmund and gave the rest of the country to Cnut. But at the end of 1016 Edmund died and Cnut became king of England, the country thereafter being under Danish rule until 1042, when the old line of Wessex was restored under Edward the Confessor.

To sum up so far, we can say that the early Scandinavian settlements (ninth century and earlier) in this country were mostly Danish and were on the eastern side of England. Norwegian settlements, occurring somewhat later (mainly in the first half of the tenth century by men who had been living in Ireland), were in the north-western counties and the North and West Ridings of Yorkshire. Few new settlements were made under the Danish kings who ruled England in the eleventh century, although a Danish trading colony grew up in London and intercourse between the two nations no doubt continued and was strengthened.

The periods reviewed above show a sequence of, at first, raiding, later settlement and consolidation, with intermingling of the English and Scandinavian races, and finally political conquest. It is doubtful whether the Scandinavian dialects could have had much effect on English during the more turbulent times, but with permanent and peaceful settlement these dialects were spoken by numerous settlers over large tracts of the country, and intermarriage as well as other intercourse between the settlers and the English would result in mutual linguistic influence. Thus took place the amalgamation of the two tongues which resulted as far as English is concerned in a language greatly enriched from Scandinavian sources but still basically of an English character. The point should be made that the English (especially northern English) and Scandinavian tongues were mutually comprehensible at this time and there is perhaps something to be gained from Joseph Wright's comparison of the linguistic situation with that which exists between present-day dialect speakers of, say, Yorkshire and Somerset.[7] There is some evidence that speakers of the two dialects learned to make 'phonemic translations' from one dialect to another, i.e. to convert a word into the form most familar to them and treat it as a native one.[8] These facts naturally assisted the ultimate complete fusion of the two dialects, although inscriptions prove that Norse was still used in some districts of England as a distinct dialect as late as the twelfth century.

The presence of the Scandinavians in England is evidenced by a number of runic inscriptions, by a large number of Scandinavian personal names, place-names and place-name elements, and by loan-words in English from the OE period onwards. It is the last-named aspect which is chiefly of interest to us here and it will be dealt with in Chapter 7, although attention should be paid at the same time to the relevant place-name material, a study of which should always be closely linked with that of local dialect. Before leaving the historical side of the Scandinavian settlements, then, it will be as well to outline very briefly the place-name evidence for such settlements in preparation for our consideration of dialectal distributions later.

The distribution of Scandinavian place-names (see Map 2) agrees, in general, with the historical evidence. According to P. H. Reaney,[9] parish-names of Danish origin are spread thickly throughout the North and East Ridings of Yorkshire, in Lincolnshire and Leicestershire, but less densely in Nottinghamshire. In Norfolk they are well represented, while in Suffolk they are well scattered but less numerous. In the West Riding of Yorkshire there is a band running from north Lancashire across the county to the North and East Ridings, with another further south, from south Lancashire to Nottinghamshire. These are less dense and separated from one another and from the counties to the north and south. Elsewhere in the Danelaw they are rare or non-existent. The greatest Danish influence is thus seen to be in the three areas of Scandinavian dominion mentioned above, namely Yorkshire, Scandinavian Mercia, and East Anglia. It is less intensive on the borders of these areas and in the counties which were first reconquered from the Danes. It should be specially noted that in Northumberland Danish influence is slight, while in Durham a considerable number of names is found only in the south, near the Tees and the Wear. The most intensive Scandinavian settlement in the eastern Danelaw was in Lincolnshire (except in Holland) and in the Wreak valley of Leicestershire. The area west of Watling Street is almost entirely free of traces of Scandinavian settlement except on the border. A count of the place-names ending in -by (< ODa bý 'village, town', etc.) in the counties of the Dane-

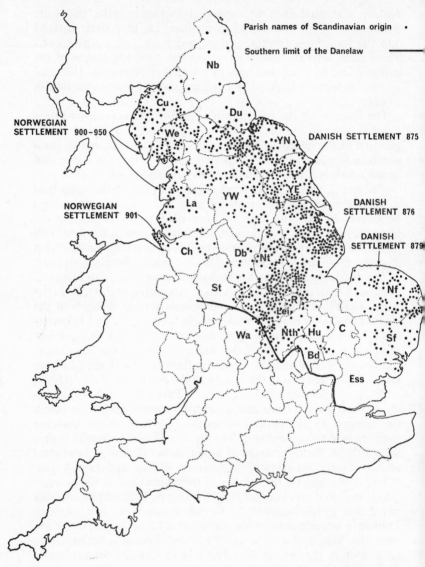

Map 2   The Scandinavian settlements

law may further be used as a rough index to the Scandinavian settlements in this area. These are as follows: Y 250 (= YNR 150,
YER 42, remainder YWR), L 260, Lei 58, Nt 21, Nth 18, Db 10,
Nf 21, Sf 3, Ess 1, C, Hu, Bd and Hrt nil, Nb nil, Du 8 (all on the Y
border).

A compact colony of Scandinavians, chiefly Norwegians, in the
Wirral is again evidenced by place-names, and the same evidence
bears witness to the strength and extent of their settlement of the
rest of the north-west, along the coastal areas north of the Mersey to
Westmorland and Cumberland, and east, beyond the Pennines, into
the West and North Ridings of Yorkshire.

By the time of the Norman Conquest the fusion of Scandinavians
and English into one people was complete, notwithstanding pockets
of Scandinavians who, as already noted, continued to speak their
own native dialect until somewhat later. The two peoples were
doubtless further welded into one in an effort to combat the new
invader from France.

The Norman Conquest

It is now generally admitted that England in 1066 was not in a
state of cultural decline, as was once thought. Indeed, some authori-
ties have seen the Norman Conquest as nothing short of a disaster,
from which the country did not recover for several hundred years.
From the point of view of English literature this certainly seems to
be borne out. The late (c. 991) OE poem *The Battle of Maldon*, for
example, shows that OE poetry still possessed life and vigour, even
though the alliterative line did not have its earlier regularity, but the
Norman Conquest brought about a decline in vernacular literary
production and also the end of the West Saxon dialect as a literary
standard. When English literature fully re-emerged from its transitional period it did so in a wide variety of different forms, with no
single dialect having precedence. Thus the *Anglo-Saxon Chronicle*
was continued at Peterborough in an east-Midland dialect until
1154, and from the east Midlands also is the *Ormulum* (c. 1200);
Cursor Mundi (c. 1275–1300) is from the north, possibly Co. Durham;
there are sermons (MS Laud 471, before 1250) in Middle Kentish;
Laȝamon's *Brut* (late twelfth century), the famous *Catherine Group*
(c. 1200–25), and the *Ancrene Riwle* (c. 1200) are from the south-
west Midlands.

Although literature never ceased to be written in English, the
Norman Conquest led to the rise of Anglo-Norman, a dialect of

French which developed as a second literary language, enjoying also a position of prestige in correspondence and legal transactions well into the fourteenth century. But in the fourteenth century one sees the reappearance of English as the sole language of literature as also of social and legal institutions. All this does not, of course, tell us much about the vexed question of the relative extents to which English and French were actually spoken during this early ME period, and by whom. It seems clear, however, that the lower classes continued to be English-speaking, since, although the Normans imposed a new superstructure on society, the total feudal pattern remained much as before. The fact that Norman landholders now ruled the estates and acquired the rents and services which their English predecessors had enjoyed surely made little difference to the linguistic habits of the farmers and their labourers, who nevertheless started to imitate the new aristocracy by such habits as giving their children French names.

At the other end of the scale there was the aristocracy, most of whom spoke French and only French at the very beginning. The Court was Norman and its language French and there was no equivalent centre of English society, the English nobility as a class having been largely destroyed by the Conquest itself. As time went on, however, the exclusive role of French could no longer be maintained and perhaps by the twelfth to thirteenth centuries many, if not most, nobles were bilingual. Between the lower and upper classes were English 'squires', modest landowners who acted as intermediaries, learning French and often aspiring to marry into the middle and lower strata of Norman society. Equally, there was a less privileged Norman element—priests and servants, for example, who were glad to marry English women. There thus existed a middle class many of whose members were bilingual.

At the end of the fourteenth century, French was still being spoken at Court, but English had by this time re-emerged as the spoken and written language of the country as a whole. It was increasingly used in literature and was gradually reinstated in all official spheres—the courts, the schools, the universities and parliament.

During the time that French was the dominant language in this country, there was a good deal of borrowing of French words into English, both spoken and written. Such borrowing conforms to the well-known pattern of what Bloomfield calls 'intimate borrowing',[10] in which the 'upper' language is spoken by the dominant privileged group, and is imitated and borrowed by users of the 'lower' language. Various factors may then lead to the extinction of one of the languages; one or more generations of bilingual speakers may intervene, then, at some period, there may come a generation which does not use one of the languages in adult life and transmits only the other to its children. In the case of England, the conquerors continued for some generations to speak their own language, but found it more and more necessary to use also that of the conquered. Once they had become merely a bilingual upper class, the way was open for the loss of the less useful upper language and the rehabilitation of the lower. It is always the lower language which borrows predominantly from the upper and this is seen to be so here. A detailed study of French loan-words is, however, not our concern in this book except in so far as such loans emerge in dialectal speech. These will be discussed in Chapter 7.

Other foreign contacts

France was not the only country with which England had intimate contacts during and subsequent to the Middle Ages. In particular, there was widespread settlement from and intercourse with the Low Countries from the Anglo-Saxon period onwards. A large number of Flemings came over with William I, and continued steadily to do so until the twelfth century. Commercial and other contacts became increasingly common: the sheep-rearing industry and wool trade were major spheres of Dutch activity in Kent, while the beginnings of Kentish market-gardening and fruit-growing in the sixteenth century, early engineering work in Dover harbour and the establishment of the glass-making industry, to mention but a few examples, are attributable to Flemish ingenuity and energy. And at all times there has been a close connexion between English and continental fishing communities. In the sixteenth century another influx from the Low Countries resulted from religious persecution on the Continent.

The close, frequent and large-scale intercourse between England and the Low Countries seems, generally speaking, to have been insufficiently appreciated. Its effects on dialect remain almost totally uninvestigated.

There has been contact with Germany since the Middle Ages, but from the dialectal point of view it is not until the seventeenth century that there is much to note. The Germans played an important part in English mining from at least the thirteenth century, when Richard of Cornwall brought German miners to work the tin mines of the county, and in the sixteenth century Henry VIII obtained German help to develop the mineral resources of England. In the seventeenth century James I brought over German workmen to the lead-mines of Yorkshire and the silver mines in Durham, and Prince Rupert brought German miners to Ecton in Staffordshire to teach the use of gunpowder in mining operations. It thus looks as if we might well be prepared to find some small German influence on the vocabulary of mining. Many of the other spheres touched by German influence are learned and scientific.

As is well known, other languages, both European and non-European, have had an influence on the English vocabulary. But these—Italian, Spanish, Portuguese, and so on—will not be discussed in this book except in passing, since their influence on dialectal English is either non-existent or negligible.

Middle English dialects

As we have already noted, in the fourteenth century English literature reasserted itself, not only pre-eminently in the works of Chaucer but also in a large number of versified romances and homilies, lyrics, mystical and devotional writings, biblical paraphrases, chronicles, debates, plays, legends—works in verse and prose of all kinds. From this time on, English writings appeared in every genre and in a great variety of dialects. Although not alone, Chaucer is the poet whose name is most closely associated with the London dialect. To mention one or two other fourteenth-century representatives of particular dialects, Middle Kentish appears outstandingly in that very dull but philologically priceless work of Dan Michel of Northgate, the *Aȝenbite of Inwyt*; Robert Mannyng of Brunne's famous manual of penance *Handlyng Synne* was written in Lincolnshire; the north-west Midlands are justly celebrated for the poems of the 'Pearl poet', namely *Sir Gawain and the Green Knight*, *Pearl*, *Patience*, and *Purity*, a group which represents the finest achievements of the fourteenth-century alliterative school of poets, noted for its employment of special types (in particular an archaic type) of poetic diction, descended, it would seem, from that of Old English; the lyrics in MS Harley 2253 were copied in Herefordshire; Langland, the author of *Piers Plowman*, hailed from the Malvern Hills; John Trevisa probably represents a Gloucestershire dialect; in the north the mystic Richard Rolle wrote in his native Yorkshire dialect.[11]

This is merely a selection of texts which can be localized with some certainty and they are supported by a vast collection of place-name forms, legal documents and the like, all bearing linguistic witness to the particular region from which they originate. Students of literature are naturally best acquainted with the literary works of the period, but these humbler items are no less valuable in providing evidence of the contemporary language of, say, Yorkshire or the west Midlands than are the texts of Richard Rolle's works and *Sir Gawain and the Green Knight*. To students of local dialect all localizable texts are of inestimable value in that they give him some idea in written form of the ancestry of the present-day (spoken) dialect of a region.

The rise of Standard English

Amidst this multiplicity of medieval local vernaculars, one dialect in particular began to rise to eminence—that of the capital, London. This dialect is traced in documents only sparingly before the four-teenth century, but by 1400 it is richly exemplified. Its linguistic features seem originally to have been a mixture of southern and south-eastern elements, but later it adopted a different character. This is generally said by scholars to be of an east-Midland variety. Recently, however, some work on ME texts (discussed further below) by Professors A. McIntosh and M. L. Samuels has been able to throw a great deal more light on this rising standard than has hitherto been possible. First of all, a (non-London) type of English can be distinguished which apparently has most claim to the title of literary standard up to 1430. This was based on the spoken dia-lects of the central Midlands, especially Northamptonshire, Hunting-donshire and Bedfordshire, and survives in a large number of manuscripts. It was copied in many outlying areas such as Somerset and Dorset. The Lollards were a powerful influence in spreading it, as is evidenced by the use of it for most of the manuscripts of Wyclif's sermons and tracts and other Lollard material. It was not, however, this type which was destined to become the written standard language of the country.

The *London* English of the time was, up to about 1370, the Essex type of dialect seen in the much earlier *English Proclamation* of Henry III (1258). After 1370, however, significant changes become evident in the surviving manuscripts, those of Chaucer's works and other items showing linguistic features of a central Midland character and thus different from those of the earlier fourteenth-century manuscripts.

After 1430 there begins a flood of government documents, written in 'chancery standard'. Showing features of yet more Midland origin than those of the previous type, it differs from Chaucerian English, and it is this dialect, not its predecessors in London English, which is the basis of modern written English. London English had thus undergone two changes in a relatively short time and was now at this stage finally adopted by government offices for regular use, while the other incipient standards were eventually ousted.

These changes—and also the presence of northern features in London dialect—are explained by immigration into the capital. A general movement to London, part of the exceptional mobility of the age, began in the thirteenth and fourteenth centuries, due largely to the concentration of economic affairs in the city. After the Norman Conquest, London had become a national centre for trading and commerce, while its Middlesex neighbour, Westminster, was already a great ecclesiastical centre, with important scriptorial resources, and ideally suited to be the home of national administration. Ekwall's work, *Studies in the Population of Medieval London* (Stockholm, 1956), in which he was able to identify some six thousand individuals who migrated to London between 1270 and 1360 (possibly only a tiny part of the whole number), shows that in the late thirteenth and early fourteenth centuries most immigrants into London came from Norfolk, with Essex and Hertfordshire next in order and then the other Home Counties. This finding, of course, agrees with the Essex and East Anglian character of the earlier fourteenth-century texts. But in the fourteenth century there was a significant change—a fresh influx of prosperous and influential immigrants took place: those from Northamptonshire and Bedfordshire increased, those from the Home Counties decreased and those from Norfolk continued. This trend of immigration from the central Midlands explains the first change in the London dialect, and its continuance explains the second change as well. Northern influence is to be explained by the presence of northerners holding high office and also by northern linguistic forms in the dialects of the central Midlands. East Anglian influence ceased after the mid-fourteenth century, although immigration continued, probably because this area was peripheral, while 'in the Central Midlands, the geographical centre of the country, a standard language was developing, progressing and easily understood all over the country: nearer the periphery, in the capital and administrative centre, a need for a language of this kind existed'.[12] We may sum up by affirming that Standard English in its written form was an upper-class dialect developed in London in late ME times mainly on the basis of the influential dialect of east-Midland immigrants.

From now on, it could be only a matter of time before dialectal traits disappeared from the written page, not only in literary works, but also in documents of a private nature. Already by the middle of the fifteenth century such demonstrably regional texts as the *Shilling-ford Letters*, written by John Shillingford, mayor of Exeter between 1447 and 1450, show few traces of Devonian character (for example there are no traces of the voicing of initial *f* and *s*). 'London' English became more and more the predominant form, and was used for all purposes by educated men of every region. And so it went on until at the end of the seventeenth century most of the surviving orthographical variations had been given up and there was more or less one norm for writing, this standard being extolled as preferable to any other types.

So far we have been referring only to a standard *written* form, but tendencies towards a standard spoken form may also go back a long way. The considerable mobility of the population in the thirteenth and fourteenth centuries—pilgrimages to shrines at home and abroad, the Crusades, which from 1095 onwards attracted large numbers of people to the Holy Land, the mixed composition of the growing universities, which brought young men together from every part of the country, the likewise mixed communities of the religious orders, the Inns of Court and royal households—seems to suggest that even as early as this local dialectal features were being weakened within some societies and groups, and the need felt for some sort of non-localized (or less strongly localized) type of speech with which to communicate with people outside one's own immediate family or circle of acquaintances. This suggestion that one type of English was felt to be 'best' is supported by the use of dialect for humorous purposes as early as the fourteenth century (see Chapter 3).

No definite evidence of such a spoken standard is, however, forthcoming before the sixteenth century. The well-known precept in *The Arte of English Poesie* (1589), in which the poet is advised to 'take the vsuall speach of the Court, and that of London and the shires lying about London within lx. myles', is one of a number of definite statements to the effect that educated, upper-class London and southern speech is by this time the model for those who wish their speech to be of the 'best' sort. Further statements by orthoe-pists in the seventeenth century bear this out by referring to the speech used in London or the universities as the best type of English

27

and equally by reacting unfavourably to regional forms of speech (cf., for example, Coote, Cooper, Sheridan, in Chapter 3). The use of dialect in literature of the early NE period to characterize rustic speakers (such as Edgar in *King Lear*) would also seem to be an indication of the growing belief that one type of English was alone superior to others.

Early Standard English should not, however, be regarded as Standard English in the modern sense: the latter is much more restricted in its permission of variants in pronunciation than was its earlier form, which apparently contained within itself social dialects and was also influenced by vulgar and regional forms.

The eighteenth century saw a movement towards 'fixing the pronunciation', its chief guiding principle being traditional spelling conventions. This is exemplified by Dr Johnson, who stated that 'for pronunciation, the best general rule is to consider those as the most elegant speakers who deviate least from the written word'. Since this time, most of the variants in pronunciation have in fact gradually disappeared, although even the late eighteenth century was still a long way from the comparative uniformity of present-day Standard English. In this late period, then, spoken Standard English was probably very much influenced by the earlier form, written Standard English. Professor Strang points out to what extent this 'highly prestigious and influential written form' has influenced spoken English of the immediate past:

Universal education since 1870...has enhanced respect for it, and for a naive concept of correctness derived from it. Education has had another kind of standardising effect during the past century. The Public Schools Act, 1864, enumerated nine schools of this type; they were relatively small and retained considerable local connections. Subsequently they have vastly increased in numbers and in size and correspondingly have reduced their local connections. They became important agencies in the transmission of a non-localised variety of English as the form with highest prestige; the adoption of this variety by the BBC in its early days naturally extended the influence of this model.[13]

The dialects in the NE period

Although provincial dialects lost importance so far as written usage was concerned, they remained, and remain, in the spoken language. Our knowledge of them since the end of the Middle Ages is derived from the statements of orthoepists and grammarians whose chief interest was often in Standard English and its uses; from spellings which, even in this period, may still indicate local dialectal features (these must be used with caution); from imitated dialect in early literature, and—later—from self-conscious attempts to imitate dialect in poems, dialogues and the like, together with the compilation of glossaries of local words.

Two facts go a long way to explaining the decline of provincial speech in the NE period. First, the rise to importance as a prestige dialect of the originally regional Standard English, as outlined above, and secondly, the not unrelated change from rural to urban living which has taken place in this country since the end of the Middle Ages.

Up to the end of the Anglo-Saxon period England had been a rural country, its people living in small villages and settlements. From the eleventh century on, a new era of urbanism began to dawn in Europe, but even by the fourteenth century, London was still the only major English city, and England continued, no doubt, to be a country of mainly rural settlements. By the fifteenth century London had a population of 40,000—a considerable number for the period, and by the end of the sixteenth century this had grown to about 200,000, i.e. one in twenty Englishmen lived there. Beside London only a very few other cities had very large populations. Even at the end of the seventeenth century, Bristol and Norwich still numbered only 30,000 and no other cities besides York and Exeter exceeded 10,000. Apart from London, the growth of such cities probably had little effect on the greater part of the population. The final and most drastic change was, however, initiated by the Industrial Revolution, whose effects in Britain were beginning to be felt at the end of the eighteenth century and reached their greatest force in the nineteenth century. Severance from the land, which was the basis of all urban population movements, had previously affected only a small minority. The needs of a rural population for manufactured products and services could be met at a simple level; manufacturing was so dispersed and on so small a scale that outside the towns it merged into rural life and did not disrupt it. But the new needs of industry, especially for coal and iron, made enormous demands on manpower, and people began to congregate on the coal areas. The first half of the nineteenth century saw a great change in the distribution of the population—away from the agricultural lands and onto the coal-fields. The same movement also saw the concentration of people in ever larger towns, some of which grew up almost overnight. By soon after 1850, the majority of the population lived in towns, by 1901 the proportion was 77 per cent, and by 1951 it was 81 per cent. The trend towards urbanization has been continued by the process of 'suburbanization', which results in larger cities encroaching upon nearby towns and small settlements, so that ultimately the urban areas coalesce in enormous sprawls.[14]

Remembering that throughout all this period Standard English was developing and growing, we must now ask what urbanization on such a scale has meant in linguistic terms. According to Professor Strang:

Our knowledge of urban speech-varieties and their origins is very limited, but it does seem to be a usual consequence of the mixing in an urban community that social stratification develops as geographical affiliations are blurred. It is, after all, natural for speakers exposed to different types of speech to wonder about the meaning of the differences, and for English speakers, at least, to try to correlate these differences with a scale of correctness or social prestige. Such an attempt is always in some measure self-fulfilling—that is to say, the view that a usage is 'the best' naturally leads to its adoption by those who want their speech to be 'the best'. Thus a consequence of urbanisation is subordination of the old local structuring of language-varieties to a new social structuring, until eventually the whole fabric of 'dialects' is altered.[15]

At first this must have been true only of London, but later, as more cities developed, true of them also:

By 1770 all regions of the country had witnessed some measure of urban concentration; the movements of population at the Industrial Revolution brought about a situation in which the norm for speakers was experience of a geographically mixed rather than an unmixed local community. Of course the inherited character of local dialects was still extremely marked, and had a special emotional status, but it was no longer the only kind of speech experienced by the majority of speakers.[16]

In the countryside, meanwhile, the old rural dialects continued except in so far as they were subject to a constant tendency towards modification in the direction of the prestige dialect, Standard English. It is this type of speech which has so far received most attention from dialectologists, a type which, because of poor communications leading to comparative isolation, has been preserved remarkably well in some areas up to the present day, and still remains as the traditional speech within the community. The fact that most dialect-speakers are nowadays bilingual (speaking their own native dialect and also a version of Standard English) and that village life is slowly breaking down (more young people migrate to the towns, and contrariwise many business people from the towns have come to live outside the towns in surrounding villages) makes it appear unlikely that this state of affairs will continue for very long except in the most remote areas.

Recent work in ME dialectology

The study of ME dialect material has been going on since the late nineteenth century, much of the earlier work being done by German scholars. A representative twentieth-century historian of the English language, the late Professor H. C. Wyld, based his own work on that of earlier writers, and himself made extensive use of place-names as one type of ME dialectal evidence that could be localized with some certainty. More recent investigations of this type, based on place- and personal-names, are exemplified by Sundby's work on Worcestershire records (see the Select Bibliography p. 172, for this and similar approaches).

But the only approach to anything like a ME dialect survey was first carried out in 1935 by Moore, Meech and Whitehall, who, from an examination of 266 localized texts, produced a dialect map showing the distribution of eleven ME phonological and morphological characteristics. They were then able to draw a second map dividing the country up into the following dialect areas—Kentish, Southern, south-east Midland, central east Midland, north-east Midland, south-west Midland, south-central west Midland, north-central west Midland, north-west Midland, northern.

A more recent, and much more satisfactory, survey is currently being carried out by Professor Angus McIntosh of Edinburgh University and Professor M. L. Samuels of Glasgow University. This survey, which began in 1952, has so far produced some highly illuminating results and shows promise of producing many more. In the first place, whereas Moore, Meech and Whitehall examined their selected texts for only eleven items, McIntosh and Samuels use hundreds, and by a far more careful use of these criteria are able to obtain results which are more precise. For example, Moore, Meech and Whitehall classify the third person plural pronoun, *hem*, etc., as forms simply having *h* or not-*h*- (i.e. as *h*- or *th*- forms), without eliciting various sub-sets of the two types. Many of these, however, have non-random geographical distributions and are therefore dialectally important, e.g. the form *hom* (an *h*- form) has a distribution of its own which does not emerge from the Moore–Meech–Whitehall treatment but which now turns out to be significant.

But McIntosh and Samuels' most important departure from the procedures of previous ME dialectologists is that they do not insist upon regarding written texts 'purely and simply as a sort of encoded form of some variety of spoken Middle English'.[17] They believe that the correct way to treat written dialectal material is first of all descriptively—to record the graphemic forms as they stand, without, for the time being, worrying about phonetic values. The contrasts in written forms, e.g. that between northern *bane* and southern *bone*, should be treated firstly as *graphemic*, not *phonetic*, contrasts. This approach is vindicated by the fact that there turn out to be regional variations between forms such as *sche* and *she*, *it* and *itt*, where the differences of spelling have no phonetic implications. Furthermore, although there are many graphemic contrasts of undoubted phonetic significance, speculation about their implications transforms them from 'verifiable pieces of information arrived at directly from the graphic substance, into debatable derivative conjuctures',[18] and renders them unsatisfactory material for entry on maps. McIntosh and Samuels' point is that, since this is an investigation into *Middle English* dialect, the basic material of which is in written form, the written forms must first of all be plotted on maps *before* any systematic phonetic interpretation can be attempted.

McIntosh and Samuels consider that at least four hundred ME texts survive which repay close examination, and that these are limited to a period 1350–1450, giving an important chronological control, as against Moore–Meech–Whitehall, who used twelfth- and thirteenth-century texts side by side with fourteenth- and fifteenth-century ones.

McIntosh and Samuels' techniques have freed them from the restriction of examining only previously localized texts. They began by using material from such texts, but then by comparing this with the total dialectal characteristics of other (unlocalized) texts, they were able to 'fit' these total dialectal characteristics into an area characterized by features of localized texts. This is what McIntosh refers to as the concept of 'fit', and it is of fundamental importance to their whole procedure. From reliable conclusions about textual provenance, based on the fit-technique, McIntosh and Samuels were able to go on and fill in their maps with a mass of information at points where hitherto there had been no information from localized texts available at all. As McIntosh says, 'This will in turn facilitate the task of further similar localisations, which, of course, as we proceed, will provide us with a series of maps with ever denser and denser coverage.'[19] Even texts 'translated' by a scribe from one dialect to another (a process which McIntosh regards as usually being very thoroughly done) can in many cases be used as evidence about the dialect of the scribe himself. The total amount of information gleaned from all the texts examined is ultimately to be published in map form.

It looks as if this new investigation of ME dialects is likely to have repercussions of the greatest significance for students of the history of the English language. 'We shall be able', writes McIntosh, 'to provide, map by map, a pretty clear and detailed account of the enormously involved and yet remarkably patterned dialectal picture in late Middle English times.'[20] Moreover, as McIntosh himself points out, it will complement the Dieth–Orton *Survey of English Dialects*, discussed in the next chapter, each survey adding to the value of the other. This last fact is one very good reason why I have thought it valuable to describe the new ME venture at some length.

The most recently published contribution towards a complete survey of ME dialects is that of G. Kristensson, *A Survey of Middle English Dialects 1290–1350: The Six Northern Counties and Lincoln-shire* (1967). This volume is intended as the first of a series, complementing *SED*, the geographical divisions chosen more or less corresponding to those used by *SED*. The investigation is based on place-names and surnames found in Lay Subsidy Rolls (and in other documents for Durham and Cheshire, for which no Subsidy Rolls exist). Such items as show a variation in form between one area and another have been mapped. This is a very thorough survey of the material chosen, and should contribute a great deal to our knowledge of ME dialects.

3 Dialect Study in England

Early interest in dialect

From an early period, writers were conscious of the existence of regional varieties of English. Trevisa's translation (1387) of Higden's universal history, the *Polychronicon* (ending originally in 1327, but continued in a later recension to 1352), notes that:

men of þe est wiþ men of þe west, as it were vndir þe same partie of heuene, acordeþ more in sownynge of speche þan men of þe norþ wiþ men of þe souþ; þerfore it is þat Mercii, þat beeþ men of myddel Engelond, as it were parteners of þe endes, vnderstondeþ bettre þe side langages, norþerne and souþerne, þan norþerne and souþerne vnderstondeþ eiþer oþer.

Al þe longage of þe Norþhumbres, and specialliche at ʒork, is so scharp, slitting, and frotynge, and vnschape, þat we souþerne men may þat longage vnneþe vnderstonde.

The last paragraph perhaps gains in force from the Gloucestershire dialect in which Trevisa's translation is couched, as well as being a somewhat embellished version of Higden's original Latin (*Tota lingua Northimborum, maxime in Eboraco, ita stridet incondita, quod nos australes eam vix intelligere possumus*). The passage derives ultimately, however, from the prologue of William of Malmesbury's *Gesta Pontificum Anglorum* (*c.* 1125), and is thus evidence of linguistic conditions some 250 years previous to Trevisa.

The use of dialect for literary purposes seems first to be recorded at the end of the fourteenth century in a fairly elaborate humorous imitation of an unspecified northern dialect in Chaucer's *Reeve's Tale*, and (about the same date or a little later) in the shepherd Mak's imitation of southern speech in the Wakefield *Second Shepherds' Play*. It is thus clear that by this time regional variation in speech was not merely a matter for comment but was (or could be) one of the distinguishing marks of a person which could be utilized for literary and dramatic ends. More significantly, Chaucer's (and possibly also the Wakefield Master's) imitation dialect suggests that one type of English is best, while other varieties are inferior. Chaucer's Cambridge students from Strother—a place

Fer in the north, I can nat telle where

are the first characters in English literature who are comic because they speak a regional, non-Standard, dialect, while Mak's assumed southern dialect perhaps implies that a 'yeoman of the king' (which is what Mak is pretending to be) would be expected to speak 'the King's'—i.e. a southern type of—English, and thus that 'southern' equalled 'Standard', a recognized official language. In all this, then, we can see the beginnings of a form of spoken Standard English.

CAXTON's comments on regional differences in language, given in the prologue to his *Eneydos* (1490), are well known, but are worth quoting again as a persuasive testimony to the current diversity in spoken and written English. The whole prologue should be read for the light it sheds on the state of contemporary English, but the following is the most relevant passage for present purposes:

And certaynly our langage now vsed varyeth ferre from that whiche was vsed and spoken whan I was borne / For we englysshe men / ben borne vnder the domynacyon of the mone, whiche is neuer stedfaste / but euer wauerynge / wexynge one season / and waneth & dyscreaseth another season / And that comyn englysshe that is spoken in one shyre varyeth from a nother. In so moche that in my dayes happened that certayn marchauntes were in a shippe in tamyse, for to haue sayled ouer the see into zelande / and for lacke of wynde, thei taryed atte forlond, and wente to lande for to refreshe them; And one of theym named sheffelde, a mercer, cam in-to an hows and axed for mete; and specyally he axyd after eggys; And the goode wyf answerde, that she coude speke no frenshe. And the marchaunt was angry, for he also coude speke no frenshe, but wolde haue hadde egges / and she vnderstode hym not / And thenne at laste a nother sayd that he wolde haue eyren / then the good wyf sayd that she vnderstod hym wel / Loo, what sholde a man in thyse dayes now wryte, egges or eyren / certaynly it is harde to playse euery man / by cause of dyuersite & chaunge of langage.

This is (excepting Trevisa) the first of a whole series of comments on dialect—merely one aspect of the vast body of opinion on the English language and its uses which becomes articulate from now on. From the sixteenth century onwards, remarks on dialect were often combined with others on the rising spoken standard,[1] usually in a disparaging way, and this emphasizes again the existence of a yardstick (namely Standard English) by which language could be judged. The Renaissance and the rise of 'national consciousness' made men more acutely aware of their national language, as opposed to the universal and anonymous Latin of the Middle Ages. Numerous opinions are expressed at this period about the vernacular vis-à-vis Latin, about the enrichment of English with loan-words, about 'aureate diction', about Standard English, about spelling, and a multitude of other topics. From this welter of comment, we have to pick out matter relevant to our own subject.

Sixteenth-century interest in dialect and also, more generally, in historical linguistics, was probably stimulated by the growing interest in antiquities: the Society of Antiquaries was founded in 1572, and the works of men like John Leland (1506?-52), John Norden (1548-1625?), William Camden (1551-1623) and others testify to these interests in 'the new spirit of creative inquiry and of crescent nationalism'.[2] Old English was also studied, sometimes by the same men who had an interest in dialect, for example Laurence Nowell (see pp. 43-4, below). Throughout this period and subsequently, scholars were constantly looking back to the roots of the language, and one may date the rise of historical linguistics in England from this time. Scholars often combined both antiquarian and linguistic pursuits, as, for example, Camden, who, in his *Britannia* (1586, and numerous later editions in Latin and English), deals not only with historical but linguistic aspects of his subject, and Sir Thomas Browne, who, besides writing his famous *Urn Burial*, wrote a tract on languages (especially OE) containing a list of Norfolk dialect words (see below). The study of antiquities and of linguistic history thus seem to have gone hand in hand from the start, and the place of dialect studies in this framework is obvious.

The study of dialect in England was taken up seriously by a small number of scholars, who are worthy of our attention as the precursors of A. J. Ellis, Joseph Wright, and, more recently, Harold Orton. Others merely noted its existence in passing, or commented on it as a form of English distinct from the Standard, but these comments, too, are valuable for the light they shed on contemporary regional dialect and its status. Obviously it is impossible to mention all who expressed opinions on dialect, and I have limited myself to a few relatively well-known writers and scholars, restricting my examples mainly to comments of a general nature. But these, I think, are representative enough to give some idea of thought on the subject during this early period. Their comments should be read in conjunction with the imitated dialect of literature of the same period.

SIR THOMAS SMITH (1513-77) is an early example. Both a scholar and a statesman, in 1542 he wrote *De Recta et Emendata Linguæ*

Graecæ Pronuntiatione, a work which was not, however, published until
1568. He was born in Essex, of an Essex father and a Lancashire
mother, and in the course of Book 2 of this work he makes many
references to English (and some to dialectal) pronunciation, and
gives English words in illustration of the sounds he wishes to be
used in Greek. Thus, for example, he says that the people of Derby
and beyond the Trent use Greek ʋ (?[yː]) more than those of the
south, and (an apparent error) that the Scots and northerners
say [byl] for *bull*.

To GEORGE PUTTENHAM, usually credited with writing *The
Arte of English Poesie* (1589), we are indebted for some general
remarks on regional dialect vis-à-vis literary English. His dictum
(in Book 3, Chapter 4) on the best type of English—'the vsuall
speach of the Court, and that of London and the shires lying about
London within lx. myles, and not much aboue'—I have already
quoted, and he observes that 'Northern-men...whether they be
noble men or gentlemen, or of their best clarkes', use a type of
English which is 'not so Courtly nor so currant as our Southerne
English is'. The same applies to any dialect used north of the Trent
and to the dialects of the far west, although Puttenham allows that
there are in every shire some 'gentlemen and others' who speak
and write as good Southern English as those of Middlesex or
Surrey, 'but not the common people of euery shire, to whom the
gentlemen, and also their learned clarkes do for the most part
condescend'.

An even clearer indication of the existence of a Standard English
to which it was desirable to conform is given by EDMUND COOTE's
spelling-book *The English Schoole-Master* (1597), published while
Coote was headmaster of the grammar school at Bury St Edmunds.
Coote seems to regard dialectal pronunciations as the chief source
of spelling errors:

I know not what can easily deceiue you in writing, vnlesse it bee by
imitating the barbarous speech of your countrie people, whereof I will
giue you a taste...Some people speake thus: the *mell* standeth on the *hell*,
for the *mill* standeth on the *hill*: so *knet* for *knit*: *bredg* for *bridg*: *knaw* for
gnaw: *knat* for *gnat*: *belk* for *belch*: *yerb* for *herb*: *griffe* for *graffe*: *yelk*
for *yolk*: *ream* for *realm*: *aferd* for *afraid*: *durt* for *dirt*, *gurt* for *girth*:
stomp for *stamp*: *ship* for *sheep*: *hafe* for *halfe*: *sample* for *exãmple*:
parfit for *perfect*; *dauter* for *daughter*: *carten* for *certaine*: *carchar* for
carcheife: *lease* for *leash*: *hur* for *hir*: *sur* and *suster* for *sir* and *sister*:
to *spat* for to *spit* etc.

So doe they commonly put *v* for *f* as *feale* for *veale*.
Take heed also you put not...*id* for *ed* as *vnitid* for *vnited*, which is
Scottish. And some ignorantly write a cup *a wine* for a cup *of wine*: and
other like absurdities.[3]

Coote does, however, allow that dialectal words may be used in
writing 'if they be peculiar termes, and not corrupting of words';
and a Northerner may use local words in private correspondence,
but it is more fitting to use 'the most knowne words' when he writes
publicly.

In 1605, a man of Dutch descent and an antiquary, RICHARD
VERSTEGAN alias ROWLANDS (*fl.* 1565–1620), published his *A
Restitution of Decayed Intelligence*, and in the course of his discussion
of the Germanic languages in Chapter 7 he comments on the changes
which have taken place so as to differentiate the Danish, Norwegian,
Swedish and Icelandic languages. Then he goes on:

This is a thing that easely may happen in so spatious a toung as this, it
beeing spoken in so many differĕt countries and regions, when wee see
that in some seueral parts of England it self, both the names of things,
and pronountiations of woords are somewhat different, and that among
the countrey people that neuer borrow any woords out of the Latin or
French, and of this different pronountiation one example in steed of many
shal suffise, as this: for pronouncing according as one would say at
London *I would eat more cheese yf I had it*, the northern man saith, *Ay
sud eat mare cheese gin ay hadet* and the westerne man saith: *Chud eat
more cheese an chad it*. Lo heer three different pronountiations in our
owne countrey in one thing, heereof many the lyke examples might be
alleaged.

RICHARD CAREW (1555–1620), well known for his *Survey of
Cornwall* (1602), was an enthusiastic user of dialect words in his
works, and brought his linguistic interests to the fore in his tract
on *The Excellency of the English Tongue* (probably written in 1595–6,
but not published until 1614). In passing, he remarks that the 'copi-
ousness' of English is shown in the diversity of dialect (social and
regional):

for wee haue court, and wee haue countrye Englishe, wee haue Northern
and Southerne, grosse and ordinary, which differ ech from other, not
only in the terminacions, but alsoe in many wordes, termes, and phrases...

And his list of expressions for getting rid of someone, although
not all of them are regional in origin, is worthy to be compared with
those elicited by question VIII.7.9 in the *Survey of English Dialects*
(To get rid of someone quickly who was being a bit of a nuisance,
you'd say:...Go away!)

Dialect usages are discussed by ALEXANDER GIL (1564/5–1635), High Master of St Paul's School, in Chapter 6 of his *Logonomia Anglica*, 1619 (2nd corrected edn., 1621). Indeed, his account of seventeenth-century dialectal pronunciation is 'the best', according to Dobson, who admits, however, that Gil probably had no exceptional knowledge of dialectal speech, and that the forms and expressions he lists were well-known dialectalisms. However, his treatment is a systematic one, aiming to characterize the speech of each of the main dialect areas. His remarks, apart from their intrinsic interest, are of value for our knowledge of the chronology of the Great Vowel Shift. Thus, in the north, he says, they use *ai* for *j* (i.e. ME *ī*), and *au* for *ou* (i.e. ME *ū*), suggesting that northern English had already reached approximately [ai] and [au] stages in the development of these two sounds, whereas in the south the first element of each diphthong had not yet been lowered to [a]. Northerners, he says, also use *ea* ([ɛə]) for *ë* ([eː]) as in *meat*, and for *o* ([ɔː]) as in *both*; and in Lincolnshire (his native county) they use *oa* (?[ɔə]) in *toes* and *hose*. In morphology, the north uses *seln* for *self* and *hez* for *hath*, while northern lexical idiosyncrasies are *sark* (for *shirt*), *gang* (for *go*), *yed* or *yöd* (for *went* and *was going* respectively).

The southern dialect has *v* for *f* and *f* for *v*, *z* for *s*, and *o* for *a* before a nasal (all well-known ME southern phonological features). It also uses *cham* for *I am* and *chil* for *I will*.

Gil states that the eastern dialect is remarkable for a 'general thinness'. His evidence on this dialect and on the speech of those he refers to as the *Mopsæ* is of very great value for our knowledge of early NE vocalic pronunciations, especially of ME *ā* and *ē̜*.[4] As eastern, he notes *fïr* for *fjer* 'fire' ([iː] < south-eastern *ē̜* < OE *ȳ*), *kiver* for *kuver* 'cover' ([ɪ] < OFr [y], a pronunciation probably still current in the eastern dialects; cf. *EDG*, §219); *ea* for *a* (as in *deans* for *dans* 'dance'); *v* for *f* (as in *velöu* for *felöu* 'fellow') and *z* for *s* (as in *zai* for *sai* 'say').

The western dialects Gil condemns as most barbarous of all, especially that of Somerset. He picks out for mention among lexical usages *sax* ('knife'), *nem* or *nim* ('take'), *vang* ('take, accept', etc.) in, e.g., *hï vangd tu mi at ðe vant* ('he fanged to me at the font', i.e. he sponsored me at baptism). He gives the phrase *hj* [an error for *hï*] *iz gön avisht* (< OE *on fiscoþe*); *z* is used for *s* as in *zit*; *throttïn* is used for *thirtin*, *narger* for *naröuer* ('narrower'); the p.p. prefix *i-* (< OE *ge-*) is retained, as in *ifrör* or *ivrör* ('frozen'), and *idü* ('done'). Finally, he comments on the old weak endings of nouns, as in *hözn* ('hosen') and *pëzn* ('peasen').

On the whole, although Gil gives only a selection of dialectal features, what he gives appears to be accurate.

The *Orthoepia Anglicana* (1640) of SIMON DAINES, a Suffolk schoolmaster, briefly castigates vulgar and dialectal forms. The author disapprovingly cites 'vulgar' usages such as *a nox, a nasse, my nuncle, thy naunt,* and cautions wariness of:

the barbarous custome of the vulgars in their pronunciation, as *shoen,* for *shoes,* an ordinary fault in some countreyes [= 'parts'], to put *N,* for *S,* and *E,* for *I*; as *mell,* for *mill*; *delited,* for *delighted,* &c. setting aside the absudities used among the vulgar in *Sommerset-shire,* and other remote places, as not worth the nominating, so much as by way of reprehension...

JOHN WALLIS (1616–1703), linguist, scientist, mathematician and cleric, published in 1653 a *Grammatica Linguæ Anglicanæ,* in which occur a few references to dialectal pronunciations, for example the use of *keen, meece, leece* (beside *kine, mice, lice*), south-eastern forms showing reflexes of ME $\bar{e}$ < OE $\bar{y}$.

An antiquarian who also had an interest in language was SIR THOMAS BROWNE (1605–82), author of the famous *Urn Burial.* We may note here his Tract 8, 'Of Languages, and Particularly of the Saxon Tongue', which contains a list of words

of common use in *Norfolk,* or peculiar to the East Angle Countries; as, *Bawnd, Bunny, Thurck, Enemmis, Sammodithee, Mawther, Kedge, Seele, Straft, Clever, Matchly, Dere, Nicked, Stingy, Noneare, Feft, Thepes, Gosgood, Kamp, Sibrit, Fangast, Sap, Cothish, Thokish, Bide owe, Paxwax*: of these and some others of no easie originals, when time will permit, the resolution may be attempted.

CHRISTOPHER COOPER (*c.* 1655–98), schoolmaster and cleric, wrote a *Grammatica Linguæ Anglicanæ,* which appeared in 1685, and in an English edition, *The English Teacher,* two years later. Chapter 19 of Part 2 of this work, 'De Barbara dialecto', warns against the use of dialectal (also colloquial, vulgar or archaic) forms such as *bushop* ('bishop'), *dud* ('did'), *leece* ('lice'), *meece* ('mice'), *nother* ('neither'), *wuts* ('oats'), *shet* ('shut'), *hwutter* ('hotter'), *yerth* ('earth'), *'ent* ('is not'), *git* ('get'), *vitles* ('victuals').

DANIEL DEFOE (1660–1731) makes some percipient remarks about local dialect in his *Tour thro' the whole Island of Great Britain* (1724–27). On Somerset:

It cannot pass my Observation here, that, when we are come this Length from *London,* the Dialect of the *English* Tongue, or the Country-way of expressing themselves, is not easily understood. It is the same in many

Parts of *England* besides, but in none in so gross a Degree, as in this Part. As this Way of boorish Speech is in *Ireland* called, *The Brogue upon the Tongue*, so here it is named *Jouring*. It is not possible to explain this fully by Writeing, because the Difference is not so much in the Orthography, as in the Tone and Accent; their abridging the Speech, *Cham*, for *I am*; *Chill* for *I will*; *Don*, for *do on*, or *put on*; and *Doff*, for *do off*, or *put off*; and the like. (5th edn., 1753)

And he goes on to retail an amusing story of a schoolboy from Martock in Somerset, whom he heard reading aloud from the Bible in the local dialect. Defoe is also the first writer to remark on the Northumbrian 'burr':

I must not quit *Northumberland* without remarking, that the Natives of this County, of the antient Race or Families, are distinguished by a *Shibboleth* upon their Tongues in pronouncing the Letter *R*, which they cannot utter without an hollow Jarring in the Throat, by which they are as plainly known, as a Foreigner is in pronouncing the *Th*: this they call the *Northumberland R*, or *Wharle*; and the Natives value themselves upon that Imperfection, because, forsooth, it shews the Antiquity of their Blood.

THOMAS SHERIDAN (1719–88), compiled *A Course of Lectures on Elocution* (1762), and in Lecture 2 of this work he makes a good many remarks on the 'vices' of 'rustic pronunciation', such speech obviously being of very inferior status in his mind, especially Cockney.

Nay in the very metropolis two different modes of pronunciation prevail, by which the inhabitants of one part of the town, are distinguished from those of the other. One is current in the city, and is called the cockney; the other at the court-end, and is called the polite pronunciation. As amongst these various dialects, one must have the preference, and become fashionable, it will of course fall to the lot of that which prevails at court, the source of fashions of all kinds. All other dialects, are sure marks, either of a provincial, rustic, pedantic, or mechanic education; and therefore have some degree of disgrace annexed to them.

He goes on to instance various Anglo-Irish pronunciations or 'defects'. As for the Cockneys, the hallmark of their speech is the frequent interchange of [v] and [w]—they call 'veal' *weal*, 'vinegar' *winigar*, and conversely 'winter' *vinter*, 'well' *vell*. Also, unstressed *-ow* is reduced to *-er*, and *r* is added to proper nouns ending in *-a*, e.g. *Belinda* > *Belinder*. However:

With respect to the rustic pronunciation, prevailing in the several counties, I mean amongst the gentry, and such as have a liberal education, there does not seem to be any general errour of this sort; their deviations being for the most part, only in certain words, sounded in a peculiar manner by each county; and which probably owe their present pronunciation, to the continuation of the old custom; which like other antiquated modes, changes more slowly in proportion to their distance from, or want of communication with the court. And these deviations not being very numerous, as was before observed, may easily be set right.

But he censures the 'dropping' of *h-*, a feature which 'is daily gaining ground among the politer part of the world'. The distinction made here between the provincialisms of the gentry and those of 'the rest' is of special interest, suggesting that a certain number of regional pronunciations were common among the upper classes.

At the end of the eighteenth century, JOHN WALKER, one-time actor become teacher and elocutionist, gave in the second edition of his *Pronouncing Dictionary* (1791) rules to be observed by the Irish and Scots for obtaining 'a just Pronunciation of English', followed by some remarks on dialect:

There is scarecely any part of England, remote from the capital, where a different system of pronunciation does not prevail. As in Wales they pronounce the sharp consonants for the flat, so in Somersetshire they pronounce many of the flat instead of the sharp: thus for *Somersetshire*, they say *Zomerzetzhire*; for *father, vather*; for *think*, THink; and for *sure, zhure.*
There are dialects peculiar to Cornwall, Lancashire, Yorkshire, and every distant county in England...

He concludes his remarks with some observations on peculiarities of Cockney pronunciation (pronouncing *w* for *v* and vice-versa, etc.).

With Walker I end this list of illustrations, since from the beginning of the nineteenth century we come face to face with new movements in philology which were to bring about an entirely different approach to dialectal—as to all linguistic—studies, culminating in the systematic and scientific description of dialects as viewed historically, and the abandonment of the old prescriptive attitude well seen, for example, in Walker himself. Furthermore, whereas pre-nineteenth-century historical work in language was merely sporadic, in the nineteenth century a continuity of scholarship was established, in which generations of men successively built up and developed their subject (see further below, pp. 46 ff.).[5]

Glossaries and early dialect literature

From a quite early period there were attempts to compile glossaries of local dialect. Such are, for example, among the earlier ones, S. Pegge's *Alphabet of Kenticisms* (1735–6), and (all in MS only) W. Chorlton's *Glossary of Provincial Words used in the Neighbourhood of Irlam o' th' Height, and Clifton, near Manchester* (1746), W. Cuming's *Collection of Words and Phrases used in Dorset* (*c.* 1750), J. Losh's *Collection of North Country Words* (1783), and J. Atkinson's *Glossary of the Provincialisms in use in Westmoreland* (*c.* 1797). In addition, numerous words, phrases, pronunciations and so on received comment in volumes of the type *The Natural History and Antiquities of...*, and *A General Survey of the Agriculture of...*, e.g. those of William Marshall.

Dialect words sometimes found their way into seventeenth- and eighteenth-century dictionaries, e.g. Stephen Skinner's *Etymologicon Linguæ Anglicanæ* (1671), the first general dictionary to list Lincolnshire dialect words; Elisha Coles's *English Dictionary* (1676); John Kersey's *Dictionarium Anglo-Britannicum* (1708); Nathan Bailey's *Universal Etymological English Dictionary* (1721). Somewhat different from these, and substantially earlier, is a work by the cleric Dean LAURENCE NOWELL (*c.* 1514–76), an eminent antiquary, one of the pioneers of OE scholarship, and a transcriber of numerous OE and Latin manuscripts.

Nowell's chief claim to fame in the field of English studies rests on his compilation of what later came to be called the *Vocabularium Saxonicum*, the first attempt at a dictionary of OE, and a source for Somner's *Dictionarium Saxonico-Latino-Anglicum* (1659). It was apparently written about 1565, and is now preserved in the Bodleian Library as MS Selden supra 63.

The *Vocabularium* is of interest for various reasons, not the least being that Nowell supplied illustrative citations for many of the words defined, the book thus being an early example of a 'citation dictionary'. But for students of local dialect, Nowell's work is of special importance in that it includes words from contemporary regional dialect, cited by the author whenever he was aware of the survival, in local dialect, of an OE word which had dropped out of use in Standard English. Being by birth and upbringing a Lancashire man, it is natural that he felt best qualified to cite words from Lancashire dialect, from which he records 173 words, but there are also seventeen words from other parts of England, some of which were added by Nowell's pupil William Lambarde. An analysis of the dialect words has shown that the collection is a very accurate one,[6] and it thus constitutes an important contribution to our knowledge of the Lancashire dialect in the early NE period, being moreover a source that was untapped by Joseph Wright in the compilation of his *English Dialect Dictionary*.

As an illustration of Nowell's contribution to dialectology in the *Vocabularium*, the following may be quoted:

Haȝan. Hawes. The frute of the white thorne or hawthorne. Lanc., hagges.

To show the usefulness of such a citation it need only be pointed out that (*a*) modern dialect forms of *haw* with medial [g] (cf. *SED* IV.11.6), e.g. *hagag, hag, haggle*, etc., are difficult to derive from OE *haga*, since OE *-ag-* regularly gives *-aw-* in modern English, thus *haw*; (*b*) the first mention of *-g-* forms in *haw* in *OED*, apart from fifteenth-century *hawghe*, is from the nineteenth century; and (*c*) here we have a *-g-* form from Lancashire attested as early as 1565, suggesting perhaps the existence of a base form with gemination, e.g. **hagga*. If a further example is needed, it is only necessary to compare *SED*'s recording (Du, La, Y) of *reckan* ('domestic crane', V.3.4/5) with:

Racateȝe. A chayne. Lanc., a racanteth is the chayne wher with the potte hangeth over the fire.[7]

JOHN RAY (1627–1705), a naturalist, famous for his systems of classification and a member of the Royal Society, produced—in addition to a collection of proverbs—*A Collection of Words not Generally Used* (1674; revised and augmented edn., 1691), the first attempt at a dialect dictionary in English. Various contributors provided Ray with material for the book (see the Preface), which is divided into two parts, dealing respectively with the north and south of England. The word is given, followed by its definition and sometimes a rough designation (usually the county) of the area in which it occurred. One of Ray's noted collaborators was Ralph Thoresby, a northern scholar, who sent a letter to Ray from Leeds, dated 27 April 1703, containing a list of local words as a supplement to or commentary on Ray's own collection.

In the eighteenth century another collection of provincialisms was made by FRANCIS GROSE (*c.* 1731–91), an antiquary and artist, author of books on military antiquities, historical and topographical works, who published a *Provincial Glossary, with a Collection of Local Proverbs, and Popular Superstitions* in 1787 (new, corrected edn., 1790), which covered the whole country—only Ray had done this before. In his preface Grose notes that:

Divers partial collections have been occasionally made...these are, in this work, all united under one alphabet, and augmented by many hundred words collected by the Editor in the different places wherein they are used.

Grose's sources were, among others, Ray's *Proverbs*, Bobbin's *Lancashire Dialect*, *The Gentleman's Magazine*, and many of the county histories. In the *Glossary*, the entries are arranged in alphabetical order, with a brief explanation and—very occasionally—citation of early forms (e.g. s.v. Yewd or Yod [< OE *eode*], quotations from Chaucer and Spenser are given), and some indication of the area of provenance—the initials N, S, W (north, south, west) or the relevant county, C meaning 'common', i.e. 'used in several counties in the same sense'. It is significant that there is no 'E' (east): 'The East country scarcely afforded a sufficiency of words to form a division.'

From the beginning of the nineteenth century, the glossaries become too frequent to exemplify, but a very full list, including most of the above, is given in the Bibliography to *EDD* (Vol. vi). Two nineteenth-century general dialect glossaries worthy of special note are J. O. Halliwell's *Dictionary of Archaic and Provincial Words* (1847), and Thomas Wright's *Dictionary of Obsolete and Provincial English* (1857).

The compilation of glossaries was accompanied by the writing of dialect poems, dialogues and other short works, intended to show the linguistic features of the dialect under consideration and, to this extent, therefore, 'linguistic' as well as 'literary' in their aim and orientation. One of the earliest was Andrew Borde's twenty-six lines of doggerel verse imitative of the Cornish dialect included in his *Fyrst Boke of the Introduction of Knowledge* (1547), and later examples include R. Brathwaite, *The Mushrome, Eglogue between Billie and Jockie* (1615; We); George Meriton, *A Yorkshire Dialogue* (1683; YNR); G. Stuart, *Joco-Serious Discourse, in Two Dialogues* (1686; Nb); *The Obliging Husband and Imperious Wife...in Witty and Ingenious Dialogues* (1717; D); *An Exmoor Scolding* and *Exmoor Courtship* (1746; D); *Norfolk Poetical Miscellany* (1744); J. Collier ('Tim Bobbin'), *View of the Lancashire Dialect* (1746); W. Hutton, *A Dialogue in the Vulgar Language of Storth and Arnside* (1760; We); R. Dawes, *The Origin of the Newcastle Burr* ('A Satirical Poem', 2nd edn., 1767); C. Anstey, *An Election Ball* (1776; So); J. Hutton, *A Tour to the Caves...in the West Riding of Yorkshire* (1781). From

45

the beginning of the nineteenth century, these works, like the glossaries, become too frequent to select from, their vogue no doubt considerably encouraged by current Romantic trends (cf., for example, J. Stagg, *The Cumbrian Minstrel; being a Poetical Miscellany of Legendary, Gothic, and Romantic Tales,* published in Manchester in 1821), but a very full list, including the above, is given in the Bibliography to *EDD* (Vol. vi).

The beginnings of systematic dialect study

As explained in Chapter 1, the earliest systematic study of dialect arose out of the controversy centring round the Neo-Grammarian principle of the inviolability of sound-laws. This controversy prompted scholars of language to test their theories on the contemporary living dialects, and led to the planning of the first linguistic atlases in Germany and France. The first, German, atlas was initiated in 1876 by Georg Wenker, but Gilliéron's *Atlas Linguistique de la France* (published 1902–12) was ultimately of greater importance for the development of linguistic geography. It is not necessary to trace the investigation of dialect carried out on the Continent, but it is helpful to realize that serious and systematic work on dialect began there,[8] and obviously gave an impetus to similar studies in England. Indeed, one of the earliest and greatest of English dialectologists, Joseph Wright, a Yorkshire miner's son who later became Professor of Comparative Philology at Oxford, was trained in the Neo-Grammarian school in Germany.

As interest in English dialect continued to grow, the English Dialect Society was founded in 1873 by W. W. Skeat, with the special intention of producing an English Dialect Dictionary. Skeat, an indefatigable philologist and dialectologist, was the first secretary of this society and himself edited many glossaries for publication by the Society. In all, eighty glossaries were printed or reprinted, but by 1896, when the *English Dialect Dictionary* was commenced, it was considered that the society's function had been fulfilled and it was wound up.

Joseph Wright's *English Dialect Dictionary* (1898–1905) drew on all the sources mentioned above, plus others such as county histories, accounts of industries (e.g. mining), agricultural surveys and natural histories. It aimed at a comprehensive inclusion of all dialect words current in Britain, or known to have been in use during the previous two hundred years. Wright intended to achieve this aim by supplementing his material from the existing glossaries with the results of a postal questionnaire sent out to 12,000 people. The problems of collecting and arranging such a vast amount of material are described in Mrs Wright's biography of her husband as well as (more briefly) in the preface to *EDD* itself. Unfortunately, the usefulness of the Dictionary is vitiated by the fact that its material is extracted from glossaries whose dates range over too long a period of time and that the designations of locality are far too vague: we need to know *precisely* where a word was recorded, and not merely its county or area. The etymologies are also often suspect. But in spite of these and other failings, *EDD*, used carefully, is an indispensable source of earlier forms for the lexicologist. It should be noted that, for one reason or another, some glossaries escaped Wright's attention for inclusion in *EDD*, and have received notice since, and secondly that the compilation of glossaries did not stop after the EDS became defunct and *EDD* was published (see the Select Bibliography, pp. 172–3).

The last part of *EDD* included Wright's *English Dialect Grammar*, also published separately in 1905. It was based on the *Dictionary*, to some extent on the enormous stock of information in A. J. Ellis's *On Early English Pronunciation* (1889; see below), and on the results of a questionnaire pamphlet sent out to more than 1200 people, the latter containing some 2400 words with instructions how to transcribe accurately the dialect pronunciation in a specially devised phonetic alphabet. As Wright admits, only comparatively few of the people who replied were of real help, since most of them had no previous experience of using a phonetic alphabet. Nor were his informants always natives of the locality from which they collected information—another likely source of error and imprecision. And again, as in *EDD*, references are far too general—'Wm.' (Westmorland), 'nw. Yks.', etc. As compared with the standards demanded of modern dialect surveys, *EDG* is greatly lacking, but Wright's aim was merely to compile a general survey of all the dialects, exhibiting their main characteristic features. In this he succeeded and although the work may be said to be both unoriginal and imprecise, because of its handy tabulation of material it is still much used by modern linguists.

EDD and *EDG* were not Wright's only labours in the field of dialect. In 1892 the English Dialect Society published his *Grammar of the Dialect of Windhill* (his own native dialect), the first systematic description of a single English dialect, which was to be the model for numerous others, many of them written by foreigners or at the encouragement of foreigners. Following Wright, all these monographs are written from an historical, diachronic point of view: they accord with the Neo-Grammarian teaching, and aim to record only 'genuine' (i.e. traditional, historical) forms, neglecting non-genuine intrusions (e.g. from Standard English). Of these early grammars and their successors, only H. Kökeritz's *Phonology of the Suffolk Dialect* (1932) includes a 'descriptive' section before going on to consider the sounds historically, and this method has since been followed in more recent monographs. As Kökeritz says (p. xiii):

My intention has been to paint a true and faithful picture of the Suff. dialect as now spoken, not to give an idealized and beautifully retouched photograph of the speech habits of very old people to the exclusion of those of the younger generations.

Although many recent monographs, and *SED* itself, are still based primarily on the speech of the over-sixties, the aim is now simply to record what is heard, not to hunt out 'pure' dialectal forms. The investigation must comprise first of all a description of the data, and secondarily an historical examination. These monographs deal either with the dialect of a single locality (like Wright's) or of a county (like Kökeritz's). A further group of monographs based on the analysis of dialect authors and gramophone recordings of the speech of British prisoners of war were undertaken by the school of Professor A. Brandl of Berlin, and range in time from 1911 to 1937, but the methods involved were obviously different ones from those of Wright and his followers.

Harold Orton's *Phonology of a South Durham Dialect* (1933) was one of the distinguished contributions in the school of Wright and has itself been the model for many more such theses and monographs, often inspired by Orton and produced from Leeds University, where he was Professor of English Language from 1947 until 1964. These more modern works are considered later in this chapter, together with *SED*.

Most of the early investigators of dialect were concerned chiefly with vocabulary. The first person to describe all the dialects of England phonetically was A. J. Ellis. Ellis's four volumes, *On Early English Pronunciation* (1869–74), were supplemented by a fifth, subtitled *The Existing Phonology of English Dialects Compared with that of West Saxon Speech*. This vast enterprise can lay claim to being the only work remotely approaching a survey of all the English dialects (including Scotland and Wales and a small portion of Ireland) before the Dieth–Orton survey. Ellis obtained information of various types from 1145 localities and 811 people, but did not actually print it all. His intention was:

> to determine with considerable accuracy the different forms *now*, or *within the last hundred years*, assumed by the descendants of the same original word in passing through the mouths of uneducated people, speaking an inherited language, in all parts of Great Britain where English is the ordinary medium of communication between peasant and peasant. (p. 1)

From this it can be seen that Ellis's bias, although 'descriptive', was also very definitely historical, and aimed to exclude anything but older forms—forms which, representing the direct traditional development of OE (ON, Fr, etc.) sounds, could be found only on the lips of 'the peasantry', and not on those of educated people.

The basic tool of Ellis's investigation was, first of all, a 'comparative specimen', containing 'at least many typical words and constructions run into sentences', which he tried to have 'translated' into the dialect of the locality under consideration. He found, however, that this did not work adequately, and four years later compiled a Classified Word List, consisting of words containing the original sounds whose reflexes he wished to record, e.g. OE *swā*, ON *sveinn*, Fr *beauté*. With this he gave a list of the principal sounds to be observed. About 1700 lists were sent out, mostly to clergymen, and about 500 were returned. In 1879 Ellis adopted a much shorter specimen called the Dialect Test, containing seventy-six words in seven sentences, the words being intended to exemplify all the principal classes of historical sounds. This is printed in *EEP* (p. 8*), with the words numbered and the addition of the original notes designed to draw his informants' attention to the points of the investigation, e.g.:

1. **So.** Note whether *s* or *z*. Note whether *o* has a vanishing *ŏŏ* after it as in London...
10. **Right.** First mark the *r*, whether it is trilled with the tip of the tongue...

The three successive methods of obtaining information were 'addressed to educated people who did not speak dialect naturally', but who tried to give accurate impressions of local pronunciation. Ellis admits that this method entailed many possibilities of error, which he himself had spent hours, days, even months and years, trying to avoid. He excuses himself from not going direct to 'the peasantry' on the grounds that dialect informants are bilingual and would be likely to adopt a refined accent if he were to visit them in person. However, he did occasionally obtain information from people such as domestic servants and railway porters, although his principal source of information was the students of Whitelands Training College for teachers in Chelsea who had been in contact from an early age with dialect speakers or who had themselves been dialect speakers in their childhood.

The disadvantages of a postal questionnaire sent to educated people acting as intermediaries are described well by Ellis in his Introduction, namely that 'the sounds may have been wrongly appreciated' (i.e. perceived); 'the sounds may have been wrongly imitated'; the type of RP used by his helpers may have been different from Ellis's own; some dialectal sounds could not be properly represented by the ordinary (Standard English) orthography, and the spellings used by the helpers in such cases were either unexplained or admitted to be inexplicable; Ellis's own interpretation of the helpers' spellings was doubtful. Added to all this is the fact that his helpers from White-lands College were untrained in dialect work—a source of errors of many different kinds (e.g. inexpert interviewing and recording)—and may have not always retained very precise impressions of the dialect they themselves knew. Finally, Ellis used, for the representation of his basic information, his 'palaeotype'. This method of notation (see Part VIII of the Preliminary Matter) cannot be described in detail here: suffice it to say that it is both tortuous and imprecise, and so has been a constant source of irritation to subsequent dialectologists. To give but one example, Ellis describes his notation (y_1) as 'a modification of Fr. u in a direction not precisely ascertained' (? IPA [ʏ]).

These deficiencies of method (many of which Ellis himself recognized) have been dwelt on at some length here, since method is of the utmost importance in the planning and supervision of any dialect survey. It should be said in conclusion, in spite of all objections, that Ellis's results are sometimes quite impressive, and even though he was working with inadequate tools, modern dialectal research often confirms his findings. Dieth's judgement of Ellis's work as 'a tragedy ... a huge store of information which every dialectologist consults, but, more often than not, rejects as inaccurate and wrong'[9] is, in my opinion, too drastic, and Dieth, if he had lived, might have wished to modify his strictures in the light of some of the results yielded by *SED*. For all Ellis's inadequacies, his book is an indispensable source of reference to the dialectologist who wants earlier confirmation of his own findings, and it was at least a beginning on which later research could build. Neither, when one gets to know it, is the book as formidable as it at first appears.

What, however, *were* Ellis's results? On the basis of the information he obtained, he was able to define six Divisions—'with sufficiently distinct differences and characters'—namely Southern, Western, Eastern, Midland, Northern, and Lowland (Scottish). These six major Divisions are further divided into forty-two Districts 'in each of which a sensible similarity of pronunciation prevails', a half of these being further broken down into Varieties and, in eight cases, even Sub-varieties. Ellis gives two maps of the Divisions and Districts, and the main part of the 900-page book, after his Preliminary Matter and Introduction, is a consideration of each District and Variety, in turn.

In addition to defining these areas and partly as a basis for them, Ellis had also drawn what he called the Ten Transverse Lines. These are isoglosses based on various items of the data, drawn horizontally across the country from coast to coast. They comprise: (1) the northern limit of the pronunciation of [ʌ] (as distinct from [ɒ]) in *some*; (2) the southern limit of the pronunciation of [ɒ] in *some*; (3) the northern limit of the 'reverted' (retroflex) *r*; (4) the southern limit of the use of *t'* for the definite article; (5) the northern limit of the use of *the* for the definite article; (6) the southern limit of [uː] in *house*; (7) the northern limit of the use of *t'* for the definite article; (8) the southern limit in northern England of *some* as an [ʌ]-type, on travelling from Scotland into England; (9) the northern limit of an [ɒ]-type in *some*; (10) the L. line—the limit between Lowland Scotch and northern English speech.

The Survey of English Dialects and other recent dialect research

We come now to a consideration of the Dieth–Orton *Survey of English Dialects*. Planned in 1946, the *Survey* was the result of a proposal made to Harold Orton (later appointed to the Chair of English Language at the University of Leeds) by Professor Eugen Dieth, of the University of Zürich. Drawing attention to the fact that many European countries already had dialect surveys, Dieth gave persuasive evidence for the need and value of such a new survey in an article in *Essays and Studies*,[10] and after five years' work the Dieth–Orton *Questionnaire for a Linguistic Atlas of England* was published in 1952, having gone through five successive revisions and much practical testing.

Following the earlier, continental atlases in aim and, to a very large extent, in method,[11] *SED* has been from the outset specifically

51

interested in a single kind of English, namely traditional vernacular—the sort of dialect normally spoken by elderly people (sixty plus) belonging to the same social class in rural communities, and in particular by those who were or had been employed in farming—'for it is amongst the rural populations that the traditional types of vernacular English are best preserved to-day'.[12] *SED* thus has an historical bias.

The basic tool of *SED*, as of any dialect survey, is its questionnaire. In accordance with the notion that the best traditional dialect is to be obtained in rural communities, the *Questionnaire* was specially biased towards farming people, contained only notions which could be universally comprehended and excluded specialized matter such as that associated with mining and fishing. The *Questionnaire* now comprises over 1300 questions, aimed at eliciting items of lexical (mostly), phonological, morphological and syntactical significance. The questions are drawn up in full, thus ensuring that the answers to each question are strictly comparable.[13] They are divided into nine books as follows: I. The Farm; II. Farming; III. Animals; IV. Nature; V. The House and Housekeeping; VI. The Human Body; VII. Numbers, Time and Weather; VIII. Social Activities; IX. States, Actions and Relations.

A few examples of questions will indicate their nature and purpose more fully; * denotes that a word is required for its phonological importance, † for its morphological importance and ‡ for its syntactical importance. Wanted lexical items are not specially marked; the words in bold type are the 'key-words', i.e. the notions to be named; ... beginning a question means 'What do you call'; □ means that a picture is shown, if necessary.

I.7.6   What do you dig the ground with? **Spade***.
III.13.16 ...the animal that makes a noise like *hee-haw*? **Donkey**.
V.1.17   Coal is very useful, but gold of course is even.... **more useful**†.
VII.1.12   How many is this? **Twenty-one***.
           If your daughter is as old as that today, you'd say she is.... **twenty-one**‡ today.

           Note the order.

Thus, by means of these four questions, the investigators aimed to elicit (1) an example of the development of ME *ă* lengthened to *ā* in open syllables; (2) the numerous local names for the donkey; (3) the comparative forms of the adjective *useful*; (4) (as well as the pronunciation of *-one*) the order of the elements in the compound numeral *twenty-one* (*one-and-twenty* sometimes occurs). In addition

to these simple questions there are one or two 'talking' questions
(including 'reverse' questions intended to bring out a variety of
meanings for one word rather than the synonyms for one notion),
such as:

IV.10.1–4   What trees have you round here? **Birch*, oak*, elm*, elder,
          willow.**
I.1.11   Rev. What's the **barn** for and where is it?
V.7.20   Rev. What do you mean by **broth**?

Naturally, the questions have produced information not strictly
limited to the purposes they were designed for, so that, for example,
the (phonological) question on *spade* has also produced lexical
variants for this notion (e.g. *shovel, spit*), and the (lexical) question
on *donkey* has produced phonetic variants in the word *donkey*
itself, especially in the stressed vowel (e.g. [ʌ], [a]). The field-workers
occasionally ran into trouble over this, as when, in response to the
question I.7.14 What do you call this (showing a picture)? **Ladder*,**
they obtained the answer *stee* in much of northern England. *Stee*
was, of course, a perfectly genuine response, but the field-workers
were under obligation to obtain *ladder* for phonological purposes
and had therefore to press their informants for it.

    The *Questionnaire* for *SED* is undoubtedly a very expert piece of
work. The compilers had had much experience in field-work themselves and used this to advantage when drawing up their list of
questions. They also had the benefit of *EDD* and numerous other
glossaries and monographs. Finally, as noted above, the *Questionnaire* was well tested and constantly revised, its original 800 questions
growing in the process to more than 1300 in its present form.
In spite of this, some questions have yielded very scant information,
e.g.:

VII.8.8   We could and would do lots of things in this world [rattle some
         coins].... **if** we had the money.

which has produced—uniformly and tediously—simply *if* (cf.
Verstegan's comparable phrases, p. 38, above). There are other
questions which one would have liked to see included, e.g. one bringing out the contrast between *catching cold* (? northern) and *catching
a cold*, questions eliciting local terms for the sparrow, the cuckoo
(northern *gowk*), the butterfly, the centipede, the clothes-horse,
dumplings, a dunghill, a parson (*priest* was recorded, according to
EDD, from the four northern counties, up until the end of the last
century), being pregnant (of a human being), the various pronuncia-

53

tions of *hang* and *sneeze*. But no questionnaire can search out everything, and at the end it is necessary to begin again, since not until one has finished does one know what to look for.[14]

Unlike some earlier questionnaires, notably those of Germany, France and Italy, the Dieth–Orton *Questionnaire* deliberately avoids asking informants to translate any words or phrases into their own dialect, and advisedly so, since questions of this nature are bound in themselves to suggest the response to the informant. Indeed, some questions in *SED* were scrupulously changed to remove any element of suggestiveness, so that in the final version, question I.1.8, for example, What do you call the place where you keep your cows? was changed to What do you call the place where you keep the animals that give you milk? so as not to suggest to the informant a response including the element *cow-*.

The Dieth–Orton *Questionnaire* has been dwelt on at some length, not only because it is the fundamental tool of *SED*, or even for its own intrinsic interest, but because in discussing it the basic philosophy and conception of the survey (and other surveys) emerge so clearly. It is now time to turn to the use of the *Questionnaire* in the field.

The field-work for *SED* was carried out by nine trained field-workers, between 1948 and 1961; on them depended the final choice of locality for investigation and of informants, although naturally some preliminary guidance was given and a general provisional network was decided on at the beginning of the survey, taking into consideration natural features and their possible influence on local dialect boundaries. Preference was given to agricultural communities that had had a fairly stable population of about five hundred inhabitants for a century or so, and newly built-up localities were avoided. Very few towns were included, although some recording was done, for example, in Leeds and Sheffield. Ultimately the network extended to 313 localities. Such a comparatively thin coverage has been criticized,[15] and indeed a closer mesh would have been in every way desirable, as the progenitors of *SED* were the first to admit. But shortage of time and money meant making the best of limited resources.

One of the great strengths of *SED* is its rigorous selection of informants who would best exemplify the type of dialect under scrutiny. They were all locally born. They were almost always over sixty, and were mostly men, since men in this country were believed to speak dialect more consistently than women. (Women were often employed to answer the domestic questions in Book V of the *Question-*

naire, however.) They were always of working-class status (often farmers and farm-workers), and of minimal education. It was necessary to avoid dialect-speakers who had been absent from the locality for many years, since they might have picked up 'foreign' speech habits; it was necessary to avoid dialect-speakers with speech-handicaps, for obvious reasons; and it was necessary (and sometimes hard) to avoid the professional raconteur. No informants were paid.

Having arrived at his selected locality with his questionnaire, the field-worker would go to the local post-office or shop and ask for the names of some of the older people who had lived in the village all their lives. He would then approach some of these and request their co-operation, and, if this were given, he would ask the questions, usually dividing them between two or three informants over a period of, say, a week, in the informants' houses (not in the local public house, as is often popularly imagined). Great care was taken to try and gain the informant's confidence, and this was fostered if the field-worker stayed on the spot and made the purpose of his visit known.

Responses to the questions were taken down by the field-workers in the International Phonetic Alphabet on specially prepared quarto sheets divided down the middle, the left-hand side being reserved for the responses proper and the right-hand side for any significant expressions from the informant's conversation. This 'incidental material', much of which has been included in the *SED* Basic Material volumes, has proved invaluable, especially in view of the fact that it emerged not in the formal framework of question and answer, but spontaneously in the course of conversation. When complete, the field-recordings were submitted to Professor Orton for scrutiny, and then returned to the field-worker for any emendations (in red ink, to distinguish them from the original recordings). Finally, they were bound separately, locality by locality, into recording-books, and these are at present deposited in the *SED* archives at Leeds University.

The objections to the 'impressionistic' method are well known: in transcribing, field-workers may inadvertently normalize what they hear from their informant, in accordance with their own usage; they may be unable to record unfamiliar sounds like, for example, [œy], accurately; and, if there are several field-workers, they may transcribe the same sound in different ways, or some may use broad transcriptions and others narrow ones. All these difficulties have been experienced by *SED*, as by other surveys,[16] as a perusal of the introductory material in Vol. iv of the Basic Material, for example, will show. However, soon after field-work started, it was decided to make tape-recordings of the unscripted speech of suitable informants an essential part of the survey. At first these recordings were of inferior quality, but by 1953 the *Survey* possessed better machines and from then onwards the programme of tape-recording was extended to every locality in the network. Thus, even if it is objected that the impressionistic recordings are in some ways unsatisfactory, there at least now exists this most valuable collection of permanent material, giving direct information on mid-twentieth-century local vernacular from one end of England to the other. Much of this material is now in the BBC's Permanent Sound-Record Library. On the recordings, the informants tell anecdotes, give personal reminiscences, discuss their school life, early years at work, various jobs such as ploughing, hedging, pig-killing, and so forth, thus at the same time providing information of value both to the folklorist and the social historian. The material was completely spontaneous, never rehearsed and never recited.

The responses to the *SED* questions have been published in tabular form, pending publication of the Linguistic Atlas; the responses to each question appear in the form of an 'article', giving the reference number, the key-word, the question, the responses listed in ordinary spelling, explanatory notes (if any), and finally the responses themselves in their phonetic form, arranged county by county and locality by locality. It should be pointed out that, although (in addition to the *Introduction*) there are in *SED* four volumes of Basic Material, namely Northern, West Midland, East Midland and Southern, these divisions are completely arbitrary and were made for convenience only. Any other method would necessarily have entailed prejudgement of the material.

This account of *SED* has of necessity been a bald and incomplete one; a whole book could be devoted to clothing the bare bones of the outline with details of informants, field-workers, the incidentals of field-work,[17] and of the history and progress of the work, which would show it to be a very live and human project, in which many people have been deeply and personally involved. At the present time, the *Survey* has ceased full-time publication and field-work for lack of funds. It need hardly be said that the full programme envisaged has not yet been accomplished. The ultimate aim is the projected *Linguistic Atlas of England* (*LAE*), providing interpretative maps of the whole country which will show important lexical, phonological and grammatical distributions. At the time of his death in 1956, Professor Dieth was preparing a series of phonological maps of the six northern counties based on the *SED* material, and this work has been continued by his former Research Assistant, Dr Eduard Kolb, now Professor of English Language in the University of Basle, and published in a beautifully produced *Phonological Atlas of the Northern Region* (Bern, 1966). But although this work is styled 'Linguistic Atlas of England', it is not, in fact, the full linguistic atlas planned as the crowning achievement of *SED*.

Leaving aside the question of the linguistic atlas, however, very little has yet been published apart from the Basic Material (in itself a mammoth task, as I can testify from personal experience). The four projected 'Companion Volumes' of selected incidental material have never been realized, and neither has the investigation of town dialects. A fishing questionnaire has been produced, however, and it is hoped that this will be used postally, and mainly for lexical information.

In addition to his joint initiation of *SED*, and his encouragement of dialectal studies outside the University, Professor Orton also initiated at Leeds University the writing of theses on dialect both at undergraduate (as part of the B.A. Honours course in English) and postgraduate levels, and this very fine collection of studies of the dialect of individual localities or counties is now housed in the archives of the Institute of Dialect and Folk Life Studies at Leeds University, founded in 1964. The existence of this Institute means that, even though money may not be at present available for the full publication of the whole projected *SED* programme, nevertheless a permanent archive has been established, and scholars can have access to the valuable collection of material there.

It would, however, be inaccurate to give the impression that recent work on English dialects has been confined to students and associates of Professor Orton. In fact, numerous monographs have been undertaken quite outside the influence of *SED* at universities up and down the country. As is probably clear from the present chapter, up until recently the diachronic approach described above has been the predominant one in linguistic and dialectal studies, but the notion of languages and dialects as systems, functioning by means of series of oppositions or contrasts, has impressed itself more and more upon modern linguists, and many recent investigators of English dialect have therefore applied the methods of modern linguistics to their work, analysing phonetic data obtained in the field in terms of distinctive or systemic sounds, and producing descriptions of the phonemic structure of a dialect, as distinct from or in addition to descriptions of the data considered in relation to an earlier (usually

ME) stage of the language.[18] It looks as if this emphasis on the synchronic study of dialect is likely to continue, in spite of formidable problems relating to phonological theory and to the methodology of dialect investigation carried out on this basis.

Structural dialectology

In American quarters especially a fairly new development has been a call for a 'structural dialectology', by which dialects might not only be described phonemically, but also grouped or distinguished on the basis of their phonemic inventories. Traditional dialectology is accustomed to trying to discover, for example, the sound of a particular vowel at a number of geographical points. But structural dialectology goes on to ask how that vowel fits into the phonemic system of each point. The call for a structural dialectology has been answered in Britain by the Linguistic Survey of Scotland, which soon after its inception decided to collect information on the *systems* of sounds of the various dialects, in the belief that in many cases useful comparisons between the pronunciations of a given word in different dialects could be made only with knowledge of the phonemic status of the sounds involved within their respective dialects, and further that the geographical distribution of sound-systems as wholes would be as significant and revealing of historical relationships as the geographical distribution of particular phonemic qualities.

The questionnaire for the Linguistic Survey of Scotland was therefore constructed, not like the Dieth–Orton *Questionnaire*, with items chosen to exemplify certain sounds of the ME period, with the aim of eliciting the present-day dialectal reflexes of these sounds, but with a word-list designed to elicit complete systems of vowels and consonants in all the Scots dialects. In this word-list, items were grouped in sections, each embodying a particular environmental frame, or context, within which sounds could be compared, and the vowel and consonant systems worked out. In other words, the contrasting features were elicited by means of 'minimal pairs'.

This short digression on the Linguistic Survey of Scotland helps to emphasize the differences between the traditional approach of *SED* and relatively new trends and methods in dialectology. In the new 'structural dialectology' attention has so far been specially paid to phonology, since this level of linguistic analysis is more amenable to description in terms of structure, but, as Weinrich's article implies (see the Select Bibliography), structural analysis is in fact envisaged as being applicable to all levels of speech.

Numerous problems have been raised by the new methods apart from those relating to phonological theory (such as whether it is possible to phonemicize for more than one dialect—or even one speaker—at a time), which inevitably have important consequences for any investigation as a whole. An obvious difficulty, as has been admitted, is that, before a method for eliciting phonological systems can be constructed, one needs to know in advance the probable total range of variation in the type of system.[19] Bilingualism in dialect speakers has also posed problems for investigators, since if an informant constantly uses two phonemic systems (i.e. that of his local dialect and that of RP), rapidly switching from one to the other, description and analysis of his speech may not be easy.[20]

In defence of traditional methods, it must be said that even before the advent of structuralism dialectologists were aware of the importance of linguistic systems, and that the concept of system is inherent in traditional approaches. It might even be argued that dialectologists of the historical school, in tracing the development of ME sounds to their present-day equivalents, are employing a structural procedure, in so far as a (postulated) ME phonemic system is the first premise of their investigations. It seems to me that dialectologists of the traditional school, while admitting the validity of the structural approach, have a duty to answer the recent charges made against them by some of the more zealous adherents of structural doctrines.

In any event, we may take heart from McDavid's assurance that 'what is most impressive is the high degree of correlation between dialect boundaries established by the two approaches'.[21] Ultimately, both structural and traditional approaches may lead us to the same conclusions (even if expressed in different terms), but possibly with a more generous view of the truth than if one method alone were used.

Research on urban dialects

Research work is in progress now on several town dialects. These are not exercises in traditional linguistic geography (which concentrates mainly on eliciting regional variations in the speech of one representative sector of the community), since they are concerned rather with linguistic variation as a result of socio-economic causes.[22] Linguistic variation has a social, as well as a regional, stratification, and these investigations have a social, rather than a geographical, basis, although the underlying regional context is important.[23] It is, indeed,

59

partially the aim of such studies to determine with what social classes the speaking of localized varieties of English is aligned.

In the early days of dialect study, urban dialects were neglected for several reasons. In the first place, England followed in the tradition of continental dialectology, the aim of which was to put sound-laws to a practical test in rural situations, and secondly the recording of English dialect has been seen as something of a rescue operation, in which priority must be given to salvaging as much as possible of traditional regional vernacular (as best exemplified in country speech) before it was too late. Town dialects have, however, been under suspicion from dialectologists because of their 'impurity',[24] that is, their traditional regional forms have been mixed with others from various sources, due to the heterogeneous and dynamic nature of urban populations. This suspicion no doubt constitutes a third reason why urban dialects have been neglected: they would not easily reveal archaic, traditional features, and would inevitably raise different problems from the rural dialects, perhaps requiring different methods of investigation. It was the aim of the Dieth–Orton investigation, nevertheless, to use basically the same methods in towns as in villages, but using a shortened questionnaire, i.e., information would be collected from informants of working-class status, who were locally born and of continuous residence, of minimal education, and over sixty years of age. The data thus collected would then complement that collected from rural areas.[25]

As it turns out, however, the methodology of urban dialectal investigation has not generally followed this course, although some scholars have produced analyses of urban dialects along traditional lines. W. Viereck's descriptive analysis of the dialect of Gateshead (Durham), part of Tyneside, is a case in point.[26] Viereck looked for the oldest features of the dialect still extant, taking the speech patterns of the lowest social classes as representative of the whole urban community. This procedure is fully justified by the composition of the Gateshead population, 89.4 per cent of its male members belonging to Social Classes III (Skilled Occupations), IV (Partly Skilled Occupations) and V (Unskilled Occupations), as defined by the 1951 Census, and only 10.6 per cent to Classes I (Professional, etc.) and II (Intermediate Occupations). Eva Sivertsen's *Cockney Phonology* is also a descriptive analysis of working-class speech in Bethnal Green.

Since the time of the original Dieth–Orton plans, however, much work has been done on urban dialects in America, and it has been felt that the methods employed there could successfully be applied in England. Moreover, many recent investigators (whether or not influenced by American ideas) have been conscious of the fact that the examination of the working-class dialect in urban contexts is not always or necessarily representative of urban society as a whole. It might be so in Oldham (Lancashire), but not in Cheltenham. Naturally, it is still possible to investigate the working-class urban population of England (as Viereck's and Sivertsen's works testify), perhaps with the aim simply of eliciting 'genuine' or traditional dialect forms, but within an urban population questions of class and related socio-economic factors will inevitably be raised. It has seemed more profitable to some scholars, therefore, to investigate urban populations as wholes, by taking random samples of speech across the community. Recent investigators of urban dialects have taken advantage of the sampling techniques developed by sociologists.

The principle underlying 'random sampling' is that informants are chosen completely at random from the whole of the population under scrutiny. The investigator can then divide his sample into classes according to his aims. A classic exercise of this sort is William Labov's *The Social Stratification of English in New York City* (Washington: Center for Applied Linguistics, 1966). Labov interviewed adult speakers of English resident for more than two years, determining their socio-economic status on the basis of the three factors occupation, education and family income, and taking as variable phonological features the presence or absence of final or preconsonantal *r*; the pronunciation of the vowel in *bad, bag, ask, pass, cash, dance*; the pronunciation of the vowel in *caught, talk, awed*, etc.; and stop, affricate or fricative articulation of [θ] and [ð]. He also developed a procedure for isolating contextual styles—'formal' speech, 'reading style', 'careful' speech, 'casual' speech—which quickly proved to have a relevance to phonological variation. Labov's work is of the utmost importance for dialectologists (and also for sociologists, whom Labov had in mind), and is already being used as the model for urban dialect research in England.

A recent English urban survey is that of Tyneside speech, currently being undertaken from the English Department of the University of Newcastle-upon-Tyne. The aim of the survey, first planned in 1963, is to determine the pattern of social distribution of the varieties of English within Newcastle (this is now being extended to Gateshead), to reclassify types of speech, especially those of a non-localized type, and to correlate speech variety with social factors.

A second survey has been made at Leeds, described by its inaugurator as 'a survey of the linguistic behaviour of Leeds as a function of socio-economic classes'.[27] It was based on a random sample of informants within the city boundaries, using a questionnaire of seventy-one questions to elicit vowel and consonant minimal word-pairs, an attempt also being made to obtain 'extended casual speech' in the Labov tradition. So far, few results have been published (though more are promised later), but Professor Houck implies in his paper that data collected on the pronunciation of the word *bud* shows that the vowel used in this word (presumably either [ʊ] or [ə]) is an indication of socio-economic class.

Very little has been published on dialect work relating to other urban centres, but a number of short articles are noted in the Select Bibliography, and investigations are now proceeding in several towns and cities. See further Chapter 9, below.

Future work in English dialectology

Aspects of English dialectology which have so far received little attention are referred to throughout this book. Further instances are not, however, lacking. There are, first of all, certain logical 'follow-ups' of the work of *SED*, one of which is the establishment of a closer-meshed survey in certain areas, especially perhaps in the transitional areas between dialects. This would enable us to pinpoint geographically the exact extent of some dialect features. Another is the investigation of certain specialized dialects—mining, fishing and so on—which is already proceeding in some quarters.

One very valuable extension of *SED* would be a re-recording (on tape) of the *SED* localities at regular intervals, say of ten years. By making comparisons between older and younger speakers,[28] we should be able to note linguistic changes, to study these changes actually taking place, and to investigate the effects on rural dialects of television, rehousing, the spread of conurbations, the disintegration of rural life, and so on. The relative extents to which men and women use local dialect is also a subject very worthy of investigation. At the same time, either a new tape-recording programme or that already carried out by *SED* would enable researchers to start work on syntactical and intonational descriptions of the dialects, areas of study impossible to carry out fully by questionnaire, and so far much neglected.[29]

Since the investigation of older regional and occupational dialects has already made headway, however, it looks as if future research in dialect studies will almost certainly take an urban and sociological direction, the former inevitably entailing the latter. There is at present an ever-growing interest in class dialect and one may reasonably expect much work to be done in this field which is still a relatively neglected one as far as England is concerned.

Little use has so far been made of the computer in English dialect studies, but some American scholars have begun to use it to produce lists and maps, with impressive results. A recent paper based on computerized material relating to the voicing of initial fricative consonants[30] shows quite clearly that this method opens up immense possibilities to future investigators handling substantial quantities of dialect data.

The dialect societies

Finally, mention should be made of the dialect societies, which foster dialect study at both academic and popular levels. The first of these, the Yorkshire Dialect Society, was founded by Joseph Wright in 1897, and its annual *Transactions* is a well-produced and substantial publication which still bears witness to the wide range of interests of its members. A similar function is fulfilled by the Journals of the Lakeland Dialect Society (founded 1938) and the Lancashire Dialect Society (founded 1951), all three testifying to the vigorous interest of northerners in their local speech. Dialect notes appear in the many and varied journals of local societies up and down the country, but no others are devoted, as are these, solely to the promulgation of interest in dialect as a subject worthy of attention in its own right. Perhaps the present writer may be permitted to express a personal view in the suggestion that it is certainly time there was a scholarly linguistic journal in Britain dealing solely with dialect.

In this chapter, we have seen how the serious study of dialect in England, although preceded firstly by much comment and then by the production of glossaries, poems, and so on, did not begin in earnest until the nineteenth century—at the time when dialect geography had its birth on the Continent. It proceeded from the collection of local words and pronunciations to the writing of systematic grammars of single dialects on historical principles and to the overall surveys of dialectal English undertaken by Ellis and by Dieth and Orton. The most recent trends are socio-linguistic, while at the same time the exclusively historical approach has to some extent given way to descriptive analysis of the synchronic type.

4   English Word Geography

Word geography is concerned with the regional distribution of expressions for various notions, e.g. the ant, the pigsty, the stream, the pantry, chitterlings, freckles, fainting, prettiness, cold, a door being ajar, etc., and in the deductions, linguistic and non-linguistic, which can be made from examining such distributions.

We have already seen how such information is collected by dialectologists. In the early days of interest in English dialect, lists of dialect words and words with special dialectal meanings for individual counties or areas were compiled by investigators, while others made glossaries for the whole country, e.g. Ray and Grose. The culmination of these activities may be seen in Joseph Wright's *EDD*. The first attempt to collect dialect words for the purpose of constructing a Linguistic Atlas of England was, however, *SED*, which assembled expressions for hundreds of notions in a network of 313 localities. Only since this investigation has it been possible accurately to plot the distribution of dialect words on a map, and the examples in this chapter and the two following will be largely drawn from *SED* (cited with their reference number, e.g. III.12.6, VII.2.14, but without further explanation). With regard to citations from *EDD*, it should be made clear at the outset that *EDD* cannot now be considered on the same footing as a work presenting more recently gathered information, although it gives useful corroborative evidence and details of earlier dialectal forms. When examples from *EDD* are cited, therefore, it will be on the understanding that forms may or may not still be current.

It is clear to the most superficial observer that the vocabulary of regional English differs very considerably area to area and also from that of Standard English. Words like *mouldy-warp, nesh, shippon*, and *glance* (with the meaning 'bounce'), to name but a very few, have in fact sometimes caused the vocabulary of a dialect to be popularly regarded as its most significant feature and the element which most sharply differentiates it from other dialects and from Standard English.

The archaism of dialectal vocabulary

Although this has been disputed (see p. 66, below), the most distinctive element of English dialectal vocabulary nevertheless consists of more or less archaic survivals from earlier times which are expressed by other (though not necessarily non-archaic) terms in Standard English. Thus, *eddish* or *arrish*, probably < OE *edisc*, is equivalent to Standard English *stubble*; *meat* and *victuals* have given way to *food*; *sull*, *sullow* < OE *sulh* has disappeared, leaving only *plough*; *dish-clout* has given way to *dish-cloth*; the verb *wed* has been largely displaced by *marry* (except in newspapers, which use it because of its brevity); the *parlour* has gone, partly, at least, because of the disappearance of the thing itself;[1] *chamber* has gone in favour of *bedroom*; *aught* and *nought* are now dialectal, while *anything* and *nothing* are the Standard English terms. All of these, and hundreds more, existed in ME (whether they came originally from OE, ON, OFr or elsewhere) and were potential components of present-day Standard English. But at some stage they were discarded from universal use, and now survive only dialectally. Others have never been in universal usage, and have always had a local distribution— the far north, west Midlands, south-west and so on. Such is, for example, the case with very many ON words, although some found their way (via a process of internal loaning) into Standard English. Very little research has been carried out into ME lexical distributional patterns, but it has been suggested that ME vocabulary was regionally quite restricted,[2] if one can judge from the rarity of occurrence of certain words, such, for example, as are found in the north-west-Midland group of poems in MS Cotton Nero A X—*Sir Gawain and the Green Knight*, *Pearl*, *Purity* and *Patience*—and in other poems written in the west-Midland alliterative tradition.[3]

The origins of dialectal vocabulary

It is not sufficient, however, simply to state that many dialect words are archaic. We must make good this assertion by pointing to the origins of several classes of words, and this is the more important in that the various origins of the vocabulary of English dialect have so far not been fully analysed. Many archaic dialectal survivals are OE in origin: almost any page of *EDD* or *SED* will produce words which, with the aid of an Anglo-Saxon dictionary, can be traced in their earlier forms in OE texts, and it was this that interested the earlier scholars of dialectal forms, e.g. Laurence Nowell.

Several words of native origin which are widespread in dialect are *meat* ('food', < OE *mete*; in use with this meaning since OE times), *learn* 'teach' < OE *leornian* ('teach' from *c.* 1200 onwards according to *OED*, but originally meaning only 'learn'), *fall* ('autumn'; first ref. *OED* 1545), *fart* < OE **feortan* (first ref. *OED c.* 1250, last ref. 1740), *spew* 'vomit' < OE *spīwan*, *barm* 'yeast' < OE *beorma*.

To take a few more examples at random, Somerset and Devon *lewze* 'pigsty' (I.1.5) is < OE *hlōse*; northern and western *delve* and northern *grave* 'dig' (I.7.8) are respectively < OE *delfan*, OE *grafan*; southern *keeve* 'tub, barrel', etc. (e.g. in Cornwall at III.12.5) is < OE *cȳf*; of the northern names for a rivulet or stream (IV.1.1), *burn* is < OE *burna*, *gote* is < OE **gota* 'water channel', *sike* is < OE *sīc*, ON *sík*; with Somerset *bache* 'slope' (IV.1.10) cf. OE *bæc* 'stream-valley'; southern and western *want* 'mole' (IV.5.4) is < OE *wand*, *wond*; northern *rackan* 'domestic crane' (V.3.4/5) is < OE *racente*; northern *greeting* 'crying' (VI.5.15) is < OE *grēotan*; northern *spelk* 'splinter' (VI.7.10) is < OE *spelc*; *atter* 'pus' at Cambridge 1 and Norfolk 7 (VI.11.9) is < OE *attor* 'poison'. In view of these and other examples given in the present chapter (plus loans from Celtic, ON and early French, discussed in Chapter 7), it is difficult to agree with H. C. Wyld that not much of present-day dialect is of any great antiquity.[4]

The dialects also contain a substantial non-native element, which we must consider in due course. Meanwhile, several other categories claim our attention.

Of special interest are words now dialectal which have a cognate Standard English form (i.e. whose Standard English counterpart has developed from the same root). The word *ant* (IV.8.12), for example, is regularly developed from OE *ǣmete*, via ME *āmete*, then *amte*, and *ante*, *ant*. But either the OE parallel Anglian form *ēmete* retained the medial vowel and became modern dialectal *emmet*—now the regular form throughout the southern counties, in most of Gl and O, all of Bk and in one or two other scattered localities—or *ant* and *emmet* are both developed from *ǣmete*, with shortening of the stressed vowel to *æ* (> ME *a*) or *e* (> ME *e*) according to dialect or to the time at which shortening took place (cf. *OED*, s.v. Ant, Emmet).

A second example is that of the parallel forms *newt* and *evet* or *eft* (IV.9.8). The OE word was *efeta*, which gave ME *euete*, *eft*, *ewt*, etc., and, by metanalysis, *a newt* from *an ewt* (see *OED*, s.v. N 3). *Eft*, *evet*, *ewt* and similar forms are now regular throughout the southern counties and in most of Gl, O, Bk, Bd, Hrt and Ess.

A further development of this type comprises dialectal words which have a cognate Standard English equivalent with a different meaning. The word *girn* is (or was, according to *EDD*) in general dialectal use, being simply a parallel, metathetic, form of *grin* (< OE *grennian*, ON *grenja*). Standard English *grin* now means 'smile', etc., but the dialectal form *girn* seems to preserve the older, basic meaning of 'draw back the lips and display the teeth...generally, or as an indication of pain or anger' (*OED*, s.v. Grin), since *EDD* gives as primary senses 'gnash the teeth in rage, snarl, be fretful, peevish, cry, whine, whimper', etc. (cf. ON *grenja* 'to howl', OSw *gränia* 'to roar, to gnash or show the teeth threateningly'). In the famous *girning-matches*, formerly a feature of rustic sports in Westmorland, the contestants simply stuck their heads through a horse-collar, the one who *girned* (i.e. distorted his face) to the judge's greatest satisfaction being declared the winner.

Mawther or *maw'r* is a widely spread dialectal word for 'a girl just growing into womanhood, esp. a great, rough, awkward wench... also used of mares, cows, and other female animals' (*EDD*). Although not accepted as such by *OED* (s.v. Mauther),[5] this may be simply a phonetic and semantic differentiation of the Standard English form *mother*.

The word *cheeld* occurs in west So, D, Co and Do, meaning 'child', except at So 10, where the [iː] form means 'girl', while [tʃaɪɫd] means 'child', and this seems to be another case in which the dialectal form has been differentiated in meaning (*EDD* gives *chiel(d)* 'girl' for west So, D and Co).

Words of obscure origin

In addition to dialect words of definitely English or foreign origin, there are a good number of which the origin is obscure, and in many ways these form one of the most interesting groups. Some of them are words which are poorly attested (e.g. only in *SED* and *EDD* or in one of them alone) and admit of no explanation for the present,[6] although one may be found in due course. Examples which seem to fall into this class are *cornutor* 'donkey' (III.13.16), found only as the second response at D 11, and otherwise utterly unknown, *cow-maid* 'urine' (I.3.10), found only at K 7, cf. *maid's-water* at K 5, *wild ducks* 'evener' (on the plough; I.8.4), found only at Brk 2, *chonnocks* 'turnips' (II.4.1), found only as the second response at St 2. The volumes of *EDD* have a special 'list of words for the present kept back from the want of further information' to which such doubtful items are relegated.

Words of imitative origin

Some words are evidently of imitative or echoic origin, like Standard English *bump*, either in English dialect or in a language (e.g. ON) from which they were adopted. Such words are often popularly seized upon to illustrate the supposed superiority in expressiveness of dialectal speech over Standard English. For example, in one report on the publication of Vol. i of *SED*, somewhat biased in this direction, attention was drawn to northern words like *shirl, skirl, skirr, slire, slur*, all meaning 'slide' (VIII.7.1—the southern terms, comprising only *skid, skidder* and *slide(r)*, are not nearly so expressive, incidentally), to the various northern expressions for a seesaw (VIII.7.2), e.g. *linkum-jinkum* and *shuggy*, for the notion of 'dull' (weather; VII.6.10), e.g. *blashy, darksome, dowly, gammy, mirky, muggy, rawky*, and for mud (VII.6.17), e.g. *blather, clarts, glaur, mire, muck, plother, puddle, sludge, slutch, sluther, sump*. It is certainly true, however, that a good many notions seem to have produced dialectal expressions which are echoic—such as hiccuping (VI.8.4—itself a word of echoic origins), a chat (VIII.3.4), slush (VII.6.16), askew (IX.1.3), tremors (VI.1.4), slippery (VII.6.14), and, as supreme examples, the various cries that animals (e.g. bulls, cows, cats) are said to make (III.10.2–7), and the words used to call animals in from the field (III.10.1).

One of the largest groups of evocative words of this type—uncollected by *SED* (unfortunately)—comprises words for women who are in some way offensive, slatternly, fat, 'loose', masculine, bibulous, domineering and so on. A very rich collection, scattered liberally through the sober pages of *EDD*, awaits scholarly attention. A brief selection,[7] although far less than enough to do justice to this fascinating subject, will illustrate the apparently imitative origin of these terms: *bamsey* (fat, red-faced woman), *bussock* (fat, heavy woman), *cloffy* (slattern, tawdrily-dressed woman), *driggle-draggle* (slovenly, untidy woman), *fiz-gig* (frivolous woman), *fuz* (fat, idle woman), *gammerstang* (hoyden), *hacky* (prostitute), *mally-mop* (dirty wench), *rompstal* (rude, romping girl), *sess* (great, fat woman), *shamnel* (masculine woman), *swammocks* (slatternly girl), *trolly* (untidy woman), *twanker* (virago), *vuddicks* (coarse, fat woman). There appear to be about 350 such expressions in *EDD*, which suggests some interesting sociological as well as linguistic conclusions!

A theory which has its attractions for dialectologists and students of non- or sub-standard forms is that which accounts for words which

Professor A. S. C. Ross has called non-imitative 'autochthonous' roots, that is, words which are not imitative, but are similarly immune to sound-laws or subject to special ones, and are 'continually liable to be regenerated at any period of the language'.[8] Professor Ross notes that such roots are of specially frequent occurrence in dialect and slang words, and gives, as one example, *chump* 'fathead, silly ass', which is not from French, and cannot have existed in OE because *č* (i.e. [tʃ]) followed by a back vowel is impossible in OE, and must therefore have come into existence at some later period.

A group of words possibly of such origin is that which includes numerous phonetically similar items meaning 'hobgoblin, object of dread', and, sometimes, also 'scarecrow', the latter presumably a semantic development from the former. In *SED* these are found at VIII.8.1 *bogey* and II.3.7 *scarecrow*. Under the first the north and north Midlands yield *boggart*, *boggin* (I.o.M.) and *bogle*, *bugabo/bowl* occurs in Sa, He, Wo and Mon, while *bogey(man)* itself is of general occurrence. For 'scarecrow' the north yields compounds in *-boggart*, *-boggle* and *-bogle*, *bugalo* and *buglug* are found at Do 5 and *bogeyman* at Bk 4; *bucca* (< Corn. *bucca*, cf. Breton *bugelien-n*, *bugelnoz*, Welsh *bwgan* and also *bwbach* 'terriculamentum') is found in west Co. To these may be added a whole host of obviously related words of similar meaning provided by *EDD* and *OED*. So, in the former, *bockie*, *bockle* (cf. *bock* v. 'to shy' of a horse—both from Co only), *boggart*, *boggin*, *boggy-bo*, *bogie*, *bogle*, *bucca* (Co only), *bug*, *bugabo(o)*, *bugan*, *bugger*, of which *boggart*, *boggy-bo*, *bogle* and *bucca* can also have the meaning of 'scarecrow'. *OED* provides *bog* sb. 2 (first ref. 1527), *boggard*, *-art* (1570), *bogle* (*c.* 1505), *bogy* (1836–40), *bucca* (as above), *bug*, sb. 1 (1388), *bugaboo* (1740), *bugbear* (1581), *buggard*, *-art* (1575), of which *bogle*, *bucca* and *bug* can also mean 'scarecrow'. A glance at the headings in *OED* reveals the uncertainty of the relationships in this group (cf. also OFr *Beugibus*, *Bugibus*, the name of a demon).

Features of dialect vocabulary

We have seen that the vocabulary of the regional dialects, like that of Standard English, consists of many English words, with an admixture of others of foreign origin, mostly ON or OFr. Several sub-groups of special interest will also appear—local birdnames, and others.

It is difficult at present to point to any large regional patterns which emerge from the study of dialectal vocabulary, however,

69

except for the distributions of ON words in the north and of the Cornish words in Cornwall, or to say why specific words fall into the patterns they do. On the other hand, some interesting tendencies can be seen at work. The constant fluctuation of dialect vocabulary can be seen in the replacement of some words by others, and in particular the ousting of dialect words by words of prestige value from Standard English. We need now to look at one or two examples in detail.

A group of words which show a history of constant 'replacement' is made up of the various expressions for 'badger' (IV.5.9). Of these, the oldest is *brock* (< OE *broc* < Common Celtic **broccos*), while *bauson* (< ME *bausen* < OFr *bausen, bauzan*) is recorded by *OED* only from *c.* 1325, and *grey* only from 'ante 1432–50' to the seventeenth century.[9] All of these have now been replaced, both in Standard English, and, to a very large extent, in dialect, by *badger*, a word of doubtful origin (probably < *badge* + *-ard*) first recorded by *OED* from 1523—'a bauson or a badger'. Of the other words, only *brock* is attested now, and this very sporadically, there being not more than some twenty occurrences recorded by *SED*, sixteen from the six northern counties—two from the Midlands, and two very isolated ones from Dorset and Essex.

The map of 'donkey' (III.13.16) shows several well-delineated areas of words like *cuddy* (the far north, penetrating southwards only into YNR), *fussock* (north and east Y), *pronkus* (mostly confined to L), *dicky* (Nf, Sf, north Ess) and *nirrup* (Ha, south-east W, Do), together with their variant forms and also more scattered words like *moke* (south-western *mokus*) and *neddy* (this by no means exhausts the list) and about twenty occurrences of *ass* up and down the country from Nb to west Sx, and from Nf to St. Whether or not these words, apart from *ass*, have always had a local distribution is open to discussion, but it seems extremely likely. *Ass* we know to have been in universal use from *c.* 1000 onwards. Whatever the individual histories of these words, both *ass* (< OE *assa*)—probably the oldest—and all the others have been superseded in Standard English by *donkey*, a word of obscure (? slang) origin, recorded by *OED* from only 1785 onwards, and perhaps originally of Essex or Suffolk origin.[10] *Donkey* has also penetrated the dialects, being distributed as an alternative to many of the local expressions throughout the length and breadth of the country. The disappearance of *ass* in both Standard English and dialect is probably due to its phonetic coalescence with *arse* in the NE period.

From their NE period of origin, *badger* and *donkey* have become Standard English terms and have then penetrated the dialects quite thoroughly. The same is the case with *cow-house* (first ref. *OED* 1530, but recorded from the late thirteenth century by *MED*, s.v. Cou, 2(d)) and *cow-shed* (first ref. *OED*, s.v. Cow, 1886). Map 3, giving some of the expressions for this notion (I.1.8), shows that these two words are widespread (*cow-shed* mostly in the Midlands and south, however), while various local expressions also occur, e.g. *-byre* (Nb, Du, Cu, north We, north Y), *mistall* (YWR), *cow-stable* (north-east Nt and east L), *beast-house* (Mon, south He), *neat-house* (south Nf, north Sf), *shippon*. The last of these, a very old word (< OE *scypen*), has a significant distribution in two completely distinct areas, occurring in the south in D, north-east Co and a small portion of west So, and in the north occupying the whole of La and Ch, protruding into the north of YWR, south We and the northern parts of the counties to the south and east of Ch. From data given in *EDD*, however, the word was at one time more widespread than this, apparently being current in almost all the western counties, from Cu down to Co, and also in Nb and Y. The two remaining areas are, therefore, isolated relics of what was once a much larger *shippon* distribution. Together with at least some of the other now local words for the cow-house, *shippon* was once in universal use (it occurs, for example, in the works of Chaucer): *cow-house* and *cow-shed* have risen in prominence and have become the accepted terms in Standard English, pushing their rivals into small (some of them isolated) pockets.[11]

From the three examples given, we are able to see not merely how some words are replaced by others—in particular, how local words are replaced by Standard English words: we are also able to see the effect in geographical terms on the local words, which survive only in isolated examples up and down the country, or in peripheral areas, while the Standard terms come to occupy great tracts of the most central parts of the country. Dialectal words (and other forms) in a situation of retreat are said to be *recessive*.

In the present state of the decay of regional dialect, it is only to be expected that words should become distorted because of their unfamiliarity. Some of the words of obscure origin listed above may be 'obscure' only because of this. This is perhaps especially true of words which were originally borrowed from French or another language, whether via Standard English or direct. It may be suggested that in some of these cases folk-etymology has been at work.

Folk-etymology is the popular interpretation of unfamiliar words in terms of more familiar ones (either semantically related or unrelated), and appears to fulfil a psychological need to explain the

Map 3   Words for the cow-house (I.1.8)

unknown by reference to what is known and familiar. An amusing example is *St Viper's Dance* 'St Vitus Dance' (VI.1.4) at Ha 5, in which the unfamiliar name *Vitus* is reinterpretated as the semantically unrelated (but phonetically similar) *viper's*. *Eggcups* for 'hiccups' (VI.8.4), found at So 3, is another. A more widely distributed example is perhaps *urge* 'retch' (VI.13.15), which, as the editors of *SED* Vol. iv point out, may simply be a metathesized form of *retch. Urge*, it is true, has a final voiced consonant, but this might well be accounted for by the widespread interpretation of *urge* as a word quite distinct from *retch*, and one moreover that has echoic qualities suggestive of the physical action involved in retching. (*EDD* gives *urge* (v. 2) also from Y, but only with the meaning of 'shake convulsively with laughter').

Finally may be mentioned various words for 'haws' (IV.11.6) in the south of England: *pig-berries, -hales, -haws, -shells* in So, W and Do, and *hogasses* (more properly *hog-hawses*, a double pl.) and *hog-hazels* in Sr, Sx and K, all of them suggesting that haws have something to do with pigs or hogs. It may simply be, however, that initially OE *haga* (or ? **hagga*, see p. 44, above) gave rise to a wide variety of forms (see the other responses at IV.11.6) including *hag-* forms which were later folk-etymologized as *hog-* forms whence there grew up a supposed connexion with the animal.

Place-name elements are as subject to folk-etymology as dialect words, and an example may be of interest.[12] To the north of the village of Newbiggin, about ten miles north of the Tyne mouth, is a tongue of land on which stands the village church, the tip of this tongue being known locally as [kəkuːspœɪnt] *kirk-house-point*. A local fisherman explained the name by volunteering the information that cock-fighting used to take place there, the first element of the name, northern *kirk-* ('church'), being misinterpreted, because of its pronunciation, as *cock-*. A similar misinterpretation accounts for the name Cock Flat (YNR) 'Church field', perhaps land held by the Church of Kirkham.[13]

It may be that it is particularly in boundary areas between dialects that words tend to disintegrate, both phonetically and semantically, and from this point of view alone a survey of these areas would be of very special interest. An example of this process occurs in central Cornwall, between the dialects of the east and west of the county. In Cornwall, as in other south-western counties, 'newt' (IV.9.8) is *evet* (also a *four-legged-evet* at Co 2—*four-legged* perhaps added to explain the word), except at Co 6, where we get *padgy-pow* (perhaps < Corn. *peswar-paw*). Throughout Cornwall the word for 'ant'

73

(IV.8.12) is *emmet*—phonetically virtually identical with *evet* except for the medial consonant—except, again, at Co 6, where *muryan* (< Corn. *muryon*) occurs. At Co 4 (central Co), *four-legged-emmet* is given for 'newt', where there has obviously been a confusion between the two very similar words. In this case, it may be suspected that *four-legged* is a necessary prefix in order to distinguish between this animal and the simple *emmet* ('ant').

The phenomenon of the break-up of words in boundary areas may be related to other facts. Professor W. N. Francis has shown how the phonemic variants of etymologically distinct forms may provide a series of easy transitional steps from one to the other across a border area.[14] He instances *swingle-tree* (part of the plough; I.8.3):

Beginning in eastern Gloucestershire and moving northeast through Oxfordshire into the northwest corner of Bucks and then swinging southeast, we encounter in order the variants *swingletree*, *swivel*, *swibbletree*, *wibbletree*, *whippletree*. A little farther north are *swelltree* and *swaytree*, with a transitional *waytree* between *swaytree* and *whippletree*, similar to the transitional *wibbletree* between *swibbletree* and *whippletree*.

Other examples could no doubt be adduced. Indeed, a similar sequence is noted below in the Yorkshire names for the starling: proceeding westward from the Yorkshire coast with *jibby*, we encounter *jippy* ([b] > [p]), *shippy* ([dʒ] > [ʃ]), *sheppy* ([ɪ] > [ɛ]), *shebby* ([p] > [b]) or *cheppy* ([ʃ] > [tʃ]), each 'easy transitional step' being made by a sound-change in a different part of the word.

Some dialectal words, admittedly few, are apparently 'blends' or 'portmanteau words', i.e. they owe their origin to a combination of two forms, being found especially in areas where two different dialectal forms are current.

Some dialects show blends of the prepositions *without* (< OE *wiþūtan*) and *bout* (< OE *būtan*, originally *be-ūtan*; V.8.10a). *Bout* 'without' is at present used in south Y and south and central La (cf. the famous Yorkshire song 'On Ilkla Moor *baht* 'at'), *be-out* (? < *be-ūtan*) at L 3/9 and at Nth 2, and *without* in most of the rest of the country. The form *bidout*, according to *SED*, occurs only at Y 11, as [bɪduːt] (designated 'old' by the informant), and looks like a blend of *without* and *bout*, which are both current in the county, *without* ubiquitously and *bout* to the south of the locality in question.[15]

A further example is perhaps to be found in one of the words for the old-fashioned earth-closet (V.1.13). *Petty*(-*hole*, -*house*) is a widespread expression for this item, attested from the north in Cu,

We, La and Y, and from the Midland counties (but not the southern ones), and is ultimately from Fr *petit* (cf. the expression *little-house* found once in K and once in Sf). *Nessy* (a shortened form of *necessary*, itself elliptical for *necessary-house, -place, -stool*) is found throughout the north of England except in Nb. *Netty*, found in Nb, Du, Cu (once) and Y (once), and stated in a Nb source in *EDD* to be a euphemism, is perhaps a (? euphemistic) blend of *petty* and *nessy*.

Finally, it has been suggested by the editors of *SED*, Vol. ii (p. 692), that the verb *reave* 'retch' (VI.13.15) is a blend of *heave* and *reach* (*retch*). *Reave* is current only at La 7 and in Gl, and at both points is surrounded by occurrences of *heave* and *reach* or *retch*, so that this explanation cannot be discounted.

Specialized vocabularies

One of the first tasks of word geography is to obtain and then to plot on maps words for notions which are known throughout the whole area under investigation, 'universals'. It will thus be possible to have for every locality in the area a strictly comparable response. It is obvious that farmers throughout England will all have names for a ladder, a spade, a lane, the eaves of a house or a stack-base, but they will not all be acquainted with notions relating to coal-mining or fishing, and such notions are generally and advisedly elicited by means of a questionnaire specially designed for the purpose. Neither may they be acquainted with words in some other specialized fields—the names for certain birds and flowers, for example—though it may be confidently expected that most country-men will be familiar with all the common, well-known species. In any case, because of the sheer numbers involved, no questionnaire could try to obtain every item, even if any investigator had time to plot them on maps: a selection must inevitably be made and the first things to be collected are, to repeat, expressions for notions which are universally familiar. In the present book, occupational dialects are discussed in Chapter 8, but here a few words may be added on the subject of other specialized, though non-occupational, vocabularies.

Bird names

SED does not ask for many bird names, confining itself to one or two species certain to be known to its informants. A full-scale survey of bird names would, however, doubtless produce some interesting results, of which the local names for the gull and the owl (IV.7.5/6) may serve as examples. *Sea-crow* is a rare alternative name for the gull, dotted up and down the country from Nb to Gl, except in the south, *sea-maw* or *-mall* is found in La, L and Nf, but *petch* only in two localities in central La. For the owl, *jenny-owl* or *-owlet* has a northern distribution (Nb, Cu, Du, the northern half of Y—*polly-owlet* at Y 19), while *meg-owl* or *-owlet* is confined to two localities in north L.

Spug or *spuggy* 'house sparrow' is not recorded by *SED*, but is certainly current in the north of England. It was recorded by *EDD* from Nb and Du and also Wa and Wo (cf. the widespread *scug* or *scuggy* 'squirrel'). *Stiggy* 'starling' seems to be a similar formation, and cf. *stoggy* 'wood-pigeon' or 'stock-dove' in Y. Perhaps these *-ggy* endings are affectionate diminutives.

Nance, in his *Glossary of Cornish Sea-Words*, cites a good many names for birds found on the Cornish coast, of which *pope* is specially interesting. It means 'puffin' in west Co (but *nath* is the word for 'puffin' in north Co, and *londoner* at Porthleven), but 'bullfinch' in Do (also the red-backed shrike in Ha, according to *EDD*).

Very little systematic research has been carried out in this field. A notable exception is the survey of Yorkshire bird names carried out in the 1950s by Mr J. C. Maycock, and published in *TYDS* (1953–6). A questionnaire was circulated, giving a list of birds for which local names were wanted, and produced names for over one hundred species, from which some useful conclusions emerged. For the house sparrow, *spuggy* was found to be common throughout Yorkshire; for the hedge-sparrow, *dunnock* was current in the Pennines and south Yorkshire, but *cuddy* throughout the North and East Ridings, with six reports of it from the West Riding (all from the Vale of York or the lower reaches of the dales). This is specially interesting in that the local *cuddy* 'sparrow' area overlaps the larger *cuddy* 'donkey' area, which penetrates Yorkshire from the north (see p. 70, above), and includes *SED* localities 1/3/6/8/14. This raises questions about the internal structures of the dialects concerned, but perhaps we may leave the solution of this problem to the structural dialectologists.[16]

The Yorkshire names for the lapwing and the starling present interesting phonetic variants: for the first, *teeafit* is usual in the North and East Ridings, but *tewit* in the West Riding (*OED*, s.v. Tewhit, states 'originally echoic'); 'starling' is *cheppy* in the extreme north-west of the county, *jibby* in the coastal areas of the North and

East Ridings, *jippy* in the wolds, the Vale of Pickering and the North Riding moors, *shebby* in the upper valleys of the Wharfe, Aire and Calder, *sheppy* in Middle Wharfedale and Airedale, and *shippy* in the Vale of York, Hambleton and the Cleveland Hills. The names thus show variation in three respects—the initial consonant [tʃ~dʒ~ʃ], the medial consonant [p~b] and the stressed vowel [ɛ~ɪ]. Proceeding westward from the coast, *jibby* gives way to *jippy*, *jippy* to *shippy*, *shippy* to *sheppy*, *sheppy* to *shebby* or to *cheppy* (cf. p. 74, above).

Plant names

The names of several weeds and wild flowers are asked for by *SED*, and here again the small amount of available material suggests that a rich harvest yet remains to be gathered. To take but one example, local names for the bindweed (II.2.4) show interesting distributions. Apart from *bindweed* and *bind*, which are of general occurrence, *convulvulus* occupies much of the north (down to north Y) and a long strip of country comprising west La, most of Ch and Sa, while *ground-ivy* occupies another well-defined area in the south-west consisting of Co and D except for the south-east. Throughout the rest of the country, names ending in *-bind* or *-wind* (*-vine* in west Sf, C, Hu, Bd and Hrt) predominate: *with(y)-wind* and *bith(y)-*, *bes-*, *beth-*, *beddy-*, *betty-wind* in most of the south, also *bell-wind* and *willy-wind*, a very large east-Midland area of *cornbind*, stretching from L and YWR to Bk, two areas of *bear-bind*, one in the west, bordering on the *convulvulus* area, and one in the south-east (parts of K and Sx), and an area of *bell-bind* in Ess and south Sf. There are besides these a good many other local names—*morning-glory*, *wandering-willy*, *Robin-run-the-dike*, and so on—but the *-bind*, *-wind* types are of special interest in that the names are significantly similar to each other both in the first and second elements, and one would very much like to know how some of them came to assume their present forms. As with other plants, a good deal of folklore probably underlies such local names as *devil's-gut*, *-nightcap*, *-twine* in the north of England.

A similar case is *couch-grass* (II.2.3). The western words *stroil*, *stroily-grass* (west So, Co, D) and *strap-grass* (east Do, west Ha), and eastern *spear-grass* (Nf and Sf) and *fowl-grass* (Nf) form peripheral areas of separate and distinct lexical forms, while the rest of the country displays numerous phonetic variants—*squitch*, *twitch*, *quitch*; *twicks*, *quicks*, *wicks*; *whilks*, *crouch* and *scutch*—all pre-

77

sumably from the OE base *cwice*. The names seem, therefore, to be of primary interest for their phonetic forms.

There is no space here to analyse the lexical and phonetic variants of the local names for goose-grass (II.2.5), charlock (II.2.6), colt's-foot (II.2.7), and cowslip, daisy and dandelion (II.2.10), but these —and no doubt others—promise to be of much interest to both dialectologists and folklorists.

Ecclesiastical words

A very interesting small group of words, uninvestigated for the most part and probably now mainly obsolete, consists of those connected with the Church. The native word *bishop* (v.) was recorded very generally by *EDD* with the meaning of 'confirm' (cf. Tyndale, writing in 1530, 'oftymes they be volowed [see below] and bishoped both in one day'), and *upraise* from Co meaning 'church' (v.). Two expressions now presumably quite obsolete are *fang to* (< ME *fangen* + *to*, a new formation, first attested *c.* 1200, formed on *fangen*, the p.p. of OE *fōn* 'take, receive, accept', etc.) 'to stand sponsor for someone in baptism', recorded by *OED* (s.v., 6 b), and in *EDD* (s.v., §6) in dialectal speech from W ('he vang'd to me at the vant', cf. Gil, p. 39, above), Do, So ('heard occasionally...but obsol[escent]') and D; and *follow* 'to baptize' (< OE *fulwian*; see *OED*, s.v. Fullought 'baptism' [< OE *ful(l)wiht*], Full v. 1, Vol-louth, Volow), last recorded as used in Gloucestershire dialect by Tyndale, writing in 1528 ('Baptism is called volowinge in many places of Englonde'; and 'The child was well volowed (saye they); yee and our vicare is as fayre a volower as ever a prest within this twenty myles') and 1530 (above).

Some local names for feast-days may still survive, at least if the celebrations attendant on the feasts still take place. *EDD* records from Wo, Sa (?), Bk, Sx and W *Cattern* (*-day* or *-tide*) 'St Catherine's Day', November 25, on which children went round begging for apples and beer, this activity giving rise to the verbal nouns *catterning* or *cattering*. *Crouchmas* is an old title for the feast of the Invention of the Holy Cross (May 3), from late OE *crūc* (< Latin *crucis*) + *-mass*. It is recorded by *OED* from 1389 up until 1706, when it is mentioned as a festival kept by Roman Catholics, and in 1891 the feast of *Crouchmas* is said to be 'quite obsolete'. *Skirisfurisday*, recorded by *EDD* from Scotland, Nb and Du, is an old northern title for Maundy Thursday, and is < ME *Skyre thuresday*, *Skyrys Thursday*, ON *Skíri-þórsdagr*, cf. ON *skírr* adj. 'clear, pure', *skíra* (= OE *fulwian*) 'to cleanse, baptize', a verb used with reference to the old Scandinavian pagan ceremony of water sprinkling, later transferred to Christian usage, and thus having a very long history. *Skirisfurisday* was used in England only up to *c.* 1670, according to *EDD*, but *OED* (s.v. Skire Thursday) gives *Skies Thursday* 1677.

These are but a few examples of local, popular designations for ecclesiastical concepts. Even if most or all of them are now obsolete, a thorough investigation would at least show when they became obsolete, and add something to our knowledge of the gradual decline in dialectal usage.

Local taboo words

Under this heading must be mentioned some words used in local areas as substitutions for names the mention of which is likely to precipitate bad luck or disaster. These are especially prevalent in fishing communities, which are notoriously superstitious. Up and down the coasts of Britain any land animal seems to be taboo to the fisherman, and this gives rise to a variety of circumlocutions for them.[17] Such was certainly the case until recently in Cornwall: no dog, even, was allowed on board a boat, and to name a *four-legger* or a *two-decker*, especially a cat, hare or rabbit, was regarded as an invitation to ill-luck. These are Mousehole expressions, but at Polperro and most other Cornish fishing ports the taboo was confined to hares and rabbits. Carew noted in 1602 that the Cornish fishermen disliked the mention of 'hares or such uncouth things', and Cornish tinners also had their taboo-names for certain animals and birds.

Another class of tabooed items relates to the Church. In fishing communities, it is often held unlucky to see a nun or a priest. In Cornwall, again, a church-tower, used as a mark in taking bearings at sea, was called a *cleeta* (< Corn. *cleghty* 'belfry', or *cleghtour* 'bell-tower'), since the mention of the word *church* at sea is held to bring the possibility of bad fishing,[18] and *steeple* may also be used from the same motive. *Tower* was a circumlocution used for St Buryan church and for Paul church in Cornwall, and *town* for Cury church. *White-choker* was similarly used in Mousehole for a priest or minister of religion, and *fore-and-after* (perhaps with reference to the Roman collar, worn 'fore and after') in Newlyn.

Children's words

A most interesting class of words showing significant regional distributions are those used by children for various notions. Some of these receive attention in Iona and Peter Opie's *The Lore and Language of Schoolchildren*, from which most of the information here is taken. A vast assortment of words denote gaining possession of an object (pp. 135–6), of which the term *bags* is probably the best-known (variants of it being *bagsy, baggy mine*). *Ballow* (*ballow that* or *I ballows that*), *barley* (*barley me that*) and *bollars* (*I bollars* or *bollar me*) seem to be all variants of one phrase, current in north-west England (YWR, La, Ch), *ferry* is also in use in YWR, *fogs* or *fog it* and *jigs it* in Manchester and elsewhere in the west Midlands, *nab it, nag it, pike I* or *prior pike* are all west-Midland terms, and there are others. Some of the same words are used for claiming precedence (pp. 137–9)—for securing a privilege or first place—*bags* and its variants again being the most common (*bags I first* and so on), used throughout southern England (but *squits* is recorded from Poplar, *lardie* from Enfield) and not at all uncommon in the north.

It is in the north of England, however, that the most distinctive terms of precedence prevail: in an area extending from Stoke-on-Trent to Lincoln and from Lincoln northwards on the eastern side of the Pennines, the operative word—in varying pronunciations—is *foggy* (*I'm foggy* = 'I have the right to be first'), while *laggy* is used to indicate that the last place is wanted. But *ferry* prevails in the towns of YWR—Bradford, Halifax, Huddersfield—the dividing line between *foggy* and *ferry* appearing to run through Sheffield, Barnsley, Wakefield and Leeds: this is a transitional area, from which both usages are recorded. *Ferry* is again in use in Furness, We and Cu, but *firsy* prevails in La.[19]

As the Opies observe (p. 141), perhaps the most important word in the schoolchild's vocabulary is his truce term, to which, interestingly, there is now no exact equivalent in adult speech. This is used, sometimes in conjunction with a sign such as crossing fingers or feet, raising the right hand and so on, to gain temporary relief from some boisterous activity, fighting, etc. Although in some places more than one term is known (*creams, creamos, creamy-olivers, ollyoxalls, olly-olly-ee, double queenie, cross kings, fingers, pax*, and also *breather* were all cited by a class at a girls' grammar school in Portsmouth, for example), on the whole there appears to be a degree of uniformity, some terms turning out to be known from other areas and not strictly native to the area under investigation, and one term usually being predominant. Map 4 gives the data for the whole country (as also for Scotland and Wales), and is believed to be true for about 90 per cent of the juvenile population. Interesting situations emerge at the points marked by rectangles, namely Knighton in

Map 4   Children's truce-terms

Radnorshire and Market Rasen in Lincolnshire, which are both on boundary areas, Knighton on the boundary between *cree* and *barley*, and Market Rasen on that between *kings* and *crosses*. Another significant point which emerged from the Opies' enquiry was that the urban children's usage is at odds with the rest of the surrounding countryside, Lincoln City being unlike the rest of the county with its *screams*, and Knighton being predominantly *cree* in a *barley* area.

Children have numerous names for nosy parkers, swankpots, cowards, sneaks and other unpopular types, but one of the epithets for a sulker or spoil-sport has a clear north-Midland distribution: this is *mardy* (< *marred* + *-y*). The northern boundary of the *mardy* area lies (very roughly) in south La and south Y, while its southern boundary extends as far south as Lei in the centre of the country. The whole area (see *Lore and Language*, fig. 8, p. 177) consists of a band from the west coast (Ch, south La) to the east (north L).

These are again only a few examples of usages that deserve a complete survey of their own. A comparison with the similar usages remembered by older people, such as the *SED* informants, from their own youth might be very revealing indeed, perhaps showing the length of time an expression had been entrenched in a certain area, or, on the other hand, its comparative newness, adoption (from another area?) and so on. To take an example, the Opies note (pp. 166–7) that sweets are referred to as *comforters*, *goodies* ('a common term'), *sucks* or *suckers* and *quenchers*, also as *candies* in Cleethorpes, which they ascribe to possible American influence (but cf. *EDD*, s.v. Candy, where it is recorded from Scotland, Ireland, Nb, Du, L and Wa; and also *OED*, which makes it clear that the word has been on record from *c.* 1420), and always *spice* in YWR. They state, however, that '"lollies" is also becoming a general term'.

A glance at the information at *SED* V.8.4 (*some sweets*) shows a wide variety of words, usually with clearly defined local distributions —*bullets*, *toffees*, *lozengers*, *c(r)ooshies*, etc. *Comforters* is not found at all, *goodies* is certainly 'a common term', though mostly found in YER, YNR, north-east We and Cu, *sucks* and *suckers* are Midland terms, *quenchers* is not mentioned at all, *candy* is found at L 8 (Old Bolingbroke), and *lollies* only in north Nth, O, east W, north Ha and west Sr (*EDD* gives it, s.v. Lolly sb. 2, for Wa, O and East Anglia, with only three quotations), there being a round dozen examples altogether. *Lollipops*, however, is found in adjacent areas to the west and east, and if *lollies* really is becoming general, it is presumably doing so from the south-east-Midland area where it has been entrenched as a traditional term for many years. Needless to say, *sweets* (first ref. *OED* 1851) and *sweeties* (ibid., 1721 N.B.) are in common use everywhere, being the sole usage in some localities, and more especially in the south of the country, both in the south-east around London and in the far south west (So, D, Co).

5   Local Accents

As we have noted, *accent* is distinguished from *dialect* as referring only to the phonetic or to the phonological level of dialectal speech. I have further suggested that there are in England today a large number of different dialects and—by implication—accents, which range from RP through various modified forms of local accent to the traditional local accents themselves, and that even speakers who habitually use a local accent are today bilingual.

We are not able today always to identify 'local' with 'traditional', since many accents are in a state of fragmentation and their tradition-al sound system may have been modified by contact with RP. It must, however, be insisted that a large number of traditional features are currently preserved in local dialect, at least in local *rural* dialect, e.g. the use of *r* in preconsonantal positions ([kaɽːt], [nɪəɽli]), the occur-rence of [ç] in *light*, *night*, and that quite a number of these features are more stable than we are sometimes led to believe.[1] Anyone who has heard the accent sometimes used by, say, Yorkshire schoolchildren knows that this is true, while there is no doubt at all that among older people an enormous amount of broad accent may still be heard in the Yorkshire dales, for example, and else-where. Old words may drop out of use, but old pronunciations tend to stick and be handed down. We shall return to this subject in Chapter 9.

Differences between accents occur on at least three levels: (1) *systemic*, i.e. one dialectal system has a different number of phonemes from another, (2) *distributional*, i.e. although two or more dialects may have identical phonemes within their systems, these are dis-tributed differently, so that in a certain context one dialect has one phoneme while in the same context another dialect has a different one, and (3) *realizational*, i.e. there is a difference between two or more dialects in the phonetic realization of their (identical) phonemic systems.[2] Examples of each of these are: (1) the absence of [ʌ] in, e.g., *butter*, *cut*, in the northern dialects, which traditionally use [ʊ] instead; (2) the use of northern [a] (= RP and southern [ɑː]) in *chaff*, *grass*, *path*, etc.; (3) the different pronunciations of the *r* phoneme in initial positions—[ʁ] in Northumberland and Durham, [ɽ] in the south-west, [r] and [ɾ] in some parts of the north, [ɹ] in south-east and Midland England. Of these types of variation, the first is obviously of the greatest importance, the second less so, and the third the least. It should, however, be observed that although realizational differences may be relatively unimportant from the systemic point of view, they may yet have important *indexal* functions in differentiating between dialects.

It is clear that dialectal description is no easy matter.[3] The theoretical and practical problems inherent in phonemic analysis of providing a description of the structures of all (or even some) English accents mean that such a description would demand a book to itself. It is, however, no part of my intention to provide a phonemic analysis of the structures of the English dialects or to make contrasts between such structures. Without a great deal more preliminary work than has at present been done, it is indeed doubtful whether this is possible.[4] My present task is made easier by the considerations that (*a*) I shall deal here only with the older 'tradition-al' element in English dialect, and the features mentioned below are all of this stratum of English, and (*b*) I believe that most readers will find a general statement of some of the differentiating factors between dialects—no matter on which of the three levels mentioned above they occur—of more immediate interest than an impossible attempt to rival A. J. Ellis in phonemic descriptions of all the dialects. For descriptions of this sort the appropriate works may be consulted. In a general treatment of the present type such descriptions are quite out of place.

The following remarks on various features of traditional regional dialect are based on data to be found in *SED*. I have tried to give such features an historical perspective by adding some observa-tions about their known antecedents. It should be noted that in expressions such as 'northern [ʊ] = southern [ʌ]' the phonetic values are generalized examples, sometimes representative of a wide variety of sounds (e.g. 'southern [ʌ]' may represent [ʌ], [ʌ], [ä], [ə], etc.). I have preferred to use this method consistently rather than to confer phonemic status upon the sounds of dialects not yet phonemically analysed, by using the traditional / /.

On the basis of various phonological criteria, the dialects of the north of England may be distinguished from those of the south. These criteria are numerous, but two are of special importance:

(1) Northern [ʊ] = southern [ʌ] in *butter, cut, gull, some*. (< ME *u*). ME *u* (pronounced [ʊ]) retains its old quality not only over all

the north of England—an area with which it is often associated—
but also in a good deal of the Midlands and sporadically in the
south, whereas the usual southern reflex is some variety of [ʌ],
the quality of the latter depending upon the area, so that in London
and the Home Counties it is a fronted type and tends towards [a].
Map 5 shows the isogloss dividing [ʊ] from [ʌ] in the word *some*
(< ME *sum*; V.8.4).

(2) Northern [a] = southern [ɑː] in *chaff, grass, path.* (< ME *a*).
The short vowel [a] followed by [f], [s] or [θ] appears in southern
English and RP as [ɑː], whereas in the north [a] is unlengthened
and unretracted. The chief difference between north and south is
one of length: to the north of Sa, Wo, Wa, Nth, Hu, C and Nf,
[a] is short, but to the south, with occasional exceptions, a long vowel
appears, [ɑː] predominating in the south-east and in south Nf,
while the rest of the south has [aː], [æː]. Present-day RP [ɑː] was
probably, in fact, adopted from the south-eastern dialects in the
eighteenth century, replacing an earlier [æː] (thus ME *a* > [æ] >
[æː] > [ɑː]) in these contexts. The map shows the isogloss dividing
the short from the long forms in *chaff* (< ME *chaf*; II.8.5).

Although they are not identical, the [ʊ ~ ʌ] and the [a ~ ɑː] isoglosses may be regarded as constituting major phonological divisions
between northern and southern England. One or two similar features,
however, deserve brief mention.

Words of the *calf, half, palm* class (containing ME *a* + *lf, lm*)
show the regular development of ME *al* + consonant (cf. *fall,
stalk*) to [ɔː] in the north and north Midlands—north of He, south
St, Lei, R, Nth, south L, C and Nf—while the southern dialects
show a special development to [aː], [æː], [ɑː] (also the RP form).

In RP, words of French origin in the *aunt, branch, dance, grant*
class are now pronounced with [ɑː], but the dialects shows great
diversity, the greatest cleavage being between those which have a
long vowel and those which have a short. In *aunt* (VIII.1.12), long
vowels [ɑː], [aː], [æː] predominate all over southern England except
in Co, north-west D and in other sporadic instances, [ɑː] itself being
most common in Nf and the south-east. (The long vowels are developed from an irregular monophthongization of ME *au* < AN *au*,
but regularly developed unmonophthongized forms with [ə] and
[ɒ] occur in the north Midlands.) The short forms predominate in
Co, north-west D, sporadically elsewhere in the south, and almost
everywhere north of Sa, St, Db, Lei, R, Nth and south L; these are
usually assumed to derive not from AN *au* but from Continental
Fr *a*. The reason for this interesting geographical distribution between

Map 5   *Some* and *chaff*

——— General southern limit of [ɔ] in *some* (V.8.4)

− − − General southern limit of a short vowel in *chaff* (II.8.5)

north and south (and for the short vowel in Co and D) is not at present clear.

The features discussed above broadly mark off northern from southern England. Within this northern dialect area, however, 'northern' proper is clearly differentiated from 'north Midlands' (and thus also 'southern', with which it shares features) by a bundle of isoglosses:

(1) Northern [uː] = north-Midland and southern [aʊ] in *cow*, *down*, *house*. (< ME *ū*).

ME *ū* began to diphthongize soon after 1400, and, developing via the stages [ou] and [əu], eventually reached NE [aʊ].

In present-day dialect, England north of the Humber (plus a small part of north L) forms a separate and distinct area in that here ME *ū* is retained undiphthongized. For the rest of the country, the *SED* material for, e.g., *house* (< OE *hūs*, ME *hous*; V.1.1) shows a bewildering profusion of forms. The first element of the diphthong may be almost any vowel sound—[ɛ], [æ], [a], [ɑ], [ɒ], [ʌ], [o], [ə], and others. The second element may show fronting or centralization ([ü], [ʏ], etc.), or may appear in a much reduced form, sometimes simply as a glide [ə] or [a]. To illustrate: La 9 [æˑəs], Y 30 [ɛəs], Db 6 [ɛ̃ːs], Lei 9 [aːˤs]. These forms appear to be most frequent in the north Midlands, as far south as St, and Lei and R, but do not occur in the south and east of England (full [o] being usual as the second element here) except in London and its environs (cf. [gɹiːnæ̃ːˤs] *green-house* at K 2, [kæː] *cow* (III.1.1) at Sr 1, [aːs] at MxL 2 [Hackney]). Sometimes the reduced second element or glide disappears altogether, and we get forms like [aːs], [ɛːs], [kaː], [kɛː] in the north Midlands (as well as London, K, Sr—as above).

(2) Northern [ɪə] = north-Midland and southern [uː], [ɒɪ] (YWR only); [o], in *fool, goose, spoon, cook, good, look*. (< ME *ǭ*). YWR is alone in showing [ɒɪ] as a reflex of ME *ǭ*. North of the Humber the dialectal developments are accounted for by the fact that northern ME *ǭ* had become a front sound, variously written *u, ui, uy, oi, oy*, sometime in the late thirteenth century. Opinion differs as to the quality of this vowel, whether [ʏː], [yː], [öː], etc., but whatever it was it has given a modern diphthong in the north of England commencing with [ɪ] (sometimes becoming [j] in Nb and Du), thus [ɪo], [ɪu], [ɪə], etc., and this occurs in ME *ǭ*-words of the RP [uː], [ʌ], or [o] types (*food, gloves, hook*). The map of the north of England shows these forms rather frequently interspersed with

RP forms, however, and there is no doubt that these very distinctively 'dialectal' sounds are now being replaced by ones more closely approximating to those of RP.

(3) Northern [ʊə] = north-Midland [ʊə], southern [əʊ], in *bone, loaf, road, stone*. (< ME *ā, ǭ*).

In the north of England OE *ā*, ON *á* were retained in ME times, whereas in the south they were rounded to *ǭ* ([ɔ:]), which was then raised to [o:] and ended up in RP as [əʊ]. The present-day reflexes are clearly differentiated between those of ME *ā* origin and those of ME *ǭ* origin. The former are represented by forms such as [ʊə], [ʊa], [ea], and occur only in the four northern counties, north La and north and east Y. The reflexes of ME *ǭ* are the forms in [ʊə], [ʊa], etc., which are distributed throughout south and west Y and central La, and also in L and east Nt (as well as some examples further south, see below). [o:] and [ɔ:] in this area are attempts to render an RP type, as are also [œ:] and [ø:] in Nb and Du.

Over the greater part of southern and Midland England [o:] < ME *ǭ* has been retained, sometimes, however, being raised to the position usually held by the reflexes of *ǭ*-words, namely [u:]. Sometimes it appears as [ɔ:], and all of these types may also be characterized by an off-glide, e.g. [ɔ:ə],[5] [o:ə]. In some areas, especially in East Anglia, the east Midlands and south-east England, ME *ǭ* results in a diphthong [ʌʊ], [oʊ], [əʊ] or the like. Occasionally (especially in the south-west) stress-shifting in an original [u:ə] diphthong (which may occur here as well as further north) has resulted in [wʊ], [wə] as in [spwʊks] *spokes* (I.9.6) at Gl 6, [gɾəɪnstwən] *grindstone* (IV.2.7) at W 3/4, etc.

(4) Northern [ʊə] = north-Midland [ɒɪ], southern [əʊ], in *coal, coat, foal, hole*. (< ME *ŏ*- lengthened).

ME *o* lengthened in open syllables gives [ʊə] throughout most of northern England (plus the usual reflexes of ME *ǭ* in the Midlands and south),[6] with [œ:] [ø:] occurring again in Nb and north Du, but with a new sound [ɒɪ] in the southern part of YWR and central La. This development accounts for the forms of a very large number of local place-names such as The Royd, Mytholmroyd (< OE **rod, **rodu* 'clearing'), North Goyts (< OE **gota* 'water channel'; cf. *SED*, i, IV.1.1) and Hoyle House (< OE, ON *hol* 'hole, hollow').[7]

(5) Northern [i:], [ʊə] = north-Midland [ɛɪ], southern [i:], in *eat, meat, speak*. (< ME *ě*- lengthened).

89

In the north-Midland dialects the reflexes of ME $\bar{ę}$ < OE $\bar{æ}$, $\bar{e}a$, are differentiated from those of ME $\bar{ę}$ < OE e lengthened in open syllables (sometimes known as '$\bar{e}_3$'), the former resulting in [ɪə], the latter in [ɛɪ]. The more northerly dialects, however, do not differentiate in this way, having [iː], [ɪə] for both ME types. There is thus in words of ME $\bar{e}_3$ origin contrast between a northern [iː], [ɪə] and north-Midland [ɛɪ].

(6) Northern [ɒ] = north-Midland and southern [aʊ] in *ground, pound*. (< ME *u*).

In words such as those cited (< OE *grund, pund*), the northern dialects do not show evidence of lengthening to OE $\bar{u}$ and thus diphthonging before [nd], whereas the rest of the country does, so that in the north, instead of a diphthong such words contain [ɒ]. The southern boundary of this area occurs in the north Midlands, but fluctuates a good deal: the southern boundary of [ɒ] in *ground* (IV.4.1) passes in a diagonal line from the mouth of the Humber through YWR, north-west to central La, while that of [ɒ] in *pound* (VII.8.2–4) virtually follows the southern county boundary of Y except for the three southernmost *SED* localities (32–4), thereafter following the boundary between Y and La up to central La. These isoglosses are thus much further south than the [uː~aʊ] isogloss, above.

(7) Northern [ɪ] = north-Midland and southern [aɪ] in *blind, find, climb*. (< ME *i*).

In words such as those cited (< OE *blind, findan, climban*), again the northern dialects do not show lengthening to OE $\bar{i}$ and thus diphthonging before [nd], [mb], whereas the rest of the country normally does, so that in the north, instead of a diphthong such words have [ɪ]. As with *ground, pound*, above, the southern boundary of this area occurs in the north Midlands, but fluctuates a good deal, so that bundles of isoglosses for both of these sounds occur in a very broad belt, which stretches from north L to central La. On the whole, however, the southern boundaries of [ɪ] follow those of [ɒ].[8]

(8) Northern [a] = north-Midland and southern [ɒ] in *long, wrong*. (< ME *-ang/-ong*).

In OE, short vowels were lengthened before the consonant groups *ld, nd, mb, ng*, etc. (cf. (6), (7), above), except when a third consonant followed or in words with reduced sentence stress, but before some of these groups the vowel became short again in ME. South of the

90

Humber, where OE $\bar{a}$ > $\bar{\varrho}$ during the eleventh and twelfth centuries, shortening usually gives o, as in RP *long, wrong*, etc. North of the Humber, however, OE $\bar{a}$ did not become $\bar{\varrho}$, and, when shortened, therefore resulted in a, thus *lang, wrang*, etc. (See *SED among* IX.2.12, *throng*, under *busy* VIII.4.11, *tongs* V.3.7 and *wrong* IX.7.1a.)

In the area which we have broadly designated 'southern', two areas of special interest emerge, marked off from each other and the remainder of the area by distinctive phonological features. One is south-west England, and the other south-east England. Predominantly south-western features are:

(1) South-western initial [v] = southern [f] in *face, farmer, feed, foal*. (< ME *f-*).

[z]	[s]	*sat, see, six, sun.* (< ME *s-*).
[ð]	[θ]	*thatch, thing, thought, thumb.* (< ME *th-*).
[ʒ]	[ʃ]	*shilling, sugar.* (< ME *sh-*).
[dɹ]	[θɹ]	*three, threw.* (< ME *thr-*).

Evidence collected in *SED* shows that the voicing of initial [f] to [v] occurs most consistently in D and its immediate neighbours, i.e. north-east Co and west So, and also in Do, part of W, and south and west Ha, to a lesser extent in east So, south and west Gl and north and west W. While these are clearly the largest solid areas having the voicing of [f], outside this there is a belt of occasional voicing. The data shows that initial [f] is the most consistently voiced of all the fricative consonants. [s] appears as [z] in a more confined area: the areas of density are more or less the same, but the outer belt of occasional voicing is more thinly covered and does not extend as far to the north and east. There is, for example, nothing shown in Sr or Wa. The areas of the voicing of initial [θ] and [ʃ] recede even further to the west.

From the sporadic examples of initial voicing found to the north and east of the areas mentioned, as well as from early spellings, it is clear that initial [f], [s], [θ] and [ʃ] tended to assume a voiced quality during the OE or early ME period everywhere south of a line approximating to Watling Street except in west Co (where the English which replaced the old Cornish language was probably a non-south-western or modified south-western variety, in which the voicing of initial fricatives was considerably weakened or even non-existent). The origin of voicing, although much debated, is obscure. Perhaps first arising in the sentence in intervocalic positions, OE initial *f, s, þ* were already pronounced [v], [z], [ð] in West Saxon speech, although this was concealed by the OE orthographic system; then the voiced equivalent of OE *sc* [ʃ] was later adopted by analogy with the other fricative consonants, and loans from French (and other languages) during the period of large-scale borrowing in ME times and subsequently had voicing extended to them on an analogical basis, since words of French origin normally remain unaffected in ME and on the whole the English words seem to have slightly more concentrated and wider distributions than the French ones in present-day dialect. There is a possibility that in some words Old or Middle Low Franconian or Dutch influence may have made a contribution to voicing (cf. Du *varken* n. 'farrow', *vader* 'father', etc.). Map 6 shows the distribution of voiced initial consonants in the words *farmer, six, thumb* and *shilling.*

In two words, namely *thatch* (II.7.6) and *thistle* (II.2.2), RP initial [θ] appears as [d]: in *thatch* in south D and east Co, and in *thistle* in D, east and central Co and west So (with outlying examples at W 6 and Bk 2). The rest of the south-western 'voicing' area has [ð] in these words, except that [v] occurs in Do. The occurrence of [d] and [v] suggests series [θ] > [ð] > [d] and [θ] > [ð] > [v], implying that the process of initial voicing had been going on in these areas long enough to allow second mutations, i.e. to [d] and [v] respectively. There is, however, a possibility that [d] in *thatch* and *thistle* may owe something to Low Dutch influence, cf. MDu *decken* v., *dac* n., Du *distel.* The closure of [ð] to [d] in these two words is not connected with the south-eastern pronunciation of RP [ð] as [d] in *the, this, they, there,* etc. (see below).

When followed by [ɾ], [θ] (in *three, threw,* etc.) may appear as [d] or [d] in the south-west, presumably developing via an intermediate stage [ðɾ], but the cluster usually remains [θɹ] in the south-east, where voicing is absent. The south-western variety of *r* is so retracted as to effect retraction of the preceding [ð], which is subsequently closed and becomes the plosive [d].

    (2) South-western [aɪ], [æɪ], [ɛɪ] = southern [a] in *ash, bag, latch.*
             (< ME *a*).
        [ɛɪ], [aɪ] = southern [ɛ] in *fresh, eggs, hedge.*
             (< ME *e*).
        [ɒɪ] = southern [ɒ] in *wash.* (< ME *a*).

Map 6   *Farmer, six, thumb* and *shilling*

——————	Limit of [v] in *farmer* (VIII.4.7)
··········	Limit of [z] in *six* (VII.1.5)
—·—·—	Limit of [ð] in *thumb* (VI.7.6)
— — —	Limit of [ʒ] in *shilling* (VII.7.5)
▲	additional examples

In the west, and more especially in the south-west, diphthongized forms [aɪ], [ɛɪ], [ɒɪ] and their variants occur before [ʃ], [tʃ], [dʒ] and [g]. The same, or similar, developments are attested in ME with, once again, a tendency to predominate in the west.

(3) The loss of [w] in *woman, wool.*
   The addition of [w] in *old, boil, poison.*
In the south-west the semi-vowels may be distributed differently from in RP. Initial [w] may be lost before [ɒ], but added (initially or after a preceding consonant) before long back vowels. Excepting west D and Co, [w] is lost in *woman* (VIII.1.6) south-west of a line enclosing Sa, Wo, south and west Wa, most of O, Gl, south and west W, south and west Ha, west Sr and west Sx. In *wool* (III.7.5) it is lost in a similar but smaller area in the south and west—and again, it is not lost in west D and Co. As for the addition of [w] as an on-glide, its present geographical distribution seems to be so sporadic from word to word that it is difficult to formulate any rule to cover it. In *old* (VIII.1.20), initial [w] occurs only in Do and the edges of the adjacent counties of So, W and Ha, plus an outlying example at D 10, but the examples of [w] in *whole* (VII.2.12), although few, are more widely dispersed over an area stretching from So to east Sx, as well as in the west Midlands. In *boiling* (V.8.6), the largest single area to show a [w] glide is W, but it also stretches into south-east Do, and by a narrow corridor through the centre of So into north and south D. There is another small area in He, Wo and Gl. In *poison(ous)* (IV.11.4/5), a [w] glide again occurs in most of W and in central and east Do. All of these latter cases, in which [w] appears as a glide, are perhaps remnants of an area which once included the whole of south-west England, an area, in fact, coextensive with that in which initial [w] disappears before [ɒ].

(4) The loss of [j] in *yeast, yes.*
   The addition of [j] in *earn, earth.*
Loss of [j] in *yeast* (V.6.2) shows the same pattern as loss of [w] in *woman, wool,* except that [j] also disappears on the other side of the country in east L and in one locality in Sf. Loss of [j] in *yes* (VIII.8.13), *yesterday* (VII.3.8) and *year* (VII.3.4/5/18) is, again, mainly restricted to the western counties, especially in the south to So, D, Co and Do, although scattered examples occur in the eastern counties. Once again, we may suggest that these forms are merely relic manifestations of a once more widespread feature.

94

Examples of the addition of initial [j] are not so easy to find. Such occur in *earned* (VIII.1.26) at W 2, Brk 4, Gl 6/7 and O 3, and in *earth* (VIII.5.8) at Ha 6. Initial [j] is common in *ear* (VI.4.1/3/4) and *hear* (V.4.2, VIII.2.6) except in the north and east, but such forms may be due not to the development of a [j] glide, but to a shift of stress in an original [ɪə] diphthong ([ɪə] > [ɪə́] > [jəː]).

Predominantly south-eastern features are:

(1) South-eastern initial [d] = southern [ð] in *that, there, these*. (< ME *th-*).

Initial [θ] apparently became voiced in unstressed words in the fourteenth century, and [ð] was then extended to stressed forms. Later, William Bulloker (*c.* 1530–90) describes a change of initial *th* (i.e. southern [ð]) to [d] in east Sx and K in *that, thorn* and *those*. In all localities where *SED* recordings were made, RP [ð] appears to be rapidly ousting the traditional [d], but a partially closed version of initial [d]—a cross between [d] and [ð]—is common in the Home Counties.

(2) South-eastern [iː] = southern [aɪ] in *hide, hive, lice, mice*. (< ME *ẹ̄* < OE *ȳ*).

In words which in OE contained *ȳ*, e.g. *hȳdan* 'hide', *hȳf* 'hive', *lȳs* 'lice', *mȳs* 'mice', the result in some dialects is [iː], since in these cases OE *ȳ* gave ME *ẹ̄* instead of *ī* and this in turn produced present-day [iː]. A consideration of the *SED* material for *lice* (IV.8.1) and *mice* (IV.5.1) shows that the present day [iː]-area is generally confined to the south-east and East Anglia, occurring in Brk, Sr, K, east Sx, Ess, north Hrt, Sf and south Nf.[9]

(3) South-eastern [ɛ] = southern [a] in *apple, cat, rack*. (< ME *a*).

RP [a], [æ] is occasionally raised to [ɛ] in Ess, Sr, K and Sx. RP [æ] was probably imported from south-eastern dialectal speech in the early NE period, and Dobson's suggestion[10] that ME *a* began to become [æ] in dialectal speech as early as the fifteenth century is substantiated by the fact that the south-eastern dialects have now taken the sound a stage further, namely to [ɛ].

(4) South-eastern [w] = southern [v] in *vinegar*. (< ME *v-*).

In parts of southern England, notably East Anglia and the south-east, initial and medial [v] may appear as [w], cf. V.7.19 *vinegar*, IV.9.4 *viper* (under *adder*), V.8.2 *victuals* (under *food*). This change goes back to ME and is evidenced in place-name spellings from much of southern England from the second half of the thirteenth century onwards. The area in which [v] > [w] was perhaps coextensive with the voicing area and may have taken place via a bilabial stage [ß]. The use of [w] for [v] was a well-known Cockney feature up to the last century.

On the other hand, [v] is heard for [w] in the south of England, and is again attested in ME spellings from the thirteenth century onwards. These early spellings may be inverted forms, but it may be assumed from the statements of various writers that early NE spellings of *v* for etymological *w* reveal hypercorrect pronunciations. I have noted from *SED* only [vætʃ] *watch* n. at So 3 (unpublished) and [vɒɪf] *wife* at K 5 (VIII.1.24), but there may be others.

Certain phonological features are peculiar to a west-Midland dialect area. Of these, the most important are:

(1) West-Midland [ŋg] = other dialects [ŋ] in *among, hang, sing, tongue*. (< ME *ng*).

In late ME, the final consonant in words such as those cited changed from [ŋg] to [ŋ], but in a west-Midland area it is still [ŋg]. For *tongue* (VI.5.4) this area stretches as far as central La in the north and as far as north Wo and north Wa in the south, while to the east it encloses the southern tip of Y, all of Db and west Lei.

(2) West-Midland [ɒ] = other dialects [a] in *man*, also *gander, hand*. (< ME *a/o* + nasal).

An examination of the vowel in *man* (VIII.1.6) shows that a west-Midland area has [ɒ] as against [a] in words in which ME *a/o* occurred before a final nasal. Before nasal consonants medieval manuscripts show an alternation between *a* and *o* from OE times onwards, and a comparison with the *man/mon* line as determined from ME sources (Moore–Meech–Whitehall) shows a very remarkable correlation between the two isoglosses.[11]

Within the main dialect areas distinguished above, several smaller areas emerge. In particular, a far northern one (comprising Northumberland and its environs) and a south-western one (comprising Devon, east Cornwall and west Somerset) should be mentioned.

The first of these areas is characterized by the retention of initial [h], whereas, with the exception of one or two dialect areas, in general the dialects lose it (see further below).

In a similar area, comprising Northumberland, north Durham and west Cumberland, perhaps originally the same area in which initial [h] is retained, and more or less coextensive with the [ʁ] area (see p. 99, below), initial [hw], as in *what, where, which, white,* is retained. In the south of England, and in RP, apart from pedagogical efforts to restore it, aspiration of initial [w] was lost at the end of the ME period.

The south-western dialects of Devon, north-east Cornwall and west Somerset are especially noted for their front-rounded articulation of [uː] and [ɒ] (viz. [y(ː)]), and of [aɒ] (viz. [œʏ] or the like) (< ME ǭ, u and iu; ME ū).

The Great Vowel Shift shows, among other things, the constant tendency of English vowels to a forward and upward movement, and the dialectal forms equivalent to RP [uː] and [ɒ] often take this a step further by showing a fronting to [y(ː)], [ö], etc. In the south-western area under discussion, words of the type *food, spoon* consistently show [yː] and those of the type *cook, good* show [y]. In this development, the *food, spoon* words are also joined by those containing ME *iu,* e.g. *few, new, tune,*[12] and the *cook, good* words by those containing ME *u* < OE *u* in words like *bull, bush* (in which [ɒ] was retained rounded on account of the phonetic context). We thus have a table:

South-western [uː] < ME ǭ ⎱ > [yː]
[iu] <   iu ⎰

[ɒ] <   ǭ ⎱ > [y]
[ɒ] <   u ⎰

These fronted vowels have been a source of much interest to dialectologists. The fronting evidently took place after the vowels in question had assumed the forms [uː], [ɒ] (as in present-day RP), and probably somewhere between 1550 and 1650.[13] There is no evidence that this fronting is the result of a Celtic substratum,[14] and in any case areas other than the south-west show fronting of various kinds.

In the same south-western area, as stated above, ME ū has given [œʏ] or the like.[15] This sound perhaps arises from an earlier diphthong ending in [ɒ] in which the second element became [ʏ] at the same time (sixteenth-seventeenth centuries) as the fronting of [ɒ] from ME ǭ, u (above), and which in turn could produce a front rounded sound [œ] as the first element, thus:

ME ū > [əu] > [εɒ] > [εʏ] > [œʏ]

Finally, there are one or two selected features which may be discussed under the heading of 'general or miscellaneous'. These are:

(1) Initial [h]

The usual development of intitial [h] in the dialects is that it is lost, but it is retained in what seem to be basically four areas. These are: a northern area comprising Nb and parts of the adjacent counties (penetrating into north Y), a south-western area comprising So and the adjacent parts of W and D (occasionally extending somewhat further afield), East Anglia and Ess and adjacent districts, and finally London, Sr, K and north Sx. In this last area, the presence of initial [h] may be due to RP influence.

(2) [θ]

The simplification of [θ] to [f] is a well-attested and widely spread phenomenon. Although generally associated with Cockney and London pronunciation (as in [sɑːfɛnd] *Southend*), it is in fact characteristic not only of the Home Counties as a whole but of areas further afield. It can, for example, be heard in Leeds. The reverse (i.e. [f] > [θ]) is not so common, but was recorded in *fellies* (I.9.9) on the Isle of Wight, while the voiced equivalent [ð] (presupposing a series [f] > [v] > [ð]) occurs in a small area of south W and west Ha.

(3) The types of *r*

The present-day dialects show various different pronunciations of *r*, no doubt reflecting a similar diversity in ME, and in the dialects *r* is often pronounced preconsonantally and finally as well as initially and before vowels.

The *SED* material for III.13.13 *rabbits* shows that the chief dialectal type is [ɹ] as in RP, which occupies the whole of England except for a small area in the far north, the south-west and occasional localities elsewhere. The next largest area is the south-western [ɾ] area, occupying Co, D, So, W and Ha. There is a small sub-area in south So in which [ɾ] is aspirated, i.e. [hɾ]; it is clear from its occurrence in *rabbits* and other words, however, that the [hɾ] is not necessarily historical, i.e. it does not necessarily represent OE *hr* as in *hring*. The material for *rabbits* does not show metathesized initial [ɾ], which occurs, for example, in [əɾːd] *red* (V.10.7) in west So and north-east D,[16] and which is sometimes aspirated, as in [həɾːd] *red* (ibid.), occurring in scattered localities in So and in W 5. The only vowels which seem amenable to the initial metathesis are [ʊ] and [ɛ], and we may assume a development:

[(h)ɽɪ]

    > [(h)ɽə] > [(h)ə˞ː]

[(h)ɽɛ]

Apart from the south-western [ɽ] area, there is a small area comprising Nb and north Du in which initial *r* is articulated as a uvular sound, phonetically [ʁ]. This sound is first mentioned by Daniel Defoe in his account of northern journeys (see p. 41, above). Lastly, initial *r* may occasionally occur—in the north only—as rolled [r]. In *rabbits* it is recorded from Cu 1, but is certainly current in other parts of the north (e.g. in Leeds).

Non-initially *r* may either be pronounced independently—[ɹ], [ɽ], etc.—or, after a vowel, it may take the form of what is known as *r*-colouring, i.e. it colours or affects the preceding vowel with an *r*-quality, but has no separate existence from the vowel. (It may be expressed thus [ə˞ː], [ə˞ː].) The *SED* material for VIII.4.7 *farmer* shows that the largest area in which *r* occurs preconsonantally is south and west of a line running diagonally from Sx through the Midlands (but avoiding the London area) up to south Ch. In this area it is almost always of an [ɽ] quality, but gives way to an [ɹ] quality in north Sr and K. This area is much more extensive than that of initial [ɽ] (above).

In La and the counties bordering it to the south and east non-initial *r* is of an [ɹ] type, but is perhaps slightly more retroflex than this transcription would suggest. Elsewhere, [ɹ] occurs occasionally in Y and L and in other counties. [r] emerges again at Cu 1 and [ʁ] in Nb and north Du. The rest of the country, apart from these areas, has now no *r* or *r*-colouring ([fɑːmə], etc.).

In the south and south-west, [ɽ], as noted above, can produce metathesis—not only initially but postconsonantally, giving rise to the well-known *purdy* 'pretty' (VI.5.18), *gurt* 'great' (IX.1.6) forms in an area extending to the north as far as Brk, south O and Bk, and to the east as far as west Sr and Sx. London, Mx and K appear to have no traces of it. It also modifies adjacent consonants [t, d, n, s, z, 1], giving them a retroflex quality as in, for example, [tʈiː] *tree*, [ʃə˞ː t̬] *shirt*, [tɛ˞ːʐ] *tears* v., [ʂ tʂɔː] *straw*, [gə˞ːɭ] *girl*.

(4) The types of *l*

l is pronounced variously, even in RP, according to the phonetic context: the *l* in *feel*, for example, occurring finally, is usually a 'dark' type ([ɫ]), while that in *illicit* is a 'clear' one, occurring, as it does, between two front vowels. But outside RP there is also a geo-

99

graphical distribution of dark and clear *l*. The *SED* material for III.7.5 *wool* (which in RP always has [ɫ]), shows that dark *l* occurs south of a line running from north He in the west, through north Wo, Wa, to the south of Db, Nt and L, and along the Nf-Sf county boundary, while the clear variety is characteristic of the area to the north of this line. In some areas, the *l* is vocalized and disappears completely—notably in Sx and parts of Sr, K and Ess, but also in east Nb and in Cu and We.[17]

(5) The development of ME [ç] and [x]

The ME palatal and velar fricatives (represented orthographically by *h*, *ȝ*, *gh*), as in *right, eight, weight; dough, enough, laugh*, gradually disappeared in pronunciation in late ME or early NE, the velar fricative sometimes, however, becoming [f] (one or the other after much fluctuation later becoming standardized—thus in present-day RP *rough* and *draught* have [f], while *bough* and *bought* do not).

The twofold development of [x] (viz. to [f] or zero) has also taken place in the dialects, but the distribution of the two types is different, so that the dialects often have [f] where RP has zero, and vice versa. There are also one or two other dialectal variants, e.g. [θ]. In all cases, the non-RP form is recessive, so that, in *trough* (< OE *trog, troh*, ME *trouȝ*, etc.; III.9.3), for example, a zero ending is registered south of a line running diagonally from K across the the country to north He, excluding, however, central and west Co and south D, with smaller areas in east Ess, Nf, R, Nb and Du and Y 6. The rest of the country has the usual [f] except for [θ] at K 4, O 3, Nf 8, Ess 9/13,[18] [ft] at Nf 13, Sf 2, Bk 2/4, [x] at Y 30 and [xf] at La 12 (on these last two, see below). *Enough* (< OE *genōg, genōh*, ME *inogh*, etc.; III.8.4a), on the other hand, shows quite a different picture: zero is registered chiefly in the east Midlands—L, R, Nth, Hu, C, Nf, Sf 2, Bd 3. It occurs in the north and west only at La 7/10, Y 5/8/26/30/31, Ch 1 and Wo 7. Over the whole of the south of England, final [f] is now regular ([xf] was recorded at La 12 and [x] at Y 21). *Cough* (< ME *coghen*, etc.; VI.8.3) and *laugh* (< OE *hlæhhan*, ME *laȝhen*, etc.; VIII.8.7, IX.2.14), possibly—like *enough* —because of their frequent use (cf. *trough*, a word now restricted mainly to agricultural communities), now show RP final [f] everywhere, except for [k] at St 5 and [xf] at La 12, in *cough*, and [xf] at La 12 in *laugh*.

In words like *dough* and *plough* the area of zero endings is not identical with that in which they occur in *trough*—not surprisingly, since here it is the [f] forms that are recessive, while zero is regular almost everywhere. Final [f] in *dough* (< OE *dāg*, *dāh*, ME *doʒ*, etc.; V.6.3), apart from sporadic occurrences, mainly occurs in the north Midlands—south La and Y, east Ch, north Db—and in south Sa and Wo. *Plough* (< OE *plōg*, *plōh*, ME *plouʒ*, etc.; I.8.1) has [f] only at Du 2/6, La 11 and sporadically throughout Y. *Shoe* (< OE *scōh*, *scō*, ME *sceoh*, *sho*, etc.; VI.14.22) has [f] in south La and Ch 2.

Occasionally ME [x] results in [k] (cf. YWR place-names such as Heckmondwike '*Hēahmund's wīc*'), and was recorded in [fɛlks] *fellies* (< OE *felg*, ME *felghe*, etc.; I.9.9) at La 9, Y 17/29 (cf. [fɛlfs] at Y 11 and [fɛlvz] at Y 28). [flɛks] occurs as a form of *fleas* (< OE *flēah*, ME *fle*, etc.; IV.8.4) in Db and La (cf. [flɛfs] in Ch, St and La, [fjɒf] (pl.) at Sa 2 and [flɛɪθ] (pl.) at La 11, also the Db place-name Belph < *Belgh*).

Finally, [ç] and [x] are occasionally retained in northern English dialects (as in Scots). Evidence for their existence in the 1930s in Crag Vale (south-west Y) and Todmorden (La) is given by B. Hedevind, *The Dialect of Dentdale*, §8:46, and [x] is recorded by *SED* from Y 21 (Heptonstall) in the incidental material forms [ɛɪmɒx], [mɒx] (beside [ɛɪmɒf]) (*hay-*)*mow* (< OE *mūga*; see I.3.18). Cf. also [x] at Y 30 and [xf] at La 12 in *trough*, above. At La 9, the informant stated that his father used to say [dɹɒxt] *drought* (VII.6.20). [ç] is recorded in *light* (V.2.12) and *night* (VII.3.11) again from Y 21. At Neston, Ch, Mr M. V. Barry recorded the pronunciation of the place-name Saughall (Domesday Book *Salhale*, *Salchale* c. 1100, *Salighale* ante 1271, < OE *salh-halh*, see *DEPN*, s.v.) as [sɔːxəl] (beside [sɔːkəl]).[19] [x] is also recorded (beside [f]) as the medial consonant in *drucken* (< ON *drukkin*) at La 9 and Y 21—the YWR/La county boundary—where it presumably arose as a secondary development from the geminate [kk]. From the above information it is clear that [x] and [ç] are still current (although rarely) in a very small area comprising the YWR/La boundary and also in Ch (Neston). Elsewhere in England, however, they have completely disappeared. An intensive search in this small area might nevertheless yield further examples.

This chapter has been chiefly occupied with describing various phonological developments characteristic of English dialects, and especially some which show significant regional patterns. In conclusion, it is relevant to summarize the definite areas and boundaries which can be said to have emerged. A. J. Ellis, working from the basis of his 'ten transverse lines', which 'divide the whole country into regions where certain pron[unciations] are prevalent',[20] was able to distinguish six great divisions—namely Southern, Western, Eastern, Midland, Northern, and Lowland (Scottish)—which were then further subdivided into forty-two dialect districts. I do not claim to attempt anything of this sort here, but it seems a fair enough prophecy that when English dialects are classified again (if they ever are), their remnants will be seen to correspond remarkably well with Ellis's results.

First of all, there are contrasting dialectal features which divide the country into two regions, north and south, although the isoglosses defining the areas are not strictly identical. The most important of these are the northern [ʊ]—southern [ʌ] line and the boundary between northern [a] and southern [ɑː], etc., in *chaff*, *grass*, *path*. Less important boundaries are those between northern [kɔːf] *calf* and southern [kɑːf], etc., and between northern [ant] *aunt* (with short vowel) and southern [ɑːnt], etc. (long vowel), while there is also a north-south division between northern clear and southern dark *l*.

A better-established boundary between north and south and one along which occurs the bundling of some historically very important isoglosses shown on Map 7 is that now beginning roughly at the mouth of the Humber and passing (roughly) along the Ouse and Wharfe valleys and out of Lancashire via the Lune and Ribble valleys. To summarize material given above (pp. 88–91), this boundary divides: (1) northern [kuː] *cow* from north-Midland and southern [kaʊ]; (2) northern [gɪəs] *goose* from north-Midland and southern [guːs], [gɒɪs]; (3) northern [lɪəf] *loaf* from north-Midland [lʊəf], southern [ləʊf]; (4) northern [kʊəl] *coal* from north-Midland [kɒl], southern [kəʊl]; (5) northern [iːt], [ɪət] *eat* from north-Midland [ɛɪt]; (6) northern [gɹɑnd] *ground* from north-Midland and southern [gɹaʊnd]; (7) northern [blɪnd] *blind* from north-Midland and southern [blaɪnd]; (8) northern [ɹaŋ] *wrong* from north-Midland and southern [ɹɒŋ].

This division probably corresponds to the ancient boundary between the Anglo-Saxon kingdoms of Northumbria and Mercia.[21] As suggested in Chapter 1, however, the north-Midland type of dialect has been gradually encroaching on the northern region for some time. Interviews conducted with young people[22] have shown that an extensive region between the rivers Wharfe and Aire was at one time purely northern, but has been penetrated during the last seventy years or so by north-Midland pronunciations, giving rise to a mixed dialect. This may be partly due to migrations of miners and

Map 7 Northern/north-Midland isoglosses

———	[kuː(z)] and [kaʊ(z)] (III.1.1)
············	[ɡɪəs] and [ɡɒɪs], [ɡuːs] (IV.6.15)
– – –	[lɪəf] and [lʊəf], [ləʊf] (V.6.9)
–·—·—	[kʊəl] and [kɒɪl], [kəʊl] (IV.4.5)
–··—··—	[iːt], [ɪət] and [ɛɪt] (VI.5.11) → indicates that [iːt], [ɪət]
	continue southwards
——+——+——	[ɡɹʊnd] and [ɡɹaʊnd] (IV.4.1)
◦◦◦◦◦◦	[blɪnd] and [blaɪnd] (VI.3.4)
-------	[ɹaŋ] and [ɹɒŋ] (IX.7.1a)

farm-labourers from the Midlands (on this boundary, see also p. 135, below).

Another dialect boundary appears to follow the course of the Watling Street, the old Roman Road which came to mark the territorial division between Alfred and Guthrum in 886. The linguistic characteristics marked off by this boundary are not all phonological, and those that are do not always strictly coincide with Watling Street, though they possibly once did. The older, dialectal, features are preserved—somewhat recessively—to the west of this boundary, while their contrasting Standard English equivalents occur to the east of it. One of the most important dialectal features probably marked off by Watling Street formerly is the voicing of initial fricative consonants [f], [s], [θ], [ʃ], which appear—now rather sporadically—in the west as [v], [z], [ð], [ʒ]. Another feature is the retroflex initial [ɽ], and retroflex *r*-colouring in words like *churn*, *farmer*, while in the east there occurs initial [ɹ] and an absence of any *r*-colouring. Initial [w] is lost before [ʊ] in the dialects to the west of Watling Street, but retained in the east, in words like *woman*, *wool*.

A south-eastern dialect division has been distinguished in respect of certain phonological features, e.g. the occurrence of [iː] in *hide*, *mice*, etc.

Finally, and cutting across the south-western (Watling Street) boundary to some extent is the west-Midland dialect boundary, corresponding well with the equivalent ME boundary in respect of the reflexes of ME *a/o* + nasal, and taking the form of a half-circle enclosing parts of some of the west-Midland counties. In addition, the northern part of this area is also characterized by the presence of a final [g] in words like *tongue*.

From the modern dialects we cannot hope to reconstruct ancient dialect divisions with any exactitude—if, indeed, at all. But certain present-day dialectal boundaries do reflect in a more or less shadowy way earlier divisions in the English language. The task of exploring these boundaries and working out their implications more precisely still awaits attention.

The regions between different dialects are of very great interest in that they often show forms characteristic of both dialects. The boundary between the north and north-Midland dialects, which runs through Yorkshire, and which has been mentioned so frequently in the present chapter, is a good case in point. Taking the reflexes of ME *ō̱* and *ǫ* as examples, it is notable how many border localities of *SED* show two entirely different sounds. In, for example,

-noon (VII.3.11/14/15) and *tooth* (VI.5.6), Y 18 shows northern [ɪə] and north-Midland [ɒɪ], as does Y 24 for *boots* (IX.8.6 and VI.14.23). In *clothes* (VI.14.19/20 and V.9.7), La 2/3, Y 12/15/16/24/28 each show the north-Midland [ʊə] beside the northern [ea], [ɛə] or [ɪə] types.

Similar results emerge from consultation of the relevant maps in Professor Kolb's *Phonological Atlas*, where the colours of red and black show up two different coexistent forms with splendid clarity. Dr Rohrer found in his investigation of this area that in Whitgift, near Goole, old people would say [stʊən] *stone* and [spʊɪn] *spoon* (i.e. north-Midland forms), but also [θɹʊat] *throat* and [muːs] *mouse* (i.e. northern forms), using a 'genuine mixed dialect'.[23] It has been suggested that a special study of these transitional areas would yield very worthwhile results,[24] and even cursory examinations of our present dialect maps give every indication of this, especially if it were possible to work with a very close-meshed network of localities within such areas.

It is thus clear that although phonological boundaries are regarded as being more stable than lexical ones (since there is less tendency to loaning on this level), phonological loans are, in fact, made both from one dialect to another and also from RP into the dialects. Such loans naturally tend to obscure original boundaries and so make dialect maps more difficult to interpret, but they are important simply because they demonstrate the influence of dialects one on another and the continuing influence of RP.

In *The Phonology of a South Durham Dialect*, the work for which was done in 1921–3, Orton had no difficulty in showing to what extent the traditional dialect of his locality (Byers Green) had disintegrated, perhaps because of population movement into the area from a very early period (see p. 138, below). Three examples are especially noteworthy:

(1) Several ME sounds, namely ME *or* + consonant (*board, horse*), *ǭ* + final *r* (*door, floor*) and *ǭ* + final or intervocalic *r* (*before, story*) appear in the dialect as [œː], which Orton tentatively derives (§§79, 121, 130) from a nineteenth-century RP [ɔː] form incorrectly reproduced by dialect speakers, i.e. 'naturalized' into their own dialect.

(2) In the area north of the Humber ME *ā* (< OE *ā*, ON *á*) traditionally results in [ɪə], [ɪa], etc., but words like *goat, road* (which south of the Humber contain ME *ǭ*, which > RP [əʊ]), Orton notes (§92), 'are always pronounced with the vowel [ō]' (= [oː]), and are obviously loan-forms from RP. In some words

105

like *bake, gate* (with ME *ā* < earlier *a* lengthened) Orton recorded [ē] (= [eː]) instead of the traditional [ɩa], corresponding to RP [ɛɩ].

(3) The traditional development of ME *ǭ* in Byers Green was [ɩə], but this was often recorded (§117) in words like *goose, moon* as [öu] (= [öɷ]), perhaps a dialectal substitution for RP [uː].[25]

Professor Hans Kurath has suggested that although the sound substitutions cited by Orton are prompted by RP, they are not accurate imitations of RP phonemes, and the replacements do not introduce any new phonemes, since all the sounds used in substitutions occur elsewhere in the dialect (e.g. [eː] in *day, wait,* etc., [oː] in *coat, rose,* etc.). Thus the integrity of the vowel system is preserved, there being no additions to it and no losses.[26]

Many other examples of such substitutions could be enumerated in the north of England. They tend no doubt to take place more especially in areas which show dialectal sounds a long way removed phonetically from the cognate RP sounds, and where dialect speakers feel it desirable to identify themselves more closely with RP. These substitutions are of great interest, since the resulting sound is usually something different both from the traditional dialectal sound and the cognate RP one, as in the examples cited here.

Local accent and sound-change

It will have become evident that, whichever way we choose to investigate dialect and in whatever form we decide to present our material, there is a close link between present-day speech sounds and their antecedents in ME and OE. The present-day dialectal boundaries between, for example, [lɩəf] and [lɷəf] *loaf* (northern/north-Midland), between [vɩʃ], [ziː], [ðʌm], [ʒɩlən] and [fɩʃ], [siː], [θʌm], [ʃʊlɩn] (south-western/eastern), and between [mɒn] and [man] (western/eastern) all correspond to a large extent with earlier boundaries defining the same features in ME. A study of present-day local accent can therefore be important for our understanding of the development of the language, and certainly the reverse is true as well. As Professor McIntosh says:

The comparative investigation of a language at two or more stages of its development produces most valuable results of all kinds. What is known about some feature in it at one stage will again and again provide the answer to some unsolved problems relating to another, and this works in both directions, from an earlier period to a later and the other way round.[27]

Thus, for example, although the voicing of initial fricative consonants is but sparingly evidenced in ME, and then only for *f* and, to a lesser extent, *s*, evidence from modern south-western dialects very strongly suggests that it prevailed over a large area, as far east as Watling Street. Contrariwise, the evidence of the modern dialects for this feature is supplemented by the ME evidence for its occurrence in south-eastern counties such as Essex, where it does not occur today. By considering both types of evidence together we are in a position to know a great deal more about both the regional distribution of this feature and also its history and development than we would with only one type of evidence at our disposal.

One topic which has so far received very little attention in the light of present-day dialectal sounds is the Great Vowel Shift and it may well be that the dialects, which, as Dobson has shown, certainly played their part in the historical development of the ME long vowels to their present-day sounds, have something of value to offer in their present-day forms for our understanding of this phenomenon. The following observations, though more in the nature of suggestions than the results of research, are put forward as a tentative contribution to this end.

First of all, it may be repeated that the dialects show the same basic tendency as is seen at work in the Great Vowel Shift for the vowels to move upward and forward, and in some cases take the process a stage further. Thus, for example, ME *ǭ*, and even ME *ǭ*, may appear as [Y:] (see pp. 89, 97, above).

Secondly, the dialects sometimes show, or may show, a stage of development equivalent to that through which the ME long vowels passed to their present-day RP forms. So, for example, [ɛɪ], [eɪ], etc., the reflexes of ME *ē̜* ([ɛ:]) in many dialects, are stages identical with that through which the vowel passed before being superseded by an [e:] (> [i:]) type, and both western [əɪ], the reflex of ME *ī*, and [e:], a dialectal reflex of ME *ā*, are identical with earlier stages of development. This is not, of course, to say that the dialectal reflexes actually are earlier RP forms, although, as Dobson admits, they may sometimes be so.[28]

One significant fact which might emerge from a consideration of these reflexes is that the north of England was probably chronologically in front of the rest of the country in the development of some of the sounds. The reflexes of ME *ā* in the north are [ɪə], [ɪa], [ɪɛ], etc., suggesting that an earlier [e:] has had time to develop further here than elsewhere. This squares well with Dobson's suggestion that ME *ā* had become [ɛ:] in the north before 1400, and that [e:]

was current in this region by the sixteenth century, whereas it was not known in RP until the beginning of the seventeenth century.[29] The same seems to be true of ME $\bar{u}$ and ME $\bar{\imath}$, which in the Midlands and north Midlands sometimes show development to a monophthong, presumably further stages from, e.g., [aʊ], [aɪ] (north of the Humber, of course, ME $\bar{u}$ remained [uː]). Again, this squares with the orthoepists' evidence of an early development in the north of England, [au] already existing in the sixteenth century[30] and [ai] being reached in this area by 1600,[31] although neither of them were used in RP before the eighteenth century. Gil (p. 39, above) in 1621 notes that in the north, dialect speakers use *au* for *ou* (i.e. ME $\bar{u}$) and *ai* for *j* (i.e. ME $\bar{\imath}$).

A case may perhaps also be made out for the west of England being ahead in some respects. Monophthongization of the reflexes of ME $\bar{\imath}$ occurs in Devon and east Cornwall, moreover here ME $\bar{u}$ seems to have had time to progress to a fronted [œʏ] diphthong, and ME $\bar{\varrho}$, as well as ME $\bar{\varrho}$, may appear as [ʏː]—all stages farther advanced than in RP. All this may simply mean no more than that the development of the ME long vowels proceeded more quickly in the north and the far west—areas remote from London and southeast England—where the impulse towards conservative pronunciations was greater. It would not be wise to theorize further now, but as the distributions of the reflexes of the ME long vowels receive more and more scholarly attention it should be possible to reach some interesting conclusions.

6 Grammatical Variation

This chapter sets out to give a brief conspectus of some of the ways in which English dialect differs from Standard English on the grammatical level. The simplest way of doing this is to consider the various parts of speech in their traditional categories.

Nouns

Apart from word-formation, the chief interest of the nouns lies in the ways in which they form their plurals and in which they fulfil their possessive function. In Standard English most nouns now form their plurals by the addition of *-s* or *-es*, the only regular survival of the old weak declension being *oxen*. In the dialects, however, the old weak plural is much commoner, though apparently not as common as at the beginning of the century and earlier (*EDG* records (§379) about thirty different nouns which had an *-(e)n* termination). Some of these are nouns which are historically weak, such as *een* 'eyes', recorded by *SED* (VI.3.1) from all the northern and some of the west-Midland counties, and *flen* 'fleas' (IV.8.4), recorded from Sa, He and Wo, but there is no longer any sign of *ashen* 'ashes', *peasen* and *pean* 'peas', or *toen* 'toes', as recorded by *EDG*. Others were originally strong nouns which in dialect have now adopted weak plural endings. *Housen* 'houses' (V.1.1) is one of these: recorded by *EDG* as general in England except in the north, its distribution is now limited to two southern areas—one in Ess and East Anglia, and one in the west stretching from He and Wo (plus one example in north Sa and a double plural in north St, see below) through Gl to O and Brk. On the other hand, *shoon* 'shoes' (VI.14.22) is recorded by *SED* only from the northern counties,[1] stretching southwards as far as Ch, Db and St. There thus seems to be no one part of the country of which weak plurals are more characteristic than others. One very curious aspect of these weak plurals is that occasionally the weak form seems to be understood also as a singular (a phenomenon also recorded in *EDG*, see §384), the singular and plural thus becoming identical in form: so in *SED een* is recorded as a singular in scattered localities in Nb, Cu, La, Y, and *shoon* at Y 13/15/22.

A small group of nouns form their plurals in Standard English by a change of vowel—*goose, geese; foot, feet; man, men; mouse, mice*, etc., but in the dialects these have sometimes had an *-s* plural extended to the singular instead. Examples are scattered and no special distribution seems to emerge—*mouses* (IV.5.1) occurs sporadically in L, So, Brk, Co and D, *foots* (VI.10.1) at L 3 and O 1, *gooses* (IV.6.15) at Sa 10.

Double plurals are common in dialect. *Bellowses* 'bellows' (V.3.10) is common throughout the north, in scattered examples in the south-west, at L 2, R 1 and Sf 4. *Hawses* 'haws' (IV.11.6) is common in East Anglia and the south-east as well as in O and at Gl 5. These exemplify plurals ending in *-s* forming a double plural by the addition of a second *-s* ending. Some nouns, however, form double plurals by adding the *-s* plural to a weak ending. *Flen* 'fleas' was mentioned above, but in other (adjacent) localities in Sa, He and Wo *flens* is recorded. *Housens* (V.1.1) occurs at St 3. In some nouns the process is reversed, i.e. the double plural is formed by adding an *-n* ending to a noun already ending in *-s*, thus *hipsen* (*hip* + *-s* + *-en*) 'hips' (IV.11.7) at O 5. Occasionally 'mutation' plurals have a second plural added, thus *mices* at R 1, Ess 1, Co 7 (plus a peculiar [mɪəsɪz] at Y 19). But I have traced no examples of the *feeten* (i.e. a mutation plural + weak *-en* ending) type in *SED*, although these are mentioned by *EDG* (§383).

Hips and *haws*, which seem especially prone to the adopting of new endings, show triple plurals in the form of *hipsens* at Brk 2 and *hawsens* at Gl 4.

One or two nouns deserve special consideration. Standard English *children* is a double plural, deriving from a southern ME form which was formed side by side with the regular (northern and north-Midland) *childre* < late OE *cildru, -a*. The regularly formed *childer* is retained in dialect (VIII.1.2) in the north Midlands, also in one locality in So (2) and two (4 and 6) in K, but of special interest is a dialectal double plural *childers* recorded from Ess 1, and a completely different type *childs* recorded from D 2 and Gl 1 (cf. ME *childes* recorded from the Towneley plays and pronounced 'exceptional' by *OED*).

Cow was in OE a mutation-plural noun, *cū, cȳ*. The plural survived in ME as *ky(e)* together with a new, double, formation, *kyn, kine*, etc., formed in the south by adding the weak *-n* ending to an already existing plural (possibly assisted by association with the collective *swine*). A further new formation, namely *cows*, does not appear until the early seventeenth century. In the dialects the regular, old plural *kye* is recorded (III.1.1) in Nb, Cu, Du, We, three localities in north Y, and in Ch and St, the now archaic double plural *kine* is recorded at Cu 6 and Y 1, and (apparently) a dialectal double plural *kyes* at Ch 1/4/5. Interestingly enough, in some of the localities which gave *kine* and *kyes*, *kye* was recorded as a singular, obviously being a new formation from the plural.[2]

Chickens is also a double plural (< OE *cicen*, pl. *cicenu*), although of a different kind, and the regular old plural *chicken* is recorded by *SED* (IV.6.11) in the south-western counties and sporadically in the western and south-eastern counties, once in La.

Pea, pl. *peas*, goes back to an OE *pise*, pl. *pisan*, in which the singular form, because it ended in -*se* was construed as a plural in early NE and a new singular formed. *Peas* is, however, still recorded as a singular form in the present-day dialects (V.7.13) in individual localities in Du, We, La, Y, Nt and O. No -*n* forms are recorded for the plural, as has already been noted.

The formation of the possessive in modern English is by the affixation of '*s*, *s*' (pl.) to a noun. This derives directly from ME -*es*, which during the ME period spread from those nouns which regularly had this ending in the genitive singular to those which originally did not. Several classes of words held out against this development—nouns which already ended in -*s*, old weak nouns with genitive singular in -*en* (OE -*an*) like *hlæfdīge* 'lady', nouns ending in -*r* and having no -*es* genitive, e.g. OE *brōþor*, *mōdor*, and some other classes. In the present-day dialects the possessive inflexion is still often omitted, especially in the north Midlands, as witness the following examples (IX.8.6/7): from Cu, *my husband people, a cow foot;* Du, *hen neb* ('beak'); We, *father shoes, a pig head;* La, *father boots, cow legs;* Y, *my father brother, this chap coat, butcher milk, four day work, another man field, my wife father;* Db, *John Dank house.*

Dialectal variation in the formation of nominal compounds of the type *dog-kennel* shows a well-defined distribution in the south-west. In this type of compound, in Standard English historical causes have produced a usage varying between a first element with or without -*s*, the former usage consisting of the simple juxtaposition of a defining noun and another noun, e.g. *schoolboy, cow-house*, the latter of a defining noun with -*s* suffix plus a second noun, e.g. *baker's boy*. In words relating to structures such as *beehive, dog-kennel, cow-house, cattle-pen, sheep-fold*, Standard English has

111

generally opted for the usage without -*s*, whereas the south-western dialects have often chosen the other variety. The following examples are mostly from Co, D and So (but all from the south-western dialects): *pig's-crow, -house, -lewze* (I.1.5); *fowls'-house, hens'-house, -run* (I.1.6); *pigeon's-house* (from west Brk), *pigeons'-holes* (I.1.7); *cows'-house* (I.1.8); *calves'-plat, -run, calves'-, pigs'-, sheeps'-meadow* (I.1.10); *barn's floor* (III.7.8).

Pronouns

1. *Personal pronouns*

The form of the 1st sg. personal pronoun *I* is virtually invariable in the dialects except for the use of *uch* in a very small area in south So.[3] The retention of [tʃ] in ME *ich* was a southern feature (northern *ic, ik > i*) even in late ME, and was used for humorous or rustic effect on the Elizabethan stage. At a later period it became confined to a much smaller area: Ellis's 'Land of Utch', Variant v of his District 4, 'occupied the angular space between the two railways which have their vertex at Yeovil, Sm., on the b[order] of Do.', and Ellis names about a dozen villages in this area which 'were named as using utch'.[4] As noted above, *uch* was recorded (but is unfortunately unpublished) by *SED* only in south So.[5] The form *us*, recorded in south So at So 13 (VIII.9.5b), may also be a reduced form of *uch*, and not the 1st pl. personal pronoun.

I is used objectively (i.e. for *me*) in emphatic contexts throughout the south-west except in Co (it is also quite rare in D and west So), as far east as west Brk (VII.5.8, IX.8.2–4). Compare the general and widespread use of *us* (i.e. the 1st pl. personal pronoun) for *me*, which is not restricted to emphatic contexts.

As regards the 1st pl. personal pronoun itself, the only significant dialectal variant is the unemphatic use of the objective form *us* for the subject *we* throughout the whole of D, in east Co, and in single localities in Wa, O and Brk (VIII.9.5, IX.7.9). On the other hand, emphatic *we* was recorded by *SED* (IX.8.1: *it's only us*) where Standard English would use *us* throughout the south of England to a lesser or greater degree, excluding Sr and K and other parts of the south-east.

Since the ME period, the 2nd personal pronoun, sg. and pl., has shown a remarkable interchange of forms, both in the standard language and in dialect. In ME, the original pl. forms *ye* (subject) and *you* (object) supplanted the sgs. *thou* and *thee* as 'pronouns of respect', *ye* at first being preserved as the subjective form, *you* as objective, the distinction later breaking down (although it is pre-served in the Authorized Version of the Bible, 1611) and *ye, you* being used indiscriminately for subject or object. In dialect, side by side with *you*, the archaic sg. forms *thou* (subject) and *thee* (object) are often preserved, as is also *ye* (southern [iː]), which may function as subject or object, sg. or pl. In the south and west, *thee* can also function as sg. subject, and (very much more rarely) *thou* as sg. object (VI.5.8, VI.14.2, VIII.2.8, VIII.3.2, IX.5.4, IX.7.2/3/5/6/7/9).[6]

Although there is not a great deal of evidence in *SED*, *he* and *him* are in certain contexts interchangeable in the south-west, i.e. *him* may be used as the subject, *he* as the object, of a sentence, in addition to which there is a third south-western form *en* ([ən], [n̩]), derived from the OE accusative pronoun *hine*, which was replaced by the dative *him* in Standard English. This form is objective (see IX.2.4 *ask him*), but occasionally emerges in situations which are regarded as subjective in Standard English. Both *him* and *en* certainly occur (although rarely) for *he* in negative-interrogative statements (i.e. in unemphatic contexts) such as...*isn't he?* (see IX.7.5, So 13, W 3), but *he* is used as object in emphatic cases only, as, for example, at VI.5.17, Co 3 *I knowed he by his voice;* VIII.1.11, So 3 *brought he up;* IX.2.4, Brk 1, Co 2, D 2/10 *ask he*. Finally, in the south-west, the pronoun *he*, when unstressed, may appear as [əːr], i.e. a form which looks like *her* (see, e.g., IX.7.5). This is, however, simply the unstressed form [ə] with the final *r*-colouring often given to this sound in such positions (cf. p. 99, above).

En is used for *it* (object) as well as for *him* in the south-west of England, beside which the forms *he, him* and occasionally *she, her* may also be used to denote an inanimate object over a rather wider area in the west but in more scattered examples: I.7.1 *to weigh it*, for example, yields *him* in the responses at Brk 5, Ch 1, Db 3, He 1/3, Wo 6; V.7.7 *to thicken it* yields *him* in the responses at He 6, and *her* at Db 4/6. The map of *en* drawn from the responses and in-cidental material from these two questions gives the form as wide-spread and general south-west of west Sx, Ha, west Brk and west Gl. *He* used for *it* (object) is much less frequent, but occurs occasion-ally, e.g. at I.7.1 *buy he* (So 11); IV.2.4 *bank he up and lay it* (*sic*; So 8), *lie he down* (Ha 3), both referring to the plashing of a hedge; *she* is recorded for *it* (object) at VIII.1.11, Co 7. There are doubtless further examples. *He* may also be used for *it* as subject, as at V.7.3 (*he's* [= *it's*] *too hot*), Brk 1, Co 5/6, Do 4/5. The full implications of the use of *he, she, him, her* for inanimate objects have not yet been ex-plored. The case of animals is ambiguous, since these may be

113

regarded in some sort of way as 'persons' or near-persons, thus seeming to justify the use of the pronouns in question.

The 3rd feminine pronoun is complicated by the fact that several forms are current in dialect, namely *she* (the origin of which is obscure: see the Select Bibliography), *hoo* or *oo* (< OE *hēo*), *shoo* (< ME *s(c)ho*, perhaps < OE *sēo*) and what appears to be the object pronoun *her*.[7] Of these, *she* is the most extensive form, covering almost all but the west Midlands and the south-western peninsula, while *shoo* is confined fairly closely to south-west Y. Occurring as it does, geographically between *she* and *hoo* forms (to the west), it looks like a blend of *she* and *hoo*, and might be explained as such. *Hoo* in the north-west Midlands covers La from a little south of the Lune, a strip of south-west Y, all but the extreme southern tip of Ch, north and central Db and the extreme north-eastern tip of St. Finally, *her* is characteristic of the central and southern west Midlands and the south-western peninsula (except west Co, where *she* is the main form). (See VI.14.14, VIII.9.5, IX.7.2/3/6/7/9/10.)

The use of *she* as object is very much less widely attested in the south-west, but there are one or two examples: III.3.6 *stock she up* (Ha 3), VIII.1.11 *brought she up* (scattered examples from Co to west Brk and west Sx). No undoubted examples of *en* as feminine object have been found, those referring to animals being again ambiguous, since in such cases, *en* may mean not 'she' but 'it'.[8]

The 3 pl. personal pronoun shows traces of dialectal interchange between *they* and *them*. *Them* is used for *they* in the south-west and in much of the west-Midland region in interrogative and interrogative-negative statements (i.e. in unemphatic contexts), as witness IX.7.2/3/5/6 (*are they? aren't they?* etc.), but apart from this, little evidence is forthcoming from *SED*. *They* is used for *them* at VIII.1.11, Ha 5 (*bring they up*). The unemphatic form *mun* occurs for *them* ('they') at IX.7.2/3/5/6 in Co 1/3, and at II.4.2 in Co 1–3, but its origin and history are obscure.[9] Finally, *EDG* (§410) records an interesting usage from Cu and north-east La, namely the use of *their* to mean 'of them', especially in the phrase *all their* 'all of them'. This appears to be unrecorded in *SED*, but no doubt owes its origin to Scandinavian grammar (ON *allir þeir*).

Two general points emerge from the above. In dialect, it is frequently possible for the personal pronouns to 'exchange' their subjective and objective roles, but the conditions under which these exchanges occur are contextually restricted, the objective form being used for the subject when the pronoun is unemphatic, and, con-

114

versely, the subject form being used as the emphatic form of the object. Secondly, in one or two cases, the plural is used for the singular: as noted above, for example, the use of *us* for *me* is widespread.

2. *Possessive*

For *my*, *I's* occurs at Ha 3 but the use of *our* is probably more widespread in dialect, corresponding to the use of *us* for *me* (above): see VIII.1.18. For *our*, the use of *us* is confined to YWR, east Ch, north Db and north St, i.e. a west-Midland area, and *we* for *our* is also recorded (albeit very sparingly) in south St:[10] see VI.3.3, VIII.8.8.

The retention of the archaic *thy* is widespread except in the east Midlands and south-east, corresponding to the use of *thou* and *thee:* see VI.5.3/4/17.

The most interesting of all the possessive pronoun forms is the neuter *its*. The old neuter form *his* was preserved down to the seventeenth century in Standard English, as witness the Authorized Version of the Bible, 'But if the salt have lost his savour, wherewith shall it be salted?' (Matthew v. 13) and also the use (*passim*) of *his*, *her* and *thereof* in an attempt to avoid the use of *its*. Beside the old form *his*, a new form *hit* arose in the fourteenth century, especially in the west-Midland dialects, and remained in common use until the early seventeenth century: the Fool in *King Lear* says 'For, you know, Nuncle The hedge-sparrow fed the cuckoo so long That it had it head bit off by it young' (I.iv.223–5). *Its* was formed, apparently in the south of England, towards the end of the sixteenth century, presumably by analogy with *his* or from the use of *it* + the *'s* of the possessive of nouns. It perhaps arose because with the loss of grammatical gender *his* was felt to be inappropriate for inanimate objects, and was probably in colloquial use for some time previous to its first appearance in books just before 1600, only gradually attaining literary recognition.

In dialect, various alternatives to *its* are still employed: first of all, a large area in the north Midlands uses the old form *it* (Y except the north, La, north Db, east Ch, north St and north L), while *his* is also apparently general in dialect (although the relevant *SED* questions, IV.6.20 and VI.1.7, since they refer respectively to a chicken and a baby, do not supply really unambiguous evidence; cf. the preliminary note in Vol. ii, IV.6.20, and Note 3 (final sentence) in Vol. iv, VI.1.7). More interesting than the use of *his*, however, is the use of periphrastic constructions. The *SED* southern material records the

115

following: at IV.6.20, *twist the neck of him* (Co 7), *cut the throat of him* (D 1), *cut the throat of en* (D 4/6/11); at VI.1.7, *the old snout of en* (viz. pig; So 13), *the guts of en* (ibid.), *put a ring in the nose of en* (viz. pig; D 6). It thus looks as if the Midland area mentioned above and a small area of the south-west preserve (or have found) ways of constructing the neuter possessive without the use of *its*.

Two further points emerge with regard to the possessive pronouns. These are the use of the archaic form *thine* ('yours'), parallel to *thou, thee, thy*, which again appears to be widespread except in the east Midlands, and the use of the forms *hisn, hern, ourn, yourn, theirn*, the final *n* presumably being adopted by analogy with *mine* and *thine*. These -*n* forms are on the whole widespread dialectally except in the north. See IX.8.5.

3. Reflexive

When we come to the reflexive pronouns, we note the widespread use of *thyself*—again parallel to *thou, thee, thy* and *thine*, and also in general usage the forms *hisself* and *theirselves* as distinct from *himself, themselves*. The forms of *self, selves* are not without their own interest. In the north and Midlands, the singular can also appear as *sen, seln*, the plural as *sen, seln*, or *sens*, all developing from ME *seluen*. (See IX.11.1/2/4.) The use of the simple personal pronoun *me, thee*, etc., for the reflexive, is found in the north and the west Midlands and occasionally elsewhere (see IX.11.1 *wash myself*). It should also be noted that a reflexive form—*yourself/you, thyself/thee*, etc.—is used in dialect in contexts where it is not so used in Standard English, e.g. in *Sit down* (VIII.3.3), *Lie down* (VIII.3.6), *play* (*play them(selves)* in La and Db; VIII.6.4).

4. Demonstrative

The demonstrative pronouns—Standard English *this, that, these, those*, etc.—show variants in dialect (XI.10.1–6). Beside the familiar *yon, yond, yonder*, used for designating an object some distance away, the north also has *thir* 'these' (of obscure origin, see *OED*, s.v.) and *tho* 'those' (< OE *þā*, ME *þo*). *Thon* 'that over there' and *thon ones* 'those over there', in use in the north, are of special interest in that *thon* appears to be a comparatively recent alteration of *yon*, the initial consonant having been assimilated to *this, that*, etc. (see *OED*, s.v. Thon); similarly *thonder* 'yonder' (IX.10.3). The south uses the well-known *thick* [ðɪk], *thicky, thuck, thucker* forms for 'this, that' (< ME *þilke*), and *theasum* 'these' (? < *these* + *them*) emerges in W, with *theseun, thoseun* at Sa 5.[11] The form *they* is also in frequent use as a demonstrative in the south. It should be observed that the *SED* forms are but a few of the much richer variety recorded in *EDG* (§§416 ff.), which the reader should certainly see.

5. *Relative*

The relative pronoun in dialect has many more forms than the Standard English *which, that, who. As, at* (? < *that* reduced form, or < ON *at* in the north), *that, what* and *who* are all in use, widely distributed, referring to persons, as well as the simple omission of the relative—*I know a man will do it for you, he's the man looks after the cows* (IX.9.5, III.3.7).[12]

Adjectives

One or two points of interest arise in connexion with dialectal forms of adjectives. In Standard English, many adjectives denoting material are formed from the noun by means of an *-en* suffix, e.g. *wooden, golden*. In the south-western dialects this *-en* ending has been extended to a larger number. At V.8.5 *bag*, the adj. *papern* 'paper' is found at So 5/10, D 6 and Do 1/3/4, and *down on the boarden floor* (i.e. a floor made of boards) is recorded from Do 1 at III.7.8.

Most adjectives in ME regularly formed their comparatives and superlatives by adding the endings *-er, -est*, but during this period the use of *more, most* plus the simple adjective arose, at first irrespective of the length of the adjective. During the NE period the present (Standard English) rule became established—namely that monosyllabic adjectives take *-er, -est*, polysyllabic adjectives use *more, most*, while for disyllabic adjectives there is no hard and fast rule, except in so far as custom has established one. In early NE it was possible to add *more, most* to the comparative and superlative pleonastically, thus in Shakespeare 'This was the most unkindest cut of all' (*Julius Caesar*, III.ii.185), and this custom survives in the dialects. *SED* V.1.17 *more useful* reveals *usefuller* occasionally in Brk and Y (adjectives ending in *-ful* regularly use the *more, most* method in Standard English), as well as *more usefuller* in Do and Y, and other double comparatives spread through the south, west and east—*more bolder, more commoner, more greener, more safer, more sweeter*, and so on. The forms of *worse, worst* (VI.12.3/5) are also worthy of special note. For *worse, worser* (an ordinary double comparative) is moderately common in the south and south-east

117

Midlands, with a treble comparative at Bd 3, namely *worserer*, and a strange form *worsener* at Y 27. For *worst*, *worsest* and *worstest* are recorded, the former at K 6 and D 3, and the latter at Bd 1/2, Brk 4, K 7 and Sx 2/3 (i.e. in the south-east and south-east Midlands). For further examples of double comparatives and superlatives and other non-Standard forms, the reader is again referred to *EDG* (§398).

Conjunctions and prepositions

Dialectal variants of the Standard English conjunctions and prepositions are really a lexical matter. *Between* (*betwixt*, etc., IX.2.11), *beside* (*by*, *broadside*, *agin*, *against*, *anenst*, etc., IX.2.5), *without* (*bout*, *bidout*, *out*, etc., V.8.10a) are all of interest, as are others. One of the best-known and most frequently quoted dialectalisms is the use of *while* for 'till' (IX.2.2/3), which is common in the north, north Midlands and east, especially in Y and La, both as conjunction and preposition, and is also recorded prepositionally as far south as Brk 4. It was formerly a more widespread usage (cf. *EDD*, s.v., and quotations from Marlowe, Shakespeare, etc., in *OED*, s.v., B.3). In the north, *till* itself is sometimes used as equivalent to Standard English *to* as a preposition with reference to place (*to the doctor's*, etc.) and in other contexts (see VI.7.9, VII.5.3/5/6, VIII.1.19, VIII.5.1). Examples emerge in Cu 1–4, but with stray examples at He 1 (VI.7.9) and Ess 2 (VII.5.6).

To cj. before a verb (IX.5.9) has a parallel archaic form *for to*, which is very widespread throughout the country, in the south often with complete absorption of the *to* (i.e. *for* appears alone). *At* is recorded at La 2, presumably < ON *at* 'to', introducing the 'infinitive of purpose' (*It's at keep the water from coming in*). This word formerly had a much wider distribution in the north of England, according to *EDD*—Cu, We, north Y and north and north-east La.

The forms of *without* prep. (V.8.10a) are of note from lexical and phonetic points of view (see p. 74 and above), but the word is also used as a conjunction meaning 'unless' throughout the west Midlands, in Y, La (loc. 6 only), L and Lei (loc. 1 only), and also in the south in scattered localities in So, K, Co, Ha and Sx.

As is well-known, the preposition *off* (IX.2.13) is frequently followed by *of* (or *on*) in dialect—*off of it*, etc.—and this is a feature which occurs throughout the country. *On* frequently does duty for *of* when followed by a vowel—*out on it*, etc. (IX.2.13/15).

118

Than (VI.12.4) is represented by a number of dialectal variants up and down the country, of which *nor* is the most widespread, being used throughout the north and (in scattered examples) the east and west Midlands. Y 29 has *as* (*they're worse as* ['than'] *stallions*), *till* occurs at Ch 4/6 and Sa 2, and *to* at So 2.

Verbs

1. *Endings of the present tense*

An important aspect of regional verb forms is that the operation of analogy has taken place on a larger scale than in Standard English, so that certain forms have a wider currency within the verb paradigm than they do in Standard English. Analogy has clearly operated on a larger scale when we find, for example, that an *-s* ending is common for other members of the paradigm, i.e. after *I, we, you, they*, or plural nouns, as well as after *thou* (reduced from *-st*), *he, she, it*. The Northumbrian dialect of OE already had *-es* for the 3 sg., whereas other dialects had *-eþ*, and *-as* for the plural (other dialects having *-aþ*), and the *-es* was also extended to the 1 sg., so that in this area the whole paradigm ended in *-s*. This was then extended in ME times to Midland areas, and these and the other dialects of present-day English may show *-s* endings for the 1 sg. and the pls. to varying extents. After plural nouns the *-s* ending is common (not so common, perhaps, in the east Midlands; see III.10.7 *bulls bellow*, etc.), but is less frequent when immediately preceded by the pronouns (see IV.6.2 (they) *keep hens*, V.2.12 *we put the light on*, VIII.5.1 *they go to church*).

The 3 sg. of the verb ended in *-eþ* in most OE dialects. This remained in ME, but was ultimately supplanted by an *-s* ending in Standard English, although the old *-eth* forms were retained up to the seventeenth century and even beyond. The *-eth* ending is now current only in the south-western dialects, and even there only to a very limited extent. *SED* records *her wear'th the trousers* from Co 1 (VI.14.14), *her'th returned* ('her hath...') from the same locality (III.1.7), *dooth* ('does') from D 9 (unpublished), and the *-eth* ending is extended to the 1 sg. in *I'th seen* ('I've seen') at D 10 (unpublished).

In the south, the *-eth* ending was sometimes lost in ME, without being replaced by an *-s* ending, thus giving a verbal form with no ending at all. Such forms are fairly familiar in the present-day southern dialects: see, for example, VI.14.14 *she wears the breeches*, from which it will be noted that uninflected forms are characteristic

119

of the south-west (So 13, W 2, Co 5/7, Do 1) and East Anglia (Nf, Sf, north Ess); and, for a somewhat different (and wider) distribution, VI.13.3 (it) *hurts*, although the examples here are perhaps not quite so certain, since the subject *it* is not given as part of the response.

In OE, the plural usually ended in -*aþ*, ME -*eth*, but in modern Standard English the plural inflection is completely lost and there is no ending. In the dialects, any trace of -*eth* endings, as recorded by *EDG* (§435) for So and D, seems to have vanished completely, an ending in -*s* is common in certain contexts (see above), but a geographically more restricted feature still present is the ending -(*e*)*n*, which already appears in the ME Midland dialects, and is usually explained as originating in the present subjunctive form. *EDG* (loc. cit.) states that this form occurs in La, Ch, St, Db, Sa, Nth, Wa, Wo, He, especially in the verb *have*, but it is obviously a recessive feature. *We putten* is recorded at Db 4 (V.2.12), *han you...?* at Ch 6, Db 7 (VI.5.8), 2 pl. *kneaden* at St 2 (V.6.4), and 3 pls. *cutten* at Ch 5 (VI.2.2) and Ch 6 (IV.4.4) and *keepen* at Db 1 (IV.6.2). Many more are, however, collected together at VIII.5.1, from which the -(*e*)*n* ending appears now to be mainly characteristic of Ch, Db and St. A consideration of IX.6.4 (*we*) *have got* extends this into south La, Sa and north Lei (see also IX.5.4 *do you*), while IX.6.1 (*I*) *have*, (*he*) *has* confirms *EDG*'s citations (loc. cit.) of 1 sgs. (and adds 3 sgs.) in -(*e*)*n* in the same west-Midland area. Note also *doen he?* at IX.5.4. For *I bin* 'I am', see below.

2. *Infinitive*

The infinitive of some of the OE weak verbs ended in -*ian*, and although the -*an* has now completely disappeared from the infinitives of all verbs both in Standard English and in the dialects, there appears to be a relic of the -*i*- left in south-western intransitive verbs. Thus, for example, at D 4 *there isn't many* (who) *can sheary* ('shear') *now* (see IX.9.5).

The use of *do* as an unstressed auxiliary with the infinitive (*I do know, they do steal*, etc.) is a well-known western feature. Precisely what historical relationship, if any, this construction bears to the use of auxiliary *do* in Standard English (in interrogative and negative statements—*do you go?, they do not go*, etc.) it is not possible to say.[13] The present distribution is a rather curious one—one area round the Severn comprising localities in Mon and Gl, one very small area in central and west Co, and a third, larger, area comprising parts of W, Do, and So. But it may be reasonably suggested that these three separate areas were once all part of a large connected area in the west (? roughly bounded on the east by Watling Street). See VIII.7.5.

3. *Participles*

The present and past participles in dialect are often preceded by the prefix *a-* ([ə]). In the pres. p. the *a-* represents OE *on* preceding the verbal noun (*on rīding(e)* 'riding', etc.), and in the p.p. it represents the OE prefix *ge-*, ME *y-*, *i-*. An examination of V.8.6 *boiling* and III.1.12 *shows signs of calving* (where various pres. ps. occur) shows *a-* before the pres. p. scattered over the Midlands, both east and west, as far north as Ch and south L, and as far west as W and Gl. It seems, however, to be missing in Ess, Sr, K, Sx and Ha. On the other hand, *a-* before the p.p. has a mainly south-western distribution: see IX.3.2 *found*, IX.3.3 *put*, IX.5.6 *done*.

One further point calls for comment in connexion with the pres. p., and that is the use of the 'expanded' tenses. These tenses—*he is waiting, they were running*, etc., have a curious ancestry. Their apparent forerunners occur in OE, but most frequently in translation of Latin constructions. They rarely occur in ME, and are still rare in Shakespeare and the Authorized Version. So in *Hamlet*, II.ii.190, *What do you read, my lord?* and Luke viii.20, *Thy mother and thy brethren stand without*, whereas modern Standard English would prefer *What are you reading...?* and *Thy mother and thy brethren are standing...* According to Jespersen, it is not until Bunyan and still later Addison that the modern rules are fully followed—'In the modern period the use of the expanded tenses has been constantly gaining ground.'[14]

It does not seem to have been generally noticed that, even today, older dialect speakers occasionally show preference for the simple over the expanded form of the verb in the present tense. An elderly relative of mine, for example, in her early years a native of Lincolnshire, would say *The kettle boils* (instead of...*is boiling*), *It rains* (instead of...*is raining*), and similar usages were recorded from an 86-year-old Kentish (female) relative of one of my students—*It rains, The sun shines, The dog sits on the doorstep*. One or two examples appear to be recorded by *SED*: at VIII.2.8, So 5 *How's get on?* may be a contracted form of *How dost (thee) get on?* (i.e. How are you getting on?), and a further (unpublished) example, from W 3, is *Don't rain now, do it?* (The use of *do* is, of course, accounted for by the fact that the first example involves an interrogative and the second a negative.) The only other example so far found in *SED* is

121

from VIII.8.5, K 5 *Shapes very well* (= 'He is shaping...' [i.e. getting on]).

4. *Past tenses and past participles*

In the formation of the p.ts. and p.ps. of verbs, again we may see the workings of analogy, and note in particular the ways in which the analogical formations have diverged from those at work in Standard English. This applies especially to the strong verbs, whose p.ts. and p.ps. are formed by a change of stem-vowel, unlike the weak verbs, which form theirs by the addition of 'dental' (-*d*, -*t*) suffixes.

In the first place, a great many originally strong verbs have adopted weak p.ts. and p.ps. in the dialects. This seems especially to be the case with verbs which in OE belonged to strong verbs of Class VII, the original 'reduplicating' verbs. Thus, for example, *know* (VI.5.17) and *grow* (IX.3.9) show that *knowed, growed* are widespread in dialect, as distinct from the Standard English strong forms *knew, grew*. The adoption of weak endings is a process which has been going on since late OE and early ME times. The weak class of verbs was numerically the stronger type and it was thus not unnatural that the strong verbs came to conform to them in forming the p.t. and p.p. with dental suffixes. Many verbs in Standard English which were originally strong are now weak, e.g. *snow, flow, bake*. The dialects have simply taken this process further. In addition to the verbs cited above, *SED* also provides weak forms for *drink* (p.t. *drinked* So 13, K 4, D 5, at V.8.1; p.p. *drinked* widespread in the south, at VI.13.11; also a weak ending joined on to the usual strong p.p., thus (very occasionally) *drunked*, in the southern counties, VI.13.11); *speak* (p.t. *speaked*, sporadically except in the north, plus an example of *spoked* in the southern counties (Sr 5); p.p. *speaked* at Sa 8, VI.5.5); *bear* (p.p. *borned* at Co 4/7; VI.5.9); *wear* (p.t. *weared* at Wo 7, D 2, Ha 7, p.t. *wored* at So 9; p.p. *weared* at La 6, Wo 3, Wa 4, So 6, Co 4, D 2/3/4/11, p.p. *wored* at So 13, Co 1/2/6 [cf. IX.3.5 p.p. *a-broked* at D 3], and p.p. *woreded* at D 6—i.e. strong p.t. + -*ed* + a second -*ed*, VI.14.14); *see* (p.t. *seed* is fairly general; VIII.2.5); *steal* (p.t. and p.p. *stealed* are widespread, *stoled* mainly in the south-west, VIII.7.5); *come* (p.t. *comed* is not very frequent, but occurs in north and south, IX.3.4); *give* (p.t. and p.p. *gived* (*gied*) are widespread, but not in the north and east, IX.8.2/3); *do* (p.p. *doed* occurs in the south-west, IX.5.6). These are only examples, considered in a very general way, but we can clearly see several distinct methods of formation: the simple addition of the weak -*d* ending to the present

122

stem (e.g. *seed*), to the past stem (e.g. *wored*), to the strong p.p. (e.g. *borned*), and (once only, namely *woreded*) to a new weak formation on the p.t. There is thus a wide range of dialectal possibilities.

On the other hand, some verbs which became weak in ME and passed thus to their modern Standard English forms, retain their old strong forms in dialect. *Creep* (IX.1.9) < OE *crēopan*, *crēap*, *crupon*, *cropen*, retains its strong p.p. *croppen* (with short -*o*-) in south La, where there is also a p.t. *crope*. The south has both p.t. and p.p. *crope* in Do and Ha (which are from the ME lengthened form of the p.t. pl. or p.p.), beside the new weak formation *creeped*. *Wash* (IX.11.1) retains a strong p.p. *washen* at Du 1.

Another familiar characteristic of ME reshuffling in the strong verbs was the levelling of the vowel of the p.t. pl. under that of the p.t. sg. and the levelling of the vowel of the p.t. sg. under that of the p.t. pl. or p.p. (these two having the same stem vowel). Thus OE *drincan* (infinitive), *dranc* (p.t. sg.), *druncon* (p.t. pl.), *gedruncen* (p.p.) has been re-formed as *drink*, *drank* (p.t.), *drunk* (p.p.), the p.t. pl. being levelled out under the sg., while OE *bītan*, *bāt*, *biton*, *gebiten* has been re-formed as *bite*, *bit*, *bitten*, the p.t. sg. being levelled out under the pl. or p.p. In either case, the result is the reduction to fewer types. The same thing has happened in the dialects, but with results often different from those of Standard English. Thus, the p.t. of *drink* is *drunk* (Standard English *drank*) in places as far apart as Y 10 and MxL 2 (V.8.1), while conversely *drank* appears fairly frequently in dialect for the p.p., except in the north and north Midlands, where we get *drunk*, or *drucken* (< ON *drukkinn*; VI.13.11); *begun* is general in dialect for the p.t. *began* (VII.6.23); *rid* is widespread for the p.t. *rode* (IX.3.10).

In ME, some strong verbs changed class, thus, for example, some of the OE Class V verbs (e.g. *sprecan*, *spræc*, *sprǣcon*, *gesprecen* 'speak') went over to Class IV (e.g. *beran*, *bær*, *bǣron*, *geboren* 'bear'), whose paradigm differed only in the stressed vowel of the p.p., being -*o*- instead of -*e*-. This -*o*- was then later extended (with lengthening) from the p.p. to the p.t. sg., thus giving modern English *spoke*, *spoken*. The same thing appears to have taken place dialectically in the south-west in *give* (IX.8.2/3) and *sit* (VIII.3.3; both Class V verbs): *give* has p.t. sg. and p.p. *gov* at Co 6, *sit* has *sot* at So 7, D 9 (p.t.), D 6/9 (p.p.).

Some of the Class V verbs show interesting archaic forms. *Give* has an unlengthened vowel in *gav* p.t. sg. in north Y. *Get* (IX.6.4) has p.p. *getten* and *gotten* in the north and the north Midlands, the former being the original regular p.p. (OE -*giten*, ME *geten*, with [g] < ON *geta*), *gotten* (with -*o*- from Class IV) being a parallel form, in use until the eighteenth century, but ousted as p.p. by the p.t. *got* from the sixteenth century onwards. *Speak* (VI.5.5) shows a rich variety of p.ts. and p.ps. in addition to the weak formations *speaked*, *spoked*, already mentioned. In the p.t. it manifests the regular old strong form *spake* (< late OE *spæc* p.t. sg.) except in the east Midlands and north (this was ultimately replaced by *spoke* after 1600, with -*o*- from Class IV). *Spak* and *spok* occur in the north (*spok* also in the south-west) as unlengthened forms of *spake*, *spoke*. The p.p. shows chiefly p.t. forms—*spoke* occurs everywhere, with the short form *spok* in the north (and south-west), the old p.t. *spake* occurs at Sr 2, and the short form *spak* at Y 17. Finally, there is *spaken* at Y 8, which looks like *spak*, with the p.p. -*en* ending added as a new formation.

One general tendency which stands out in the dialectal forms of verbs is that towards a reduction of the parts of the verbs, perhaps on the analogy of verbs like *cut* and *put*, which, in Standard English, have only the one form in present tense, p.t. and p.p. Thus *begin* (VII.6.23) and *ride* (IX.3.10) apparently show forms of *begin* and *ride* as p.ts. in the south, *see* of *see* more generally (VIII.2.5), and similarly *come* (IX.3.4).

The weak class of verbs does not on the whole now display forms as exotic as those of the strong verbs. *Reach* (VI.7.15), however, shows strong forms in Nth, namely p.t. *roach* and p.p. *roached* (with the weak -*ed* ending, however) at Nth 5, apparently being formed on analogy with the p.t. of Class I verbs (*write–wrote*).

The general observation must again be made that the present-day dialects are very much poorer in forms than they used to be. *EDG* (§§425–34), listing only forms which diverge from Standard English, gives a vast number and variety, and this work should be consulted to get a fuller picture of the extremely diverse verb forms which once existed in dialect.

The forms of the verb *to be* show much complexity and cannot be presented here in any detail, but reference should be made to the appropriate sections of *SED* (see Be in the Index of Key-Words). As a single interesting specimen, however, from information given at IX.7.7 *I am* the country may be clearly seen to be divided into two—*I be* (*bin*) and *I am*—by a line roughly parallel with Watling Street. *I is* in the north may be a Scandinavian intrusion, as suggested below (p. 135), with the English form on either side. *I bin* in a small western area comprising Sa and its environs shows the -*n* ending characteristic of some west-Midland dialects (see p. 120, above). *I are* along the *I be/I am* boundary and in the south-east is an enigma.

Syntax

Syntax is an unwieldy subject which dialectologists have fought shy of. This section will confine itself to citing one or two examples of syntactical divergence from Standard English. Indeed, such is the overlap between the various levels of speech—in this case morphology and syntax—that some examples have already been mentioned above, e.g. the use of auxiliary *do* in forming simple statements, and the preference of a simple verb over an expanded form.

An interesting construction which differs from Standard English usage is the negative command. Whereas Standard English uses the auxiliary *do* for this—*Do not go*, etc.—there is a small amount of evidence in the south-west that such constructions can be formed without *do*, merely using emphatic *not*. So, at So 8, *SED* records *not put no sugar in* and *not wait* (IX.7.11), and at D 6 *not go* (ibid.).

A number of divergences from Standard English usage centring around the pronouns are evidenced in the *SED* material, especially around the indirect interrogative forms of the pronoun. IX.9.6 requires as a response a dialect equivalent of (that's the chap...) *whose uncle was drowned*, and provides a rich variety of methods of expressing the notion *whose*: *as/at/that his uncle was drowned*, *'s uncle what was drowned*, *that was his uncle drowned*, *what's uncle drowned self*, and (with omission of the pronoun) simply *his uncle was drowned*.

An examination of phrases for *have you got toothache?* (VI.5.8) reveals that the use of the definite article before an ailment is very widespread in dialect, while the question (VII.1.17) About how many calves does a cow have? About... reveals the widespread occurrence of the indefinite article *a* before a numeral. The use of the definite article before *church* (VIII.5.1) and *school* (VIII.6.1; *go to the church/the school*) is also attested in the north.

7   The Foreign Element in English Dialect

In Chapter 4 attention was drawn to the large native element in English dialect vocabulary, which coexists with a substantial element of non-native origin. This is now to be considered. We need to see what proportion and what sort of dialect vocabulary is of non-English stock and to note its regional distributions. Following the method of Chapter 2, the various items will be dealt with in chronological order—Celtic, Scandinavian, French and others.

The Celtic element

Contrary to popular, and somewhat romantic, opinion, a large proportion of English dialect vocabulary does not consist of words of Celtic origin. Indeed, the Celtic element in dialectal English, whether Brittonic (Welsh, Cornish) or Goidelic (Irish, Manx), except in a very few special areas, namely the Isle of Man (not discussed here), the Welsh border and west Cornwall, is negligible. Only two or three words go back to early times, being mediated into present-day dialect through Old and Middle English. Thus, *ass* (< OE *assa*), mentioned above (p. 70), probably came into OE from Old Welsh or Old Irish (ultimately from Latin); *brat* 'apron' is recorded by *SED* (V.11.2) throughout Cu, We, La (as well as in Man) and west Y, with single occurrences in the neighbouring counties of Nb, Du, Ch and Db. Its former distribution was apparently wider (see *EDD*). The word occurs once in OE (Northumbrian), as *bratt* in the *Lindisfarne Gospels*, *c.* 950, and was probably adopted from Old Irish *brat(t)* 'cloth', especially as a covering for the body—'plaid, mantle, cloak'; *brock*, also mentioned above (p. 70), is from a Common Celtic **broccos*, via OE *broc*.

There is also a group of words (found at I.1.5/6/9) all ultimately going back to a Common Celtic **krāu̯o*, and emerging variously as *cree* in (*pig-*)*cree* 'pigsty' and *hen-cree* 'hen-house' (Nb and Du), as *crew* in *pig-crew* (Cu 1, La 5–7, Db 4), *hen-crew* (La 5–7), *crew*, *crews*, *crewyard* ('straw-yard', L, Nt, Lei, R, Nth, west Nf), and as *crow* in *pig's-crow* (Co 6/7). The whole family of words presents a fascinating complex: the northern and Midland forms derive either directly from Brittonic sources (cf. Middle Welsh *creu*), or from Brittonic sources mediated through OE, or from Goidelic sources (Old Irish *cró*) mediated through ON (ON *kró*), while in Co *crow* is < Corn. *crow* (cf. Breton *kraou*, Welsh *crau*, *craw*). The various members of this group also occur in scattered place-names, the element *crow*, however, being quite well attested in place-names of Cornish origin.[1]

Sock 'ploughshare' (I.8.7) is derived by *OED* from OFr *soc*, 'commonly regarded as of Celtic origin'. It may be, however, that *sock*— found in Nb, Du, Cu, We, north and east Y, La, Ch, Sa and north He—is directly from Celtic sources (cf. Old Irish *socc*, Welsh *swch*)

As might be expected, most Celtic words are found along the 'Celtic border', either Welsh or Cornish. So, for example, *mochyns* 'pigs' (< Welsh *mochyn* pl. + -*s* ending, giving, in effect, a double pl.) is found at Ch 4 (III.8.1), and *brithin* 'stye on the eye' (VI.3.10) at Sa 1 is presumably < Welsh *llefrithen* with the same meaning. Both of these localities are on the north Welsh border. A much more widespread dialect word, however, is *tallet* (with numerous variant forms), which occurs as 'hay-loft' in *SED* at I.3.18, distributed over an area stretching from north-east Co, through D, (most of) So, Gl, O, Mon, He, Wo and Sa, with single examples in north-east Do, south W, south-west Brk, and north and south-west Ha. The immediate origin of the word is Welsh *taflawd*, -*od*, ultimately from medieval Latin *tabulat*- (< *tabulare* 'to board, floor', etc., < *tabula* 'board, plank'); it perhaps spread from Wales via the agency of travelling folk such as casual harvest labourers and drovers during the ME period and subsequently.[2]

A word should be said here about the well-known 'sheep-counting numerals', a traditional method of counting apparently once common in the north of England and southern Scotland, as well as in more scattered areas of England and also abroad. To give but one example from a very large selection assembled in the course of a recent study,[3] the following, recorded from Grassington (Y) in the last century, although evidently much distorted from an original series, show obvious affinities with the Welsh numerals: [jan], [tiən], [tɛðəɹə], [pɛðəɹə], [pip], [siːzə], [liːnə], [katəɹə], [kɔːn], [dik], cf. modern Welsh *un, dau/dwy, tri/tair, pedwar/pedair, pump, chwech, saith, wyth, naw, deg*. Various theories have been advanced to account for the origin of these numerals (of which reliable first-hand evidence is negligible or non-existent, since informants who use them appear to be extremely elusive)—namely that they represent a survival from

Old Welsh, or that they were a medieval importation from Scotland or from Wales. The last seems inherently more likely, though much research remains to be done on these strange numerals. They may, in fact, not have been used originally for counting sheep at all, but in children's games or rhymes.

Evidence for Welsh phonetic influence on dialectal English is very slight, and is probably restricted to one or two localities in Mon. Mon 4 occasionally shows strong aspiration of initial [p], [t], [k], as in [pʰɪdʒɪnz] (IV.7.3), [kʰaɹəts] (V.7.18), [tʰoːz] (VI.10.3), [rabɪtʰ] (III.13.13), and the last word also contains a very rare example of rolled [r], as distinct from the more usual [ɹ] of this locality. Mon 4 and 5 occasionally have gemination of medial consonants, as in [applz] (IV.11.8), [haddə] *adder* (IV.9.4), [hɪkkᾰpɪn] (VI.8.4), [ɹạbbɪts] (III.13.13), which may owe something to Welsh lengthened *pp, tt, cc*, occurring medially between vowels after accented syllables, but a smaller area further north (Ch 2, Db 1/4), where Welsh influence seems less likely, shows similar gemination (see IV.1.8 *boggy*, IV.11.8 *apples*, VI.3.8 *peeping*). The use of the Welsh diphthong [ɪuː] for more usual English [juː] occurs in *tune* (VI.5.19) at Sa 1/9, localities on the Welsh border, but the same diphthong also occurs in this word at Db 5, and indeed is a fairly widespread—probably archaic— diphthong in words formerly containing ME *iu*. Apart from these few features from Mon (the evidence from further north is doubtful), there appears to be nothing in English dialect attributable to Welsh phonetic influence.

By far the largest corpus of Celtic words in English dialect at the present-day, however, is to be found in west Cornwall, and even here they are now not numerous—according to *SED*, anyway—although many have no doubt been lost,[4] and many probably still exist in fishing and mining terminology and as names of flowers, birds, and so on (cf., for example, Nance's *Glossary*, in which numerous fishing terms of Corn. origin are listed), and so were not elicited by *SED*, with its questionnaire of 'universal' notions. The words that *were* found by *SED* were given in localities 6, 7, 5 and 4, locality 6 having by far the greatest number. There were also one or two from localities 2 and 3. They are thus mostly confined to the extreme west of the county, where Cornish was last spoken, with an occasional example further east.

The Cornish loan-words in the dialect of west Co are mostly (but not exclusively) the names of things: *bannel* 'a broom' (< Corn. *banal* coll., 'broom flower or plant, besom'; unpublished); *bucca* 'scarecrow' (< Corn. *bucca*; II.3.7); *clunk* 'to swallow' and *clunker* 'windpipe' (probably < Corn. *collenky* 'to swallow down', with the noun subsequently derived by means of the English *-er* suffix added to the base; VI.6.5); *dram* 'swath' (< Corn. *dram*; II.9.4); *fuggan* 'pastry dinner-cake' (< Corn. *fügen*; unp.); *gook* 'bonnet' (presumably < Corn. *cūgh* 'head-covering', etc.; VI.14.1); *griglans* 'heather' (< Corn. *grüglon*; I.3.15); *groushans* 'dregs' (< Corn. *growjyon*; V.8.15); *gurgoe* 'warren' (< Corn. *gorgē*, pl. *gorgow* 'low or broken-down hedge'; unp.); *hoggan* 'pastry cake' (< Corn. *hogen*; unp.); *kewny* 'rancid' (< Corn. *kewnÿek* 'mossy, mouldy, hoary'; V.7.9); *muryans* 'ants' (< Corn. *muryon* coll.; IV.8.12/13); *padgy-pow* 'newt' (< Corn. *peswar-paw* < *peswar* 'four' + *paw* 'foot'; IV.9.8); *pig's-crow* 'pigsty' (< Corn. *crow*, see above; I.1.5); *rab* 'gravel' (cf. Corn. *rabmen* 'granite gravel'; unp.); *scaw* 'elder-tree' (< Corn. *scaw* coll.; IV.10.6); *stank* 'to walk, trample, step (on, in)' (< Corn. *stankya*; unp.); *tidden* 'tender' (< Corn. *tyn*, later *tidn* 'tight, firm, rigid', etc.; unp.); *whidden* 'weakling' (of a litter of pigs; < Corn. *gwyn*, later *gwidden* 'white'; III.8.4). It will be noted that many of these words have undergone various modifications in their transition to English dialect, some of them, for example, attaching an English plural *-s* to what is a collective form (e.g. *muryon*).

Some of the Cornish loan-words are not ultimately Cornish, in fact, but Latin, French or English, mediated into English dialect via Cornish. From a very early period indeed, Cornish showed itself to be susceptible to foreign influence, and the extant medieval and later literature abounds in words and phrases from all three languages, together with chunks of verse in French and English. It therefore comes as no surprise to meet words of this type. Examples are: *bulhorns* 'snails' (< Corn. *bulhorn*, a late Cornish word, adapted from an English dialectal nickname for the snail; IV.9.3);[5] *bullies* 'cobbles' (< Corn. *būly*, ultimately < Fr *boulet* 'small globe, sphere or ball', possibly via English; unp.); *bussa* 'salting-trough, bread-bin' (probably < ME *busse* < OFr *buce, busse* 'barrel' and medieval Latin *bussa*; III.12.5, V.9.2); *croust* 'snack' (< Corn. *crowst* < OFr *crouste*, Latin *crusta*, possibly via English; VII.5.11); *flam-new* 'brand-new' (*flam-* < Corn. *flam* 'flame' < Latin *flamma*; VI.14.24); *gawky* 'stupid' (< Corn. *gōky* < ME *gōki* < *gōk* 'cuckoo' < ON *gaukr*; see *MED*, s.v. *gōkī*; VI.1.5); *geeking* 'gaping' (< Corn. *gÿky* 'to peep', perhaps < English *keek*; VI.3.7/8); *hoggans* 'haws' (< Corn. *hogan* [+ English pl. *-s*], probably < OE *haga* + Corn. singulative suffix *-an*; IV.11.6); *peeth* 'well' (cf. Latin *puteus*, but the etymological difficulties are great—? < a Vulgar Latin *putteus; unp.).

It should again be stated that the list as given from *SED* need not be regarded as exhaustive. There may be, and there certainly once were, more Cornish words in English dialect. But a number of them are probably non-Celtic in origin, and, like those listed above, themselves loans in Cornish before making their final appearance in English dialect.

With regard to Cornish phonetic influence upon English dialect, the dubious possibility of explaining south-western front-rounded vowels ([ʏ:], etc.) by a Celtic substratum is mentioned above (p. 97): there is really nothing or almost nothing in Co, D or west So that can be satisfactorily attributed to the influence of Celtic phonology—which is very natural, considering the length of time that the Celtic languages have been dead in those parts. In the remote west of Co, Cornish lingered on in the mouths of one or two peasant speakers until the eighteenth century, but in so enfeebled a condition that one would hardly have thought it able to bring any phonological influence to bear on English. One word, however, may perhaps echo an older Cornish pronunciation, and this is *plaeth* 'plaice', a pronunciation found, according to Nance (*Glossary*), at Mousehole. As Nance observes, in Middle Cornish, words of French origin ending in [s] are sometimes spelled with *th* in the manuscripts, e.g. *fath* 'face', *grath* 'grace', *plath* 'place' (beside *fas, gras, plas*), suggesting an actual pronunciation with [θ]. In this instance it appears that the [θ] ending of the Cornish word has been preserved in local fishermen's dialect.

The Scandinavian element

The linguistic result of the Scandinavian invasions and settlement was the introduction into the English lexicon of a good number of Scandinavian words, and perhaps also a certain amount of phonological influence. This effect, although it must have started in the OE period, hardly becomes apparent until the ME period, partly because late OE literature was written chiefly in the West Saxon dialect, in which Scandinavian influence was likely to be least prominent. Many borrowings—chiefly restricted to the intimate part of the vocabulary[6]—became part of universal English usage, and survive in Standard English—e.g. *both, husband, outlaw, Riding, skin, window, wrong*—and some of these ultimately ousted their English synonyms or cognate phonological forms: so, for example, ON *taka* 'take' ousted OE *niman* (which did, in fact, survive sporadically up to the seventeenth century, from *c.* 1600 with the meaning of 'steal', see *OED*, *EDD*, s.v. Nim), ON *kasta* 'throw' ousted OE *weorpan* (and was later itself generally superseded except in special collocations [see *OED*, *EDD*, s.v.] by *throw* < OE *þrāwan*, originally meaning 'turn, twist'), ON *bón* 'prayer' ousted OE *bēn*, ON *egg* 'egg' ousted OE *æg*, ON *ketill* 'kettle' ousted OE *cietel* (see Note 7, below), ON *stakkr* 'stack' ousted OE *hrēac* 'rick' (which does, however, still prevail in the south and west of England in dialectal English; see II.7.1, II.9.13), and, most notable of all, the ON pronouns *þeir*, *þeira*, *þeim* 'they, their, them' ousted the equivalent OE pronouns *hīe*, *hīera*, *hem*. On the other hand, it should be noted that sometimes the struggle resulted in the disappearance of the Scandinavian form, thus, for example, OE *gāt* 'goat' survived ON *geit*, and OE *fisc* 'fish' survived ON *fiskr*. Sometimes cognate forms from ON and OE existed side by side, and ultimately both made their way into Standard English, but with different meanings, thus *leap* (< OE *hlēapan*) and *lope* (< ON *hlaupa*).

To the dialectologist, one of the most interesting types of such coexistence is that of English and Scandinavian cognates in which the Scandinavian form survives only in dialect, while the English is the Standard English form, e.g. *yard* (< OE *geard*) and *garth* (< ON *garðr*), *elm* (< OE *elm*) and *holm* (< ON *álmr*), *chest* (< OE *cest*, *cist*) and *kist* (< ON *kista*). Historically, such cognate pairs may be classified in several groups, of which the following are of special note.

(1) Scandinavian [k], English [tʃ]. In the neighbourhood of palatal vowels, Germanic *k* was a palatal sound in OE, and thereafter became [tʃ], whereas it remained as [k] in ON. Although it is often difficult to decide whether an ON word was simply borrowed or whether its English cognate was influenced by it, such forms as *kirk*, *kirn*, *kist* in the northern dialects are obviously the result of ON influence of some kind, while their English equivalents *church*, *churn*, *chest* are the Standard English norms.[7]

The present-day dialectal distribution of *kirk* (ON *kirkja* = OE *cirice*) is very limited, according to *SED* (VIII.5.1) occurring only in Nb, We, Cu, north La and YNR, and even here, except in Nb, it was usually given only with qualification (i.e. 'rare', 'obsolete', 'old', etc.). Modern place-names containing the element *kirk* as far south as Nf, Sf and Ess testify to its much wider range in ME, although from the references in *OED* it seems that the word became restricted to the north at an early period. The distribution of *kirn* (ON *kirna* = OE *cyren*; V.5.5) is somewhat wider, but is restricted to the northern counties.

131

ON k in final position, in *flick* 'flitch' (ON *flikki* 'patch' = OE *flicce*; III.12.3), *sike* 'such' (ON *slíkr* = OE *swylc*, etc.; VIII.9.7) and *birk* 'birch' (ON *birki* = OE *bierce*; IV.10.1), has a wider distribution, extending into L as well as up to Nb (and in *flitch* being recorded in Db, Nt, Lei, and even in Wa, Bd, So and W),[8] while *beck* 'brook' (ON *bekkr* = OE *bece*; IV.1.1) stretches right into south Nf (it is recorded by *EDD* from Sx!).[9] It is not found in Nb at all, and its occurrence throughout Du is probably due to influence coming from more definitely Scandinavian areas, since the county has no early examples in place-names, and when it does occur it replaces an earlier *-burn* (< OE *burna*, etc.).[10] *Sark* 'shirt' (ON *serkr* = OE *serc*; VI.14.8) has a distribution now limited to the far north, namely Nb, north Cu, south Du, but formerly had a much wider distribution: *EDD* records it from Nb, Du, Cu, We, Y, La (also ? Sx—probably an error).

(2) Scandinavian [sk], English [ʃ]. Germanic [sk] was a palatal sound in OE, and thereafter became [ʃ], whereas [sk] remained in ON. Words containing [sk], of which there are few in Standard English but an enormous number in dialect,[11] are therefore often considered to be of certain Scandinavian origin or to have been influenced by Scandinavian [sk], but may, in fact, sometimes have a different provenance, namely one of the Low Dutch dialects. Words such as *skell* 'shell' (ON *skel* = OE *sciell*) and *skift* 'shift' v. (ON *skipta* = OE *sciftan*), both recorded by *EDD* from the northern counties, are pretty certainly directly from ON sources or the result of ON phonological influence, whereas *skelving(s)* 'cart-frame', etc., recorded by *SED* (I.10.5/6) from Cu only, and presumably a derivative of *skelf* 'shelf', may be of Low Dutch origin (cf. Du, LG *schelf*, and see *OED*, s.v. Shelf).

One word of definite ON origin is the element *scale-* or *skell-* in *scale-*, *skell-board* or *-boose* 'partition' (between cow-stalls; I.3.2). *Scale-*, *skell-* is < ON *skáli* 'hut, shelter', etc. The word is found in a typical distributional pattern (see below) throughout north and east Y, north La, We, south and west Cu.

In final position, [sk] occurs in *mask* 'mash' (the tea; V.8.9) in the four northern counties, but is sometimes reduced to [st] or [s] (cf. Sw *mäska*, Da *mæske*; OE *māsc-* n.). A comparison may be made with northern *pace-* or (perhaps by folk-etymology) *paste-eggs* 'Easter eggs' (VII.4.9). The first element of this compound is probably from ON *páskar* (pl.) < Latin *pascha* (final [k] being retained in northern England at first and then lost, giving a fifteenth-century form *paas* and finally modern *pace*). According to *OED*, the word is first recorded in Andrew Wyntoun, *c.* 1425 ('the sextene day efftyr Pase'), but the compound *pace-egg* itself does not appear until 1579. It has a fairly full northern distribution in Nb, Cu, Du, We, La, Y, and north Db.

(3) Scandinavian [g], English [ʤ]. Germanic medial *gg* was palatal in OE in the neighbourhood of palatal vowels, and ultimately became [ʤ], written *cg*, whereas in ON it remained *gg* [gː]. The words *brig* 'bridge' (ON *bryggja* 'landing-stage, gangway' = OE *brycg*; IV.1.2), *lig* 'lie' v. (ON *liggja* = OE *licgan*; VIII.3.6) and *rig* 'ridge' (ON *hryggr* = OE *hrycg*; II.3.2) have fairly full distributions in the north, except that *lig* is not found in Nb or north Cu, north and east Du. None of them are found in south La, but they are attested fully throughout most of Y, extending into L, and *rig* extends southward as far as south Nf.

(4) Scandinavian initial [g], English [j]. Before palatal vowels, Germanic initial *g* was a palatal sound [j] in OE, but [g] in ON. *Garth*, occurring alone and in various compounds at I.1.3 (*farmyard*), I.1.4 (*stackyard*), I.1.9 (*straw-yard*) and I.1.10 (*paddock*) is < ON *garðr*. *Garth* is not current in north Nb or in La and central west Y, but is otherwise fairly evenly distributed throughout the north as far south as YWR. (Cf. *garn* 'yarn', < ON *garn*, recorded by *EDD* from Nb, Du, Cu, We, Y, La and St.)

(5) Scandinavian [kk], English [ŋk]. In at least one word, the northern dialects show a Scandinavian form with assimilation of Germanic [n] to a following [k] (whereas there was no such assimilation in OE), namely *drunken* (VI.13.11). Forms of *drucken* (with medial [k]) predominate in the four northern counties, in north La and west Y. There is also one example in south-east La, and this area—the south La–YWR boundary—is especially interesting in that it also has forms with medial [f] and medial [x], presumably both of these arising as further developments from the geminate [kk] (cf. further, p. 101, above).

(6) Various cognate vowels. *Bairns* (ON *barn* = OE *bearn*; VIII.1.2) has a very wide distribution, being current to the north-east of a line running from north La, enclosing the whole of Y, north Nt and the whole of L, with one single example in east St. It may well be, in this particular area, that ON *barn* reinforced OE *bearn*, thus accounting for its very wide currency over a large area of the country.

Loup 'jump' (ON *hlaupa* = OE *hlēapan*; IV.2.10) is a word widely current throughout the whole of the north, including L (note, however, that in central La and YWR it is often replaced by or exists side by side with the cognate *leap*).

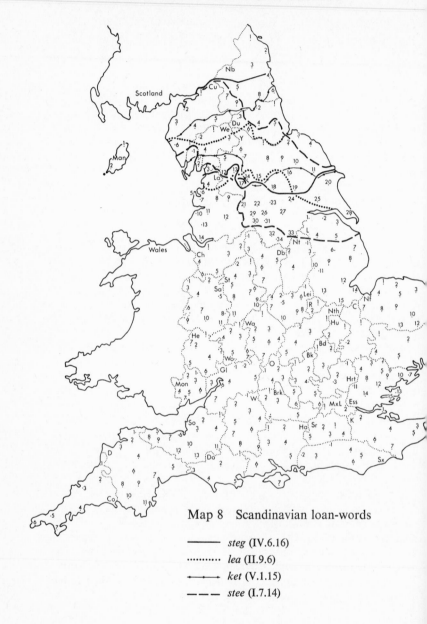

Map 8   Scandinavian loan-words

———— *steg* (IV.6.16)

·········· *lea* (II.9.6)

←———→ *ket* (V.1.15)

— — — *stee* (I.7.14)

Lake 'play' (ON *leika* = OE *lācan*; VIII.6.4) is likewise current throughout the whole north except in most of Nb and south La.

On the whole, as may be seen from Map 8, the most familiar distribution shown by the Scandinavian loans in English dialect at the present time is a broad (sometimes diagonal) band across the north of England, its northern and southern boundaries fluctuating quite considerably from word to word. Thus *steg* 'gander' (< ON *steggi, steggr*; IV.6.16) occurs in south Nb, Cu, We, Du, north La and the northern half of Y. *Lea* 'scythe' (< ON *lé*; II.9.6) occurs in west Cu, south We, north La, south Du (locality 6) and north Y. *Lait* 'to look for' (< ON *leita*; III.13.18) occurs in west Cu, We, north La (one example) and the northern half of Y. *Flay-crow* 'scarecrow' (< ON *fleyja* + *crow*; II.3.7) occurs in south Nb, Cu, Du (three scattered examples), We, north La and most of Y. *Ket* 'rubbish' (< ON *kjǫt* 'flesh'; V.1.15) occurs in south Cu, We, south-east Nb, south Du (loc. 6), north La and north Y; *brant* 'steep' (probably < Sw, ODa *brant*; IV.1.11) occurs in south Cu, south-west Nb, west Du, We, north and central La and north and east Y; *slaip* 'slippery' (< ON *sleipr*; VII.6.14) occurs in Cu, south Du, We, north and central La, most of Y, north Db and north L; *stee* 'ladder' (< ON *stige, stege*; I.7.14) occurs in Cu, south Du, We, north La, most of Y and north L; *I is* 'I am' (< ON *ek es*; e.g. IX.7.7) occurs in south Nb, Du, Cu, We, north La, and north and east Y. To the north and south of these areas, English words are current. Professor Kolb has drawn attention to the fact that the southern boundaries of many of these words coincide neatly enough with those of some of the phonological isoglosses discussed above (pp. 89–91),[12] and similarly their northern boundaries coincide with the southern limit of Nb [h], [hw] and [ʁ].

Some Scandinavian loans do not, however, show this distribution. In addition to examples already cited, *neave* 'fist' (< ON *hnefi*; VI.7.4), for example, occurs throughout the entire north from Nb southwards. The present distribution of *lathe* 'barn' (< ON *hlaða*; I.1.11) is south-west Cu (locality 6), north We, and a narrow western strip from north to south Y (although according to *EDD*, it formerly occurred in Nb, Du, Cu, We, Y, La, Db, Nt, L and Nth). *Lops* 'fleas' (< ME *loppe* < Da *loppe*, Sw *loppa*, from the root of *hlaupa* 'to jump'; IV.8.4) now occurs only in north-eastern England—in south Nb, Du, north and east Y and north L, although, according to *EDD*, it once occurred in Nb, Du, Cu, We, Y and L. There is, however, one stray example on the La coast (locality 5). *Kay-fisted, -pawed*, etc. 'left-handed' (< Da *kei*; VI.7.13), occurring only in

135

central La, one locality (30) in YWR, and north Ch, has an even more limited distribution, while *unheppen* 'clumsy' (< *un-* + ON *heppinn* 'lucky, dexterous', cf. Norw *unheppen*; VI.7.14) occurs throughout L, but apart from this only at Y 25, a locality just on the other side of the river Humber.

Some other Scandinavian loans in dialect occur only in scattered northern areas: *haver* 'oats' (< ON *hafre*; II.5.1) occurs in Cu and We, and, in compounds, occasionally in west Y and at La 3; *ings* 'low-lying land' (< ON *eng*; IV.1.7) occurs only in Y, and *carr*(*s*) with the same meaning (cf. Da *kær*, *kjær*, Sw *kærr*, Norw *kjær*, *kjerr*; IV.1.7) in south Du, east Y, north L and La 5; *feal*, *felt* 'hide' (< ON *fela*; VIII.7.6) occurs at We 3 and otherwise only in north Y, although *EDD* attests a much wider, mostly northern, distribution (the *-t*/*-d* forms are difficult to explain); *stern* 'stars' (< ON *stjarna*, pl. *stjǫrnur*; VII.6.3) occurs only at Nb 8 (in the south) and Cu 3. (*Starn* at O 2 is perhaps *star* + weak *-n* plural ending.)

It is relevant to mention that there are a good many words apparently of Scandinavian origin that are not (or, in some cases, formerly were not, according to *EDD*) restricted to the north—often being in fact widely distributed—but yet are dialectal (as distinct from having a place within Standard English). So, for example, *agate* 'on the way, afoot' (< *a-* + ON *gata* 'way', ME *on gate*); *ding* 'knock, strike, beat' (< ME *dingen*, cf. ON *dengja* 'to hammer'); *gape* 'yawn' (< ON *gapa*; VI.13.4, cf. *gawp* with the same meaning, and also meaning 'stare' at VI.3.7); *hell* 'pour' (probably < ON *hella*; V.8.8, but now recorded from Do only); *lafter* or *laughter* 'brood of chickens' (< ON **lahtr*, *láttr*; IV.6.12, but now recorded only from the north); *lugs* 'ears' (? cf. Sw *lugg* 'forelock'; VI.4.1/4, recorded by *SED* from the south as well as the north); *rab* 'gravel' (< Sw dialectal *rabbe* 'remnants of a stone wall', according to *EDD*, inexplicably recorded—but unpublished—only from Co by *SED*, and from Co and Nb by *EDD*); *skep* 'feed basket, straw beehive' (< ON *skeppa*; IV.8.8(b)). The explanation of such words may lie in the fact that some of them are not Scandinavian at all, but are derived from lost OE cognates, or perhaps that internal loaning from ON dialects was more widespread than has been thought.

This review of the various distributions of the Scandinavian loans in dialect prompts some remarks on the differences which emerge between them, although reasons for these differences are not easy to find. It is too simple to rely solely on Gilliéron's celebrated dictum that 'every word has its own history', although this factor is no doubt basic. Comparing, for example, *kirk* and *bairn*, why has *kirk* receded so drastically and *bairn* hardly at all? Is one in more constant use? Is one felt to be more 'acceptable' than the other? Perhaps in this particular case, *kirk* has been largely replaced from an early period by southern and official *church*,[13] while *bairn*, belonging to a more intimate part of the vocabulary, has survived. Since *bairn* shows such a wide distribution (cf. *beck*), it is also tempting to assume that this is an English word anyway, merely reinforced by its Scandinavian cognate. Such questions demand answers, which in turn demand research.

The patterning we find is, however, undoubtedly due to historical causes and is consonant with the place-name evidence for the Scandinavian settlements: in the latter part of the ninth century there appear to have been three Danish dominions—Yorkshire (with parts of the adjoining districts), East Anglia and Scandinavian Mercia (which included the Five Boroughs of Lincoln, Stamford, Leicester, Derby and Nottingham). At the beginning of the tenth century there were fresh incursions into the west, this time from Norwegians. Northumberland and Durham are on the edge of the Yorkshire kingdom and thus only to a limited extent share its present-day dialectal characteristics, which no doubt spread out into adjoining areas from those regions which had been more completely Scandinavianized. Dialect words in Cumberland, Westmorland and north Lancashire must be due either to the Norwegians or to loaning from the adjacent easterly areas. As with other dialect words, it is necessary to take into account both increasing spread (i.e. loans from adjacent districts) and recession, taking place either at different times or, in some cases, perhaps simultaneously.

It is probable—especially in view of the place-name and ME evidence for some of them—that all the Scandinavian words given here originally had a much wider distribution in a southerly direction, but have tended to recede to the north as time has gone on and Standard English has become a more powerful factor. Many of them have apparently receded as far as the Humber–Ribble boundary, a dialectal boundary of some standing. In Northumberland and Durham, however, it is significant that the distributions are limited, and this is partly because these were not originally areas of Scandinavian settlement, and partly also on account of dialectal disintegration: Orton's examples of changes which were evidenced in the traditional reflexes of the ME long vowels at Byers Green even in 1920 (pp. 105–6, above) are instructive, as is also his comment that words of Scandinavian origin were rare at this locality.[14] Orton ascribes this dialectal disintegration mainly to the enormous rise in the population of the whole area since as far back as 1801, the coal industry in particular being the means of bringing into Durham considerable numbers of workmen and their families from Ireland, Scotland, Wales, Yorkshire, Lancashire and the Midlands. Together with such settlement we should also remember the substantial migrations from the county to London and elsewhere, especially during periods of depression.

On account of these and no doubt other factors, we are in many instances left with the familiar band of ON forms spread across the country, as seen, for example, in *steg*, etc. (above). But clearly much scholarly attention needs to be applied to the problems merely mentioned here before a really adequate answer can be found in each individual case.

Some other ON words are mentioned in the treatment of fishing dialect in Chapter 8.

The French element

In some ways consideration of the French element in English dialect presents much greater difficulty than does the Scandinavian element, not only because so little research has so far been done on it, but also because on the whole words of French origin show no particular territorial distribution and are related to no special categories. Any discussion of them is, therefore, likely to be extremely selective, based merely on what seem to be the most interesting examples.

In the sphere of farming, *court* or *back-court* (< OFr *cort*, etc.; I.1.3) refers, as it does in *Piers Plowman* (see *OED*, s.v. Court sb. 1, I.1), to a farm-yard in W, D, east Co and Ha 3, alternating in the southern and south-western part of England with the native expressions *barton* and *yard* (compounded and alone). *Court-yard* occurs in the same sense at Wa 5 and O 3. *Place* (uncompounded) adds several dialectal meanings to those current in Standard English, namely 'farmstead' (I.1.2) at K 5—and also at Man 2 (note that *EDD* also gives it as meaning 'farm or small holding', and as 'court-yard, barton' from K only) and 'cow-stall' (I.3.1) at D 2, Sf 3, Bd 3.

On the domestic level, the words *chamber* (< Fr *chambre*) and *parlour* (< OFr *parleor*) both have widespread dialectal distributions although they are now obsolete or obsolescent in Standard English. *Chamber* has denoted various rooms from ME times onwards, including the *bed-chamber* (first ref. *OED* 1362). But from the seventeenth century this word existed side by side with *bedroom* (first ref.

OED 1616). The latter is now universal in Standard English, while *chamber* meaning 'bedroom' (V.2.3) occurs frequently up and down the country in dialectal usage.

The dialects show a number of words for the 'best room' in the house (V.2.2), many of them compounds with first element *front-*, suggestive of the actual structure of the house, others merely *room* or *house* (*hall* only in west Co). Like *chamber*, *parlour* has a widespread distribution in dialect. It is recorded by *OED* as the 'best room' from 1469 onwards, but has now been replaced in Standard English by various other words such as *lounge* (first ref. *OED* 1775)— though this has an obsolescent ring now—and *sitting-room* (first ref. *OED* 1806). It is interesting to note that in the south-east (Ess, Sr, K, Sx—also at Mon 4) this last expression is used for the living-room (V.2.1) as well as for the sitting-room, perhaps indicative of sociological changes in the Home Counties area.

In answer to the question at *SED* V.2.6 Where do you keep your food? both *larder* (< OFr *lardier*, AN *larder*) and *pantony* ~ *pantry* (< AN *panetrie*, OFr *paneterie*) were attested—side by side with words like *milk-house*, *buttery*, etc.—both of them on record in English since the beginning of the fourteenth century.

Vault (< OFr *voute*, *volte*) can mean a brick-lined well made for a cess-pool in one locality in W (I.3.11), or the actual box in an earth-closet (V.1.13) more widely attested in the same county. The other more widespread expressions for this notion are worth noting: *necessary* or *nessy*, *netty*, *petty*, *privy*, contrasting with the more obviously Germanic and less euphemistic *shit-hole*, *-house* (cf. ON *skíta* v., *skítr* n.). The word *planching* (ultimately < Fr *planche* 'plank'; cf. ONFr *planke*, whence English *plank*), apparently meaning an upstairs or bedroom floor, is recorded (V.2.7) throughout Co, and raises questions about the construction of the older type of house in the county,[15] while a *causen* (< *causey* [< ONFr *caucie*] 'cobbled street, paved area', etc., + adjectival *-en*), i.e. flagged, floor was mentioned at D 11 (V.2.7).

Launder(*ing*) 'gutter' (< *lavender* [< OFr *lavendier*] 'launderer'; V.1.6) occurs in areas as far apart as Y (only at locality 7), Db and Co (the usual word in the centre and west of the county; the east has *shoot* (locality 1), *shooting* (2), common words for his notion in south-west England), although *EDD* records it from Nb, Y, St, Db, So, D and Co. This former distribution suggests that the word may have been adopted from mining usage, and indeed *OED* records it (from 1667) firstly as a trough for water, especially in mining, for washing the ore clean from dirt, and only as a gutter for rainwater

from the end of the nineteenth century. The sense-change 'launderer'
—'water-trough in mining'—'household gutter' is noteworthy (see
OED, s.v. Launder, Lavender sb. l).

The words for 'funnel' (V.9.3) show an interesting distribution.
Funnel itself is a French word (< OFr **founil*, ultimately < Latin
infundibulum < *infundere* 'to pour in'), and is the Standard English
expression, as well as being the usual word throughout south-east
England, much of the north and east, and Co, D and west So.
Tunnel (< OFr *tonel*, modern Fr *tonneau*) occupies We, much of
west Y, north Nt and north L, while various words having OE
tunne 'tun' as the first element occupy the rest of the country:
tundish has a west-Midland distribution, and was used by Shakespeare, *tunniger* occurs in a small area in the south-west, comprising
most of So and Do and D 5, and *tunning-dish* occurs only in three
localities in south Ch and north Sa, and at Wa 3. Here the French
words seem to have pushed the native words over to the west of the
country.

Rummage 'rubbish' (< Fr *arrumage*; V.1.15) has a south-western
distribution comprising part of west So, most of D and north-east
Co. Two words for 'basket', *flask* or *flasket* and *maund*, are both of
French origin. The first, meaning 'clothes-basket' (V.9.7), is < OFr
flasque, flasquet, and is the usual term in west So, D and Co as well
as other parts of the west and south-west, while *maund* 'feed-basket'
(for horses; III.5.4) is < OFr *mande* (< MDu *mande*), unless
immediately from MDu or MLG, and has a similar distribution
(So, D, Co). (*Corn-*)*hutch* (< Fr *huche*) is the common term for a
corn-bin (I.7.4) in west So, D and Co, as well as in parts of Sf and
Ess, while *coffer* (< OFr *cof(f)re*) alternates with *bing* (< Da *bing*
'bin') in Ch, Sa and St, and the usual words farther north are *bing*
and *kist* (< ON *kista*). *Corn-ark* (< OE *arc*) occurs at St 1/3.

Several dialectal words for food or meals are French in origin.
Among them, *victuals* (< OFr *vitaille*), now obsolete in Standard
English, is current in scattered places in southern England (V.8.2,
VIII.1.26); *bever* 'snack' (< OFr *beivre* 'drinking, drink') is re-
corded by *SED* from the south-east, extending into O 4 and Wa 6
(VII.5.11).

Vermin (< OFr *vermin*), pronounced [vaːmɪnt], is used to mean
'pus' (VI.11.9) at Y 16, while *humour* (< AN *(h)umour*) expresses
the same notion in scattered localities (Sr to Co, also once in Wa)
in the south. *Piss* n. (from the v., ME *pissen* < OFr *pissier*) is a word
still widespread throughout the dialects (I.3.10, VI.8.8), although
now 'vulgar' in Standard English.

THE FOREIGN ELEMENT IN ENGLISH DIALECT

Saucy 'slippery' (< *sauce* [< Fr *sauce*] + -*y*) is attested (VII.6.14) only from Do 4 and Hrt 1, and *glance* 'bounce' (perhaps ultimately < OFr *glaichier*; VIII.7.3) only from one or two places in Co and D.

Words of French origin often show some interesting phonetic features in dialect, especially those belonging to the original word which have been lost in Standard English. So, for example, *mushroom* (< Fr *mousseron*; II.2.11) and *April* (< OFr *avrill*, but refashioned after Latin *aprilis*; VII.3.3) still show stress on the second syllable in some cases, whereas in Standard English such words have conformed to the Germanic stress-pattern of first syllable stress. *SED* actually records second-syllable stress for *mushroom* only in the south. When *April* has this sort of stress, the second syllable is sometimes long, containing not the usual [ə] or [ɪ], but [iː].

Mushroom shows two other features worthy of note, namely the retention in the south of the original final -*n* (note, too, the shortened version *roons* at Gl 6) and the medial unstressed [ə]—*musheroom*.

The word *cushion* (V.2.10) exists in two ME types: ME *quisschen* < AN *quissine*, OFr *coissin*, *cuissin*, and ME *cusshyn*, *cushon* < Fr *cussin*, *coussin*. Only the second of these survives in Standard English, but the dialectal forms sometimes derive from the first. Forms with initial [w] only (< northern ME *whishin*) emerge at Cu 4, We 3/4, La 5/8/9, Y 5–8/13/14/21/22/29; Cu 3 has [kw] and Y 15 zero ([ɒʃɪn])! All of these except Cu 3, We 3 and Y 15 have vowel nucleus [ɪ], and at Y 30 is recorded [kwiːʃɪn].

Fester v. (< OFr *festre* n.; VI.11.8) is very interesting. The north shows [ɪə] in this word at Cu 6, La 1/5–8 and Y 5/6/9/13/14/15/17/21/29, [ˡiː] at We 1/3, and [iː] at We 2 and La 9. The south shows [ʏː] at Co 1/2, D 2–4/6/7/9/11, [ʏ] at D 5/10 and [juː] at Do 3 (the east and west Midlands have no specially significant forms here).

Low Dutch words

Apart from one or two occasional words of other origins,[16] the only other non-native elements in English dialectal vocabulary worthy of mention are those of Low Dutch (which includes Flemish, Dutch, Frisian and Low German) and German. It is very possible that the Low Countries and Germany exercised most of their influence in certain specialized spheres in which their people were active, and indeed some loans from these regions are dealt with under mining and fishing dialects, below. There are, however, some dialect words of other types which apparently owe their origin to the Low Countries. *Brandis* 'gridiron' (V.7.4) at D 6/7 may owe something to Du

141

brandijzer ('branding-iron'), since the English form (OE *brandīsen*) is so rarely attested (nothing is on record between *c.* 1000 and 1874, according to *OED*, which describes the word's history in the intervening years as 'uncertain'!), and may have died out after the OE period, later being borrowed from Du. *Flitter-mouse* 'bat' (IV.7.7), found at odd places in Y, K, Sx and Nf (cf. *flitter-bat* in Sx, *flinter-bat* in K), is apparently 'in imitation of' Du *vledermuis* or German *fledermaus* (*OED*). *Grift* 'channel shaped out by water for itself', recorded by *EDD* from north L, may be < Du *grift*, related to *griff* 'deep, narrow valley or chasm'. *Grill* v. 'snarl, snap like a dog, grin', recorded by *EDD* from Sf and D, may be < MDu *grillen*. *Groop* 'drain in the cow-house' (I.3.8), recorded widely from Nb to Nf and St, is < MDu *groepe*. *Keeking* 'peeping' (VI.3.8), recorded from Nb and north Cu, is perhaps < MDu *kieken* or LG *kîken*.

Pad 'path' (< Du, LG *pad* = OE *pæþ*; IV.3.11), found today in Nt and east Db, L, Lei, R, north-east Nth, and occasionally in Hu, Nf, Ch and Sa, though, according to *EDD*, formerly of a far wider distribution, is a specially interesting case. The first mention of this word in *OED* is 1567, and it is stated to be a 'word orig. of vagabonds' cant, introduced like other words of the class in 16th c.'. But as found in English dialect, the word has no suggestion of slang or 'low' usage and seems to have been borrowed into the dialects as the ordinary word for 'path'.

Rean 'furrow' (II.3.1), recorded in the north and west, may be from Du *reen*, *reyn* 'limit, bound', if not from ON *rein* 'strip of land'. *Slap* 'opening in a hedge, fence, etc.', recorded by *EDD* (sb. 4) from Nb and So (as well as Scotland, Ireland, Pembrokeshire), is < MDu or MLG *slop* 'opening, gap, narrow passage'. *Stull* 'large piece of anything edible' (e.g. bread), recorded by *EDD* from Hrt and East Anglia (and still in use), may be from Frisian *stulle* 'piece, lump' (cf. German dialectal *stollen* 'slice of bread').

Finally, as noted in Chapter 5, in some cases at least, dialect words containing initial [v] for RP [f] may owe something to Low Dutch influence, as may also initial [d] in *thatch*, *thistle*.

Some German words are discussed under Mining Vocabulary, in Chapter 8.

8 Occupational Dialects

One of the criticisms sometimes made of *SED* is that the notions for which it aims to secure dialectal expressions are nearly all 'universals', i.e. notions such as are familiar to countrymen the length and breadth of England, most of whom are naturally farmers or farm-workers, or who have had experience of farming in some way or another. It does not ask for words for special notions, for example such as might be included in a questionnaire specifically designed to obtain miners' or fishermens' language.[1] But dialect surveys cannot deal with everything, and very obviously the first and most important objects of their attention must be such universally known things as streams, hills, farm-buildings, domestic paraphernalia and so on, leaving more specialized matters to be dealt with later and in a specialized way.

Apart from farming, two of the oldest industries in Britain are mining and fishing, and it is not surprising that the attention of dialectologists has tended to turn to these in preference to industries such as textiles, boots and shoes, brewing, and car or aeroplane construction, since here they can expect to find the old and interesting words characteristic of an earlier stratum of speech. This is not to say that archaic or otherwise interesting words are not to be found in the vocabularies associated with other industries—almost certainly they are—but so far very little research has been done in these fields, and it is more profitable to concentrate here on mining and fishing terminologies as examples of specialized vocabularies, components of which may have regional distributions.

Mining

There are, of course, diverse types of mining, of which in Britain the most familiar and widely spread is coal-mining. The vocabulary relating to this industry has been the object of a recent study by Dr Peter Wright (see the Select Bibliography), as part of a full-scale investigation of industrial language. In addition to localities in Scotland and Wales, Dr Wright pursued his investigations in

Northumberland, Cumberland, Yorkshire, Lancashire, Nottinghamshire, Shropshire, Kent, Somerset and the Forest of Dean, using a questionnaire of eighty-one questions asking for lexical items.

One difficulty of the study of coal-mining vocabulary is that the industry is far less stable than, say, farming: there have been frequent and large-scale movements of miners between coalfields, creating, one would expect, lexical diversity. Such, for example, are the recent large migrations from Durham to the Yorkshire–Derbyshire–Nottinghamshire coalfields and more especially the opening up of the Kent coalfield in 1908, which drew part of its labour force from the fishing industry and from the other coal-fields. A number of additional reasons underlie the complexity of the coal-mining vocabulary up and down the country—social factors not least among them. This complexity takes several forms. In the first place, there often seem to be a large number of words for the same notion in a small area. Thus Dr Wright records for 'stint, the amount of work allotted to a miner', *stint*, *pog* and *sneck* from Yorkshire West Riding pits within a ten-mile radius of each other, while even within a single locality, namely Warsop (Nt), the first response obtained for 'stallman' was *chargeman*, the second *stallman* and finally the old word *butty*. Secondly, changing conditions in the mines have meant the employment of new words (denoting new or changed 'referents'), adding even greater diversity, so that, for example, *stint* is apparently losing ground in favour of words like *cycle*, suggestive of the modern methods.

On the other hand, the tracing of national distributional patterns is difficult because one word often seems to be used up and down the country. Thus, for example, for 'miner's working place' *stint* was recorded in both Nt and K and *stall* in Y, Nt, Sa and the Forest of Dean; and for 'water-channel' *garland* was recorded in north Wales as well as in So. But such widely dispersed examples are no new thing to dialectologists, and may simply mean that all the available evidence has not so far been collected or that words migrated with the miners from one coalfield to the other. The comparatively small number of coal-mining areas also means that a close-meshed network of localities cannot be established, as was possible with the agricultural communities used as a basis for *SED*, and this in turn means that any geographical pattern which one attempts to establish necessarily looks disappointingly incomplete.

An impressive result of a study of mining vocabulary is that it yields a fair number of words which are used also in agricultural contexts (hence recorded in *SED*), some of which appear to be old. Thus, for example, a steel bucket is known as a *hopper* in Y and the Forest of Dean and *hoppet* in Nt, and as a *skip* in So: cf. *SED* II.3.6 *sowing-basket* and III.5.4 *basket* (for carrying horse-feed in). A tub is known as a *corf* in Y: cf. *OED*, s.v., where it is recorded (mainly from Scotland) from 1483 onwards, but specifically in mining use only from 1653 (Manlove, see below). 'Lunch' is variously *piece, snap, jock, tommy, bait, crowdy* or *grub*, many of which were recorded from the agricultural communities in *SED* (VII.5.11/12). The occurrence of some of these words in coal-mining suggests some interesting conclusions about the origin of such usages, and in particular the possibility of their transference at an early date from agricultural contexts—although some of them of course, may have always had a wide currency. Cf. also *grove* discussed under lead-mining. The coal-mining industry may not be unique in this respect: the Yorkshire steel term *strickle* (an instrument used to smooth the outside wall of a mould) is < OE *stricel* (an instrument used for smoothing corn in a measure), and *skip* (small wheeled container to charge the furnace) and *hopper* (container for receiving the ore and passing it into the furnace) are known here too.[2]

Lead-mining has been an industry in this country from the Roman period, and some of the most famous of the mines are in Derbyshire. From very early times, miners have been regarded as special groups within the community, and have been allowed their own laws. In Derbyshire these were the subject of a study in verse by Edward Manlove, a seventeenth-century Steward of the Wirksworth Wapen-take Barmote Courts in the county and probably in his day the greatest authority on matters connected with the Peak lead mining. Manlove's object in his poem, which was published in 1653, was to place on record the curious and antiquated mineral laws granted to the miners by custom, and it is still considered one of the most authentic historical records of mining in this area. Towards the end of the poem there is a section dealing with nothing but miners' terms, and this is worth quoting in full for its dialectal interest:

> Bunnings, Polings, Stemples, Forks, and Slyder,
> Stoprice, Tokings, Sole-trees, Roach and Ryder,
> Water-holes, Wind-holes, Veyns, Coe-shafts and Woughs
> Main Rakes, Cross Rakes, Brown-henns, Budles and Soughs,
> Break-offs, and Buckers, Randum of the Rake,
> Freeing, and Chasing of the Stole to th' Stake,
> Starting of oar, Smilting, and Driving Drifts,
> Primgaps, Roof-works, Flat-works, Pipe-works, Shifts,

Cauke, Sparr, Lid-stones, Twitches, Daulings, and Pees,
Fell, Bous, and Knock-barke, Forstid-Oar, and Tees,
Bing-place, Barmoot Court, Barghmaster, and Stowes,
Crosses, Holes, Hange-benches, Turntree, and Coes,
Founder-meers, Taker-meers, Lot, Cope, and Sumps,
Stickings and Stringes of oar, Wash-oar and Pumps,
Corfes, Clivies, Deads, Meers, Groves, Rake-soil, the Gange,
Binge oar, a Spindle, a Lampturn, a Fange,
Fleaks, Knockings, Coestid, Trunks and Sparks of oar,
Sole of the Rake, Smytham, and many more.

Some of these expressions, like *grove* (the mine itself)[3] and *forks* (pieces of wood used to keep the side up in soft places) are probably simply words in universal currency used in special senses, but others possibly have more exotic origins (although little research has so far been done on them). For example, it has been suggested that some of the terms owe their origin to Germans, brought over by the English government in the sixteenth and seventeenth centuries to give instruction in working the mines:[4] *toadstone* is possibly < German *todtes gestein* 'dead rock'; *barmaster*, earlier *barghmaster* ('a local judge among miners'), is < German *bergmeister* ('mine-master'), < *berg-* 'mining', which possibly also gives rise to Derbyshire dialectal *barghmote*, *barmote* 'hall or court for mining trials' and *barman*; and other similarities have been pointed out between *loch* 'hole, cavity in a vein' and German *loch*, *trogues* 'wooden drains' and German *trog* 'trough', *slickensides* 'smooth sides lying face to face' and German *schlichten-seiten* 'smooth sides' (although for this last, *OED* gives a derivation from *slicken*, the dialectal variant of *slick* adj. + *side*), *kibble* 'a tub' and German *kübel*, *stemple* 'wooden beam' and German *stempel*. *Coe*, with reference to the little hut built over the mine-shaft as a protection to the shaft, is probably < MDu, MLG *couwe*, in the same sense, < Latin *cavea* 'hollow, stall, cage, coop'.

Fishing and nautical

The fishing industry closely resembles the mining industry in that there has been large-scale movement of workers from one part of the country to another, resulting in the transference of words from one part to another (see below).

Very little research has been done on the dialects of fishing communities, apart from R. M. Nance's *Glossary of Cornish Sea-Words*,[5] although a valuable start has again been made by Dr Peter Wright, who has published a short fishing questionnaire in *TYDS* (1964) and (with **G. B.** Smith) some of the results achieved with it in the *Journal of the Lancashire Dialect Society* (1967; see Select Bibliography), and by the University of Leeds, which has in the last few years produced a questionnaire of seventy-five items. Such questionnaires need not be completely restricted to questions requiring lexical responses. There may be, for example, phonological peculiarities of a regional type associated with fishermen's dialect no less than with farming dialect: this is borne out by pronunciations such as *kelk* 'church', *colk* 'cork', *folk* 'fork' and *polk* 'pork', found at Filey and Staithes on the Yorkshire coast, *soyle* 'seal', found in Cornwall (see Nance, *Glossary*, s.v.), and *floo* 'fluke' (of the anchor) from the Lancashire coast (cf. *OED*, s.v. Pea³: 'Seamen by custom drop the k in *peak* and *fluke*, which they pronounce *pea* and *flue*' (1833)).

Not surprisingly, however, fishing dialect has been sought primarily for its lexical interest, for it yields a rich variety of terms. The dialect names for the fish themselves are legion, as the following small selection from *EDD* shows: *Atterpile* or *utterpile* (a small fish with venemous spines) was recorded by *EDD* (s.v. Atter-pile) from north-east La only, and designated 'obsolete', but was found in 1967 by Dr Wright at Grange (La); < OE *ātor, attor* 'poison' + ME *pīle* 'quill, dart' (cf. *atter* 'pus' at C 1, Nf 7; VI.11.9); *becker* 'species of bream' was recorded from Co (Polperro, according to Nance, *Glossary*, who suggests ? cf. Fr *bécard* 'female salmon'); *bret* 'turbot' is cited from the north, Y, L, East Anglia, Sx and the west; the word is of uncertain derivation, but is recorded from *c.* 1460 onwards, cf. *OED*, s.v., which gives 'turbot' or 'brill', depending on locality (Dr Wright recorded *brit* from La meaning 'sansker'); *clam* 'starfish' (sb. 4) is recorded from Nb, Y, C, K and Co, also *cramp* from Penzance, according to Nance (? variants of *clamp*); *cuvvins* 'periwinkles, sea-snails' (Cu, Y) is perhaps < Norw dialectal *kuvung* 'sea-snail'; *ged* 'pike' (Nb, Cu) is < ON *gedda*; *gyte* 'spawn of herrings' (Nb) is < ON *gýta* 'spawn'; *queen* (sb. 2) 'common scallop' (Sx, D, Co, the south-west): cf. *gweans* 'periwinkles, scallops' (Co only; < Corn. *gwihan* 'periwinkle') and *squin* in Sx and Do; *rauning-pollack* (Co—Polperro, according to Nance, who also gives *rauner* 'coal-fish' from Porthleven, Marazion): west-country *rawn, rean* 'ravening' (cf. *EDD*, s.v. Rawn v. 'eat greedily') < OFr *raviner*. Earlier forms have *l*, however—*rawlin*, etc., see *OED*, s.v. Rawlin pollack; *saith(e)* 'mature coal-fish' (Nb) < ON *seiðr*; *tub* '(sapphirine) gurnard' (Co, D, So, also Cu [1794]). From

147

Co, Nance cites, among numerous others, *minnick* (*ray*) 'long-nosed skate' (St Ives; < Corn. *mynek* 'long-muzzled'); *zebedee*, referring to various sorts of crab.

Fishing gear and techniques and associated matters show a great many local expressions. Dr Wright found numerous Lancashire expressions for making nets: *braid* (< OE *bregdan*, cf. *breed*(*y*) from Co [Nance]) at Fleetwood, Lytham and Marshside (but *braid* is recorded in this sense or as 'to mend nets' by *EDD* from Nf, Do, Co, D and East Anglia); *knit* at Flookburgh and Morecambe, also *casting on* at Flookburgh 'to begin net-making'. *Beet* 'to mend nets' is recorded as general by *EDD* (< OE *bētan* 'to amend', etc.), and Nance also mentions that in Newlyn the needle used is a *beetle*; *EDD* also records *cantor* 'small frame of wood on which a fisherman keeps his line' from Co (Nance gives Newlyn, Mousehole, Sennen): cf. Breton *kantol*; *dor-line* is recorded by *EDD* from Nb— 'the line used for catching mackerel' (cf. ON *dorg* 'angler's tackle, rod and line, etc., for trout or small fish'); *gange* or *ginge* 'to fasten a hook to a fishing-line' is recorded from Co (perhaps cf. Fr *ganse* 'braid'); the verb *kip* 'to catch fish by means of line and chopsticks' is recorded from Nf and is perhaps < ON *kippa* 'to pull' (cf. Norw dialectal *kippa* 'to fish with a rod' and also MDu *kippen* 'to catch, grip'); see *OED* Kip v., Kip-(hook, -net); *taum*, more generally 'a rope', is recorded as 'fishing line' (especially of horse-hair; < ON *taumr* 'rein, line, bridle') from Nb, Du, Cu, We, Y, Lakeland, north-east La and Db. To these, Nance adds, among others, *cowl rooz* (a call) 'shoot the net' (< Corn. *towl ros*), used in the St Ives seine fishery; *lagging* 'splashing made by surfacing fish'; *ouga* 'stench of fish rubbish'; *pole-end* 'outer end of a net' ('a wooden pole was formerly used to extend this'); *skwinch* (from Mousehole and Newlyn) 'small twine used to fasten drift-nets together'.

Natural features and phenomena play a substantial part in the vocabulary of fishing communities. *Air* 'sandbank', recorded by *EDD* (sb. 2) from We and La, is < ON *eyrr*; and *meal* (sb. 3), also 'sand-bank, -hill', recorded by *EDD* from Lakeland, La, Ch, L and East Anglia, is likewise an ON word *melr*; *out-wen* 'backwater, ebb of the tide', recorded from L, is perhaps < an Old Scandinavian **útvetni* (cf. Da *vand* 'water'), and a *wake* (sb. 2) is a stretch of open water in East Anglia (cf. Sw *vak* 'hole in the ice'). *Judas-heaps*, recorded by *EDD* and Nance from Co only, are 'treacherous rocks near the sea-coast'. The names for a creek would repay investigation: *wick* is a well-known one—recorded by *EDD* (sb. 2) from Y, Lakeland and the north, and having its origin in ON *vík*; also in the north, Dr Wright recorded from La *bight* and *channel, bight* perhaps < OE *byht* 'bend' (cf. OE *būgan* 'to bow, bend'), while *pill* < OE *pyll* 'pool' is recorded by *EDD* (sb. 3) from Wo, He, Gl, So and Co.

Indications of impending bad weather are signified by a *mockson* or *dogging* 'end of rainbow' in La; and the word is *ragg(l)ing* (*for rain*) in Co (Nance), when the wind blows as it does before a change from dry to wet (cf. La, Y, Db *raggy* 'stormy and cold, with drizzling rain', or, as a verb, 'to rain slightly'—*EDD*, s.v. Rag sb. 2 and v. 2).

The small selection of words given above has already revealed a number that are of Scandinavian origin. A great many more could be added, words like *ouse* (recorded by *EDD* from the north, Y and L) 'to bale out a boat' < ON *ausa* 'to pump, especially a ship'; and *ouskerry, howskelly* (Nb) 'baling utensil' < ON *ausker*; *skane* (north Y) 'to cut shell-fish out of the shell' < ON *skeina*. There also appear to be a fair number of Dutch sea-words, as one might expect: Nance cites *caboose* 'iron stove used in a fishing-boat' < Du *kabuis* (see *OED*, s.v.); *callaminks* 'fisherman's jumper' (Newlyn) < Du *kalamink* (a woollen stuff); *hand skoon* 'fishermen's fingerless gloves' < Du *hand schoen*; and both Nance and *EDD* cite *cob* (*EDD* sb. 2) as a name given to a species of gull (Y, East Anglia, K, Sx, D), or as 'young gull' (St Ives), cf. Frisian, Du *kobbe*; *drive* 'to fish with drift nets' (a form of fishing perhaps invented by the Dutch, or at least copied from them; see *EDD* Driving (East Anglia, Nf, Co), hence *driver, driving-boat, -nets* (Co only)); perhaps < Du *drijven* 'to float'; *train(-oil)* 'fish-oil' (Co only) < Du *traan*.

One or two other languages have also loaned words connected with the sea: in Co, *burdon* 'runner-and-fall of a lugger's foremast' is perhaps < Spanish *burda*; and *fermade, fair-maid* or *fumade* 'salted pilchard' < Spanish *fumado* 'smoked' (until the late sixteenth century pilchards underwent treatment by smoke as part of the curing process for export to Spain and Italy, these being called *fumados* in Spain); *composant* 'St Elmo's fire' is a version of *corposant* < Portuguese *corpo santo* 'holy body' (so called from its resemblance to an aureole or nimbus). This last word is also recorded from K by *EDD*.

Of very special interest are words which are widely distributed around the English coastline, suggestive of the movement of fishermen from one place to another within the industry. Such are (Nance): *barvil* 'fishing-apron' < OE *bearm* 'lap' + *fell* 'skin' (*EDD* cites from Co, K, USA): cf. *barm-skin* and *barm-cloth* '(leather) apron' from the north of England, and *barm-, berm-skin* 'fishing-apron'

149

from Sf; *composant* (above); *corve* or *corb* 'floating stock-box' < Du or LG *korf* (Co, east coast; cf. *EDD* Corf); *drive* (above); *jabber* 'jaw of a fish', ? cf. OE *ceafl* (Co, west So); *kiff* 'kittiwake' (cf. Sx *skiff* 'tern'); *lurker* 'small boat used by the master-seiner in pilchard-seining' (cf. Nb *lurky* 'shore-boat, hobbler'); *stoiting* 'leaping of fish out of the water' (Co, East Anglia), perhaps < Du *stuiten* 'to rebound'; *yockey* 'sailing drifter' (nickname from St Ives, Co; Nf *jockey*, whence they formerly came for the Cornish herring season).

Finally, one example of a phonological item apparently restricted to a local fisherman's dialect is that of the development of a 'parasitic nasal consonant' in certain contexts: this phenomenon is characteristic of the dialect of Marshside, an old fishing village near Southport, on the southern side of the Ribble estuary, Lancashire. The dialect was investigated by Dr Peter Wright in 1948–51, and he observed that, at the end of a sense group, [b], [d], [g] are often, and [tʃ], [dʒ] occasionally, followed by syllabic nasal consonants, [n] after [d] and [dʒ], [ŋ] after [g], and [m] after [b] and [tʃ], thus: [sɒndːn] *sand*, [kabɪdʒn] *cabbage*, [pɪgːŋ] *pig*, [pɒbːm] *pub*, [maːˑtʃm] *March*. The feature can also take place before the plural inflexion [z], thus [saɪdːnẕ] *sides*, [bagːŋẕ] *bags*. Dr Wright suggests that, since parasitic nasals usually follow a lengthened consonant (such lengthening being frequent in the dialect), the tendency thus shown towards heavy consonantal stress is also responsible for the parasitic nasal, intermediate stages in its development perhaps being consonantal lengthening or the development of [ə] after a lengthened consonant, as in his examples [stɒbː] and [stɒbːə] *stub* 'side-post of a gate'. Dr Wright observed the same phenomena at Banks, another fishing village two miles east of Marshside, but in both places only among the older generation. He suggests that slight traces of them may remain in Fleetwood dialect (elderly Fleetwood inshore fishermen are descendants of Marshsiders who migrated to Fleetwood about 1840–60), viz. [dɒgɪn] *doggin* 'end of rainbow' (above) ? < Marshside [dɒgːŋ] *dog*, and the nickname *Bobbins* ? < [bɒbːm] *Bob*.

Space has not permitted the discussion of fishermen's dialect in any detail, but enough has perhaps been said to encourage investigation of it both from the lexical and other aspects. In particular, the few indications that we have suggest that the phonological characteristics of many fishing dialects would be a very rewarding subject for study, since they may preserve archaic features not found in inland dialects. See further under Local Taboo Words, above, p. 79.

The specialized dialects of mining, fishing and other industries take on historical perspective when research is carried out into early records. Such items as local account books, wills, inventories and the like are of great value in supplementing the present-day record of specialized vocabulary, and one or two works of interest in this field are mentioned in the Select Bibliography.

9   Social Class and the Dialects

Are there any general conclusions that emerge from our consideration of dialect in the foregoing chapters? On the basis of his investigation of the phonology of English rural dialects, A. J. Ellis was able to distinguish six major areas in the country, some of which are still reflected in present-day dialectal divisions. There is, for example, no doubt at all that the northern dialects are still separated from those of the Midlands by important isoglosses. It may therefore be said first of all that traditional dialect areas may still be traced with some definiteness. The older rural types of speech still preserve features which divide dialect from dialect, and even the modified forms of dialect make it quite clear that there are still marked regional differences to be heard in the speech of both old and young people.

As stated in Chapter 1, however, dialectal variation in a language may be social as distinct from or as well as regional. Linguists speak of the language having a 'vertical' (social) as well as a 'horizontal' (regional) stratification. For example, the sound [ɒɪ] in words like *die, fire, write* may act as a class indicator as well as a regional indicator, suggesting a speaker of lower to middle-class status as well as of southern origins, while according to Professor A. S. C. Ross numerous lexical features are immediately indicative of either middle- or upper-class speech.[1]

Our basic premise, roughly put, is then that different types of English are used by different strata of society, and studies like those of Professor Ross and others in the field of sociological linguistics emphasize the importance of investigating these varying usages, not only from the theoretical aspect but from the practical or vocational point of view. Some scholars have, for example, examined the ways in which children of different social classes are variously able (or unable) to use Standard English in speech and writing. Now, the difference revealed by the way in which various social classes use the personal pronoun, for instance,[2] is not a matter of linguistic geography, and so is not our concern here. The linguistic geographer is, however, interested in the correlation between certain classes and regional dialect, and likewise in the correlation or non-correlation of other classes with non-regional dialect.

In England today one type of English enjoys a greater prestige than any other. This is the non-regional form Standard English, including the most socially acceptable form of pronunciation, RP. It is widely felt that this is the type of English, sometimes identified with 'BBC English', which is 'best' or 'most correct',[3] and it is fairly safe to say that it is in general use today among the upper classes and the upper middle classes. On the other hand, the regional dialects are still very largely used by the working classes and lower middle classes.[4] To quote Professor Strang, there is:

a high degree of correlation between working-class status and use of a localised variety of English—much higher than the degree of correlation between non-working-class status and use of a non-localised variety of English.[5]

In case these remarks should be taken to imply a gross oversimplification of the present-day social and linguistic situation, it must be said that clear-cut distinctions between the classes named above do not, of course, exist. Sharp divisions between classes in England are disappearing, and with them the sharp divisions between Standard English and non-Standard English. Many schoolteachers, for example, members of a professional class, come from working-class backgrounds and have marked regional dialects which they have no wish to abandon or modify. On the other hand, generally speaking, the more marked features of regional dialect, especially in the south, and in urban populations, are disappearing. There thus appears to be (1) modification in the class system itself, chiefly by a breakdown of the barriers between one class and another, (2) a certain degree of acceptance of regional dialect, though often in a modified form, in professional and other circles, and (3) modification of the regional dialects in a Standard English direction. Having sketched what seems to be the general present-day situation, let us now consider the relationship between Standard English and the dialects a little more closely.

That Standard English is gaining ground at the expense of the regional dialects has been amply demonstrated in this book. In Chapter 4, for instance, the example of *donkey* showed how this word of comparatively recent origin has become not only the sole term for the animal in use in Standard English, but has also largely ousted the local words of the regional dialects. The fact that this word—like others—was itself earlier dialectal in origin makes no difference at all, since Standard English has frequently adopted words, pronunciations and morphological forms from the dialects, which have then come to enjoy a prestige usage and ultimately ousted other dialectal forms.

The fact that Standard English is steadily gaining ground, and has been for some time, is an indication of its position of prestige, and contrariwise of the lowly status of regional dialect. This situation is reflected in statements by dialect speakers themselves, who will frequently refer to some dialect forms as 'slang', for instance. In Cornwall, I have heard the voicing of initial [f] to [v] described as such, and there is a general feeling among dialect speakers that the traditional forms are unworthy, vulgar, and for intimate use only. Indeed, as Professor Orton has pointed out, even the older speakers of traditional dialect in England today are bilingual and can use a Standard English form of speech, or one approximating to it, as well as their own native dialect.[6] And this form which approximates to Standard English is used with strangers or when the occasion otherwise seems especially to demand it, while the dialect is reserved for intimate or family circles. The switch (sometimes accidental) from one form to another is a point made much of in literature, as when, for example, we are told in Chapter 3 of *Tess of the d'Urbervilles* (1891) that:

Mrs Durbeyfield habitually spoke the dialect; her daughter, who had passed the Sixth Standard in the National School under a London-trained mistress, spoke two languages: the dialect at home, more or less; ordinary English abroad and to persons of quality.

or when Joe Lampton, in John Braine's *Room at the Top* (1957), suddenly finds himself relapsing, during an angry exchange with his future father-in-law, into broad Yorkshire dialect, a dialect he had (we assume) previously abandoned for a form of Standard English.

Another indication of the relative status of Standard English and regional dialect is to be found in the constant revision of dialectal forms in accordance with what is thought to be Standard English usage, often resulting in forms which belong to neither. On the phonological level, several examples of this, taken from Professor Orton's work on Byers Green (Du), were mentioned in Chapter 5, namely the use of [œː] in *horse, door, story* for a possible earlier [ɔː], the use of [oː] in *road* and [eː] in *gate* in place of traditional [ɪa], [ɪə], and the use of [öɷ] in place of [ɪə] in *goose, moon*. For the same purpose, hypercorrect forms such as [bʌtʃə] *butcher* occur in the north and Midlands, where it is desired to replace traditional [ɷ] with

154

Standard English [ʌ], while the hypercorrect use of initial [h] in words like *arm* and *off* is a widespread and familiar feature in dialectal and non-Standard usage. All of these features stem from the desire to use what is considered the 'best' type of English, namely Standard English.

Although little investigation into the speech habits of the upper and middle classes has been done in England, a beginning has been made in the United States. In the linguistic survey of the Eastern States, the usage of the social extremes—the 'folk' and the 'cultured' —as well as that of the middle class was systematically investigated, and Professor Hans Kurath has recently emphasized that one of the major tasks confronting dialectologists at the present day is to supply a record of middle- and upper-class linguistic usage for those European countries in which 'folk usage' has already been recorded. In particular, he stresses the need for investigation of the regional usages of the middle class:

Without reliable, detailed knowledge of usage on this social level, the influence of cultivated speech upon folk speech, and vice versa, cannot be traced in realistic fashion, since the social extremes do not influence each other directly. It is the middle group that mediates between them.[7]

Professor Kurath is also able to cite part of a significant passage from H. C. Wyld's *History of Modern Colloquial English* which is so relevant to present purposes that it is worth quoting here more fully:

It is much to be regretted that during the last twenty or thirty years a series of observations into the speech of old people speaking the best English of the first half of the last century was not made in a systematic way. These old people, both by their own actual usage, and by their recollections of that of their own elders, could have shed a very valuable light on much that is now obscure...It is remarkable that while the English of illiterate elderly peasants has often been examined, with the view of recording for posterity the rugged accents of the agricultural community, and even of the inhabitants of slum villages in colliery and industrial districts, it has not been thought worth while to preserve the passing fashions of speech of the courtly and polite of a former day, and those whose good fortune it was to be in a position to record these at first hand have neglected their opportunity. (pp. 186–7)

The best examples of the relation between regional and social varieties of English will be found in towns and cities, whose populations are more often than those of rural communities representative of different social classes, and where linguistic stratification on the social as well as the regional level may be expected to occur.[8] Most traditional dialectology has so far restricted itself, as Wyld observed, to the working-classes of rural communities—Ellis's 'peasants'—and so it is unlikely that the data obtained from such investigations will provide us with much material of a 'socio-regional' nature.

Unfortunately, so little research has been done on urban dialects in this country that very few results are available for scrutiny. Certainly there is nothing yet published approaching Labov's work on New York City speech. There has, however, been a recent investigation dealing with the speech of the Urban District of Cannock (St).[9] In this work, from an examination of eighty informants, selected at random, Dr C. D. Heath has been able to draw some most enlightening conclusions about the influences on the speech of Cannock inhabitants, which he determined to be income group, sex, length of schooling, and social class, the last being basic to the other three. On linguistic grounds Dr Heath classified his informants into six groups: those with (A) a two-thirds majority of local features (i.e. those of Cannock Urban District—CUD); (B) a five per cent majority; (C) less than fifty per cent of both CUD and RP features; (D) a 50 per cent majority of RP features; (E) a two-thirds majority of RP features; (F) a majority of features not describable in terms of RP and CUD. When these were classified on a non-linguistic basis, the five groups then turned out to be: (A) men in skilled manual or semi-skilled occupations; (B) women in skilled manual or semi-skilled occupations; (C) and (D) men and women in skilled non-manual occupations; (E) men and women in intermediate occupations, with more than minimum education.

In the lowest social classes (A) and (B), whereas the men tended to speak in a CUD manner, the women already seemed to make some modification in the direction of the prestige dialect (RP), in particular using [ʌ] and [ɒ] correctly (e.g. in *cut, put*), being more careful with [h], and using [äɪ] instead of [ăɪ] (*die, fire, write*). In the non-manual workers (C) and (D), in addition the front vowels and diphthongs were found to be modified, and in the two last classes there was alternation between [a] and [ɑ:] in *laugh, dance, glass* (only [ɑ:] was used in (E)), the phoneme /ɪ/ was [ɪ] and not [ɪ̣] (a CUD feature) and the back vowels and diphthongs were also altered (e.g. [əɒ] instead of [ɔ̣ɒ] (*coat, post*), [ʉu] by the side of [əu] (*boot, loose*)).

The result, roughly speaking, is to show scientifically that dialectal features are stronger in men than in women and in the lower classes than in the others. What is now needed is a large number of comparable investigations to reveal for other areas in what sectors of the community local dialect is primarily being modified and in what order the dialectal characteristics disappear—i.e. which are the most stable, which the most easily lost.

Some similar research has, in fact, been carried out by Dr P. J. Trudgill on the speech of Norwich people,[10] using a random sample of sixty informants, which was then divided into five social groups from lower working-class to middle middle class. Dr Trudgill examined his informants for a number of 'variables', e.g. the pronunciation of [ɒ], [a], [aɪ], and found that, although the speech of Norwich is clearly founded on East Norfolk rural speech, it has become increasingly differentiated from rural speech over the years, both by influence from RP and from other sources (London and the Home Counties). The linguistic situation in Norwich is obviously of some complexity, but Dr Trudgill suggests that the introduction of RP forms is effected in the first place by middle-class women, while the introduction of non-Standard forms from outside is effected in the first place by working-class males in general, and by those of the middle working class in particular.

Both of the investigations mentioned use dialect material such as that collected from rural areas by *SED*, in order to identify the traditional, rural forms of the dialect of the area. They then set out to show, among other things, to what extent urban dialect partakes of the nature of this dialect, to what extent it has been modified by Standard English (and also by the introduction of non-Standard forms from other areas), and what sectors of the population were responsible for the changes involved. Such investigations are of very great importance—not least because by making detailed records of the speech of an urban 'sample' it may be possible to see linguistic change actually in progress, and to study the ways in which this takes place.

Chapter 1

1. H. Orton, 'An English Dialect Survey: Linguistic Atlas of England', *Orbis*, ix (1960), 331.
2. Op. cit., 332.
3. *The Use of English* (London, 1962), p. 95.
4. *An Introduction to Modern Linguistics* (London, 1936), p. vi.
5. Op. cit., p. 146.
6. This raises the whole question of division into separate dialects. For the use of statistical correlation methods, see Weinreich (Note 8, below), 397–8, and also D. W. Reed, 'Establishing and Evaluating Social Boundaries in English', in *Studies in Languages and Linguistics in Honor of Charles C. Fries*, ed. A. H. Marckwardt (Ann Arbor, 1964), pp. 241–8.
7. By E. J. Dobson, *English Pronunciation 1500–1700* (2nd edn., Oxford, 1968), i, §50, who suggests that ME *a* before *f*, *s*, *th* remained [a], instead of becoming [æ] as usual, and was then lengthened to [aː], from which both dialectal [æː] and Standard English [ɑː] could easily develop.
8. 'Is a Structural Dialectology Possible?', *Word*, x (1954), 397.

Chapter 2

1. According to A. Campbell, *Old English Grammar* (Oxford, 1959), §5, linguistic differentiation was apparently not sharp among the continental tribes in question and was virtually limited to matters of vocabulary. The distinctions between the various OE dialects thus developed mainly in England, owing to geographical isolation. The same point is made by F. M. Stenton, *Anglo-Saxon England* (3rd rev. edn., Oxford, 1971), pp. 9–10.
2. This subject is treated fully by A. McIntosh, 'The Analysis of Written Middle English', *Trans. Phil. Soc.* (1956), 26–55.
3. By K. Sisam, *Studies in the History of Old English Literature* (Oxford, 1953), p. 138.
4. But *walh* in place-names must be carefully distinguished from elements such as *wall* 'wall', *wald* 'woodland', etc. Also, on many occasions—perhaps usually—*walh* may mean 'serf' rather than 'foreigner' (but perhaps the two were often synonymous). Further examples are given by K. Cameron, *English Place-Names* (London, 1961), pp. 42–3, and P. H. Reaney, *The Origin of English Place-Names* (London, 1960), pp. 83 ff.
5. *Language and History in Early Britain* (Edinburgh, 1953), pp. 221 ff.
6. See W. G. Hoskins, *The Westward Expansion of Wessex* (Leicester University Press Occasional Paper No. 13, 1960), pp. 20–1. The Dorset evidence is, however, disputed by Jackson, op. cit., p. 239.

7. J. and E. M. Wright, *An Elementary Middle English Grammar* (2nd rev. edn., Oxford, 1928), §158. It is often stated that Scandinavians and northern English dialect speakers are still to varying extents mutually intelligible, but, while admitting that many single words are similar in the two language-families, the more extravagant of these claims must surely be dismissed, along with various others (e.g. the alleged 'purity' or 'Anglo-Saxonism' of some dialects) as dialectal mythology.
8. On this process in place-names, see Reaney, op. cit., pp. 165–9.
9. Op. cit., pp. 179 ff.
10. L. Bloomfield, *Language* (New York, 1933), Chap. 26.
11. This does not, of course, imply that *all manuscripts* of these works (where more than one text exists) are from the same areas as the authors and their original works.
12. M. L. Samuels, 'Some Applications of Middle English Dialectology', *English Studies*, xliv (1963), 91.
13. *A History of English* (London, 1970), p. 75 (cf. also §26).
14. This summary is based on E. Jones, *Towns and Cities* (Oxford Paperbacks University Series, 1966), pp. 24–34.
15. Op. cit., p. 105.
16. Ibid.
17. A. McIntosh, 'A New Approach to Middle English Dialectology', *English Studies*, xliv (1963), 3.
18. Op. cit., 4.
19. Op. cit., 7.
20. Op. cit., 10.

Chapter 3

1. For many such references, see E. J. Dobson, 'Early Modern Standard English', *Trans. Phil. Soc.* (1955), 25–54.
2. F. E. Halliday (ed.), *Richard Carew of Antony: The Survey of Cornwall* (London, 1953), p. 49.
3. E. J. Dobson, *English Pronunciation 1500–1700* (2nd edn., Oxford, 1968), i, 36–7, shows in some detail, however, that many of the pronunciations given by Coote are 'clearly not dialectal', but 'merely forms which Coote did not like, generally because they departed from the orthography'.
4. For a detailed discussion of these, see Dobson, *English Pronunciation*, i, 147–52.
5. See R. H. Robins, *A Short History of Linguistics* (London, 1967), Chap. 7.
6. A. H. Marckwardt, 'An Unnoted Source of English Dialect Vocabulary', *JEGP*, xlvi (1947), 177–82.
7. Nowell's *racanteth*, which is unrecorded by *SED*, is < OE *racentēah* < *racente* + *tēah*, *tēag* 'tie', n., whereas in fact the *SED* -*e*- forms may be < ON *rekendi, rekendr* (pl.). *OED*'s last example of *rakenteie*, from Nottingham records, is from 1517. *EDD* has *reckan-tooth, racenteth* from the north.
8. As early as 1864 the Professor of Comparative Philology in the University of Zürich lectured on Swiss German once a week: see E. Dieth, 'A New Survey of English Dialects', *Essays and Studies*, xxxii (1946), 78, Note 1.
9. Op. cit., 76.
10. Op. cit., 74–104.
11. According to G. Bottiglioni, 'Linguistic Geography: Achievements, Methods

and Orientations', *Word*, x (1954), 375–87, the 'master of linguistic geography' (375) is Jules Gilliéron (who, with E. Edmont, published the *Atlas Linguistique de la France*, Paris, 1902–12, and the *Atlas Linguistique de la Corse*, Paris, 1914–15). 'Linguistic geography draws its origin from Gilliéron's *Atlas*' (379). Gilliéron's methods and departures from them in subsequent linguistic atlases are discussed by Bottiglioni.

12. H. Orton, *Introduction* to *SED* (Leeds, 1962), §1. 2.

13. The pros and cons of this have been much debated, and the followers of the *SED* procedure labelled 'rigorists' by Bottiglioni as distinct from the 'free collectors'. For a review of the advantages and disadvantages, see Bottiglioni, op. cit., 384–6. The *SED* method (which has much to commend it) is defended by Orton in *Orbis*, ix, 333.

14. On the numerous objections which have been raised to aspects of the questionnaire for the American Atlas, see the interesting note (1) in R. I. McDavid Jr, 'Structural Linguistics and Linguistic Geography', *Orbis*, x (1961), 42.

15. But the criticism has been answered by E. Dieth in H. Orton and E. Dieth, 'The New Survey of Dialectal English', *English Studies Today*, ed. C. L. Wrenn and G. Bullough (Oxford, 1951), pp. 68–9. Incidentally, the advantages of a postal questionnaire for the purposes of lexical investigation (especially the possibility of gaining a denser coverage) have been convincingly argued by Professor A. McIntosh in *An Introduction to a Survey of Scottish Dialects* (Edinburgh, 1952), pp. 77 ff. See further J. Catford, 'The Linguistic Survey of Scotland', *Orbis*, vi (1957), 113–14.

16. See W. G. Moulton, 'Structural Dialectology', *Language*, xliv (1968), 461–3.

17. For the human side of the *SED* investigations, see P. Wright and F. Rohrer, 'Early Work for the Survey of English Dialects: The Academic and Human Sides', *LSE*, N.S. ii (1968), 7–13. My own most notable experience was being mistaken, while doing field-work in Cornwall, for an escaped convict!

18. On the other hand, it is only fair to point out that the 'traditional' dialect monographs very frequently embody both types of description, giving a synopsis of the development of the ME sounds and a straightforward synchronic description of the phonology of the present-day dialect. B. Hedevind's *The Dialect of Dentdale* (Uppsala, 1967), originally a Leeds doctoral dissertation, is a prime example of such a treatment. In the face of much modern criticism of 'historical' studies, note should be made of Professor McIntosh's belief that 'there are many excellent reasons for their prosecution', a point which he goes on to elaborate, op. cit., pp. 14–15.

19. Cf. McDavid, 'Structural Linguistics', 42, Note (2).

20. Eva Sivertsen's remarks on dialectal vacillation under the heading 'Is a Synchronic Structural Analysis Possible?' also seem to be very relevant here. See *Cockney Phonology* (Oslo, 1960), §7.14.

21. Op. cit., 46.

22. Cf. B. M. H. Strang, 'I have said that my Survey is linguistic, not dialectal, and I should not venture to call myself a dialectologist', in 'The Tyneside Linguistic Survey', *Zeitschrift für Mundartforschung*, Beihefte, Neue Folge, Heft iv (1968), 794.

23. Cf. R. I. McDavid Jr, 'Two Studies of Dialects of English', *LSE*, N.S. ii (1968), 27.

24. Orton's comments on the confusion which had overtaken the traditional phonological system of Oldham (Lancashire), as exposed by K. J. Schilling's *Grammar of the Dialect of Oldham* (Darmstadt, 1906), are very revealing in

this connexion: 'If ever a warning were needed to adopt the most cautious possible attitude in studying the dialect of a large town, we have one here in this example of a debased regional dialect. Schilling was himself aware of the adulteration of the Oldham vernacular...' See 'The Isolative Treatment... of OE *ě* Lengthened in Open Syllables in Middle English', *LSE*, vii–viii (1952), 109, Note 21.

25. See H. Orton, *Introduction* to *SED* (Leeds, 1962), p. 46.
26. W. Viereck, *Phonematische Analyse des Dialekts von Gateshead-upon-Tyne Co. Durham* (Hamburg, 1966).
27. C. L. Houck, 'Methodology of an Urban Speech Survey', *LSE*, N.S. ii (1968), 115.
28. At least one thesis has already attempted this. See J. R. Hurford, 'The Speech of one Family: A Phonetic Comparison of the Three Generations in a Family of East Londoners' (unpublished Ph.D. dissertation of the University of London, 1967).
29. But see C. Haldenby, 'Intonation in Lincolnshire Dialect' (unpublished M.A. dissertation of the University of Leeds, 1959); and F. Rohrer, *Untersuchungen zur Intonation der Dialekte von Dorset, Gloucester, Westmorland, Northumberland, Yorkshire, Lincoln und Norfolk* (dissertation for the University of Zürich, 1952).
30. W. N. Francis, J. Svartvik and G. M. Rubin, 'Computer-produced Representation of Dialectal Variation: Initial Fricatives in Southern British English', a paper read at the International Conference on Computational Linguistics in Stockholm, 1969. See also J. Svartvik, 'Computational Linguistics Comes of Age', *Times Literary Supplement*, 23 July 1970, 821–3.

Chapter 4

1. The same could be said of numerous dialect words, e.g. the names of the parts on the old wooden plough. See *SED* I.8.1–9, and K. Sandred, 'Notes on the Distribution of some Plough Terms in Modern English Dialects', *Studia Neophilologica*, xl (1968), 80–93.
2. See H. C. Wyld, *A History of Modern Colloquial English* (3rd edn., London, 1936), p. 13.
3. See J. P. Oakden and E. R. Innes, *Alliterative Poetry in Middle English: A Survey of the Traditions* (Manchester, 1935), Chap. 8.
4. Op. cit., p. 13.
5. But accepted by E. J. Dobson: see *English Pronunciation 1500–1700* (2nd edn., Oxford, 1968), ii, 592–3.
6. Some of these—found in one source only—may be errors, as, in fact, is sometimes suggested by the editors of *SED*. Such is possibly *urrins* (? 'earrings') 'earwigs', recorded at K 1 (IV.8.11), but at Co 4 *four-legged-emmet* ('newt'; IV.9.8), where *-evet* would be expected, and given the comment '? i.'s [= informant's] error for «-ɛvʌt»' by the editors, is perfectly correct, although due to confusion (see pp. 73–4, above).
7. I must thank Mr J. Koster for collecting a very large sample of these from *EDD* for me.
8. See 'The Middle English Poem on the Names of a Hare', *Proceedings of the Leeds Philosophical and Literary Society, Literary and Historical Section*, iii (1935), 347–77.
9. But *grey* was said to be 'a common term' in Devon as late as 1937, according to W. W. Gill, 'Some Devonshire Words', *Notes and Queries*, 29 May 1937, 391.

10. It is given as an Essex or Suffolk word in *The Gentleman's Magazine*, lxiii (1793), 1083.
11. For a full discussion of the distribution of this word, see M. F. Wakelin, 'Names for the Cow-house in Devon and Cornwall', *Devon and Cornwall Notes and Queries*, xxxi (1968), 52–6; reprinted in *Studia Neophilologica*, xlii (1970), 348–52.
12. I owe this example to Professor Orton.
13. See *SED*, i, VIII.5.1, and A. H. Smith, *The Place-Names of the North Riding of Yorkshire* (Cambridge, 1928), p. 68.
14. 'Some Dialect Isoglosses in England', *American Speech*, xxxiv (1959), 248–9.
15. Cf. L. R. Palmer, *An Introduction to Modern Linguistics* (London, 1936), pp. 144–5 and fig. 18, who gives a map, based on material in *EEP*, showing forms of [biðɑːt] and [biðuːt] in south Yorkshire.
16. Two similar examples are the use of *sitting-room*, which appears to mean both 'living-room' and 'sitting-room' at a number of *SED* localities (V.2.1/2; see p. 139, above), and (a phonological example) the occurrence of the same vowel in *fleas* (IV.8.4) as in *flies* (IV.8.5) over a considerable part of the north of England.
17. Cf. the ME poem on the names of the hare, mentioned in Note 8, above, in which some names, e.g. *euele-i-met* 'evil met', *make-fare* 'make flee', þe *der þat no-mon ne-dar nemnen* 'the animal that no-one dare name', may result from a similar taboo. No such names are now on record in *SED*.
18. See Nance, *Glossary*, s.v., and cf. the use of *bell-house* instead of *kirk* by Scottish fishermen.
19. The relationship between *foggy*, *ferry* and *firsy* is obscure.

Chapter 5

1. Cf. J. C. Wells, 'Local Accents in England and Wales', *Journal of Linguistics*, vi (1970), §8.1, who implies that much of the material collected by *SED* is mainly of historical (rather than contemporary) validity.
2. Cf. A. C. Gimson, *An Introduction to the Pronunciation of English* (2nd rev. edn., London, 1970), §5.36.
3. Cf. Miss Sivertsen's remarks, referred to in Chap. 3, Note 20, above.
4. Cf. R. I. McDavid Jr, 'Structural Linguistics and Linguistic Geography', *Orbis*, x (1961), 42, Note (2).
5. Cf. Gil (p. 39, above), writing in 1621, who states that *oa* (perhaps [ɔə]) is used in Lincolnshire in *toes* and *hose*. Except in south L (localities 13–15), this has now become [ʊə] or [oə], according to the *SED* transcriptions at VI.10.3 *toes*. See Dobson, *English Pronunciation*, ii, 673, Note 4.
6. But note [ʊə] in the word *foal-foot* 'colt's-foot' (II.2.7) at Cu 5, viz. [fʊəlfɒt]; and pronunciations [fiəl], [fɛəl] *foal* are noted by F. Rohrer in seven villages between Leeds and Ripon: 'The Border between the Northern and North-Midland Dialects in Yorkshire', *TYDS*, viii, Part 1 (1950), 35.
7. See A. H. Smith, *The Place-Names of the West Riding of Yorkshire* (Cambridge, 1961–3), vii, 86–7. The spread of the [ɒɪ] sound beyond the river Wharfe, traditionally its northern boundary, in place of the northern [ɔə], is attested in sporadic place-name spellings.
8. There is also, however, a south-western distribution of [ʊ] in *climb*, in So, W, Do, Co, D, west Brk and west Ha, plus one example at Sa 7, with *climmer* in So and D, and *clem* in one So locality (13).

9. ME *ę̄* < OE *ȳ* probably occurred much further afield than this, however. Cf. perhaps an [iː] type in *cows, cow* (III.1.1; ? < ME *kē* < OE *cȳ*) at Ch 4, for instance. Ellis, *EEP*, p. 825, notes [iː] in *kite* (< OE *cȳta*) from Y, and in *sky* (< ON *skȳ*) from near Bradford.
10. See *English Pronunciation*, ii, 545 ff., and especially 548.
11. An area in the west Midlands, greatly varying in extent from word to word, shows [ɒ] (= RP [a]) in other positions, however, not only before nasals. See, e.g., IV.5.3 *rat* (*rot* has a very wide distribution in the west Midlands), IV.11.8 *apples*, V.1.9 *latch* (at Mon 1 only). It should further be noted that in ME there is little correlation in regional distribution between *a/o* + single nasal (*mon*, etc.) and + nasal followed by a consonant (*honde*, etc.), *o* being common in the latter everywhere in the south.
12. It is, of course, also true that ME *ǭ* and *iu* fall together in other areas. But often they are kept apart: two good examples of *SED* localities which distinguish sharply between them are Nf 7 and Db 4.
13. I have discussed the evidence for this in my forthcoming book on dialect boundaries in Cornwall.
14. Also discussed in the book mentioned in the previous note.
15. See *SED*, iv, 15 ff., where information is cited from tape-recorded responses in this area. The field-worker usually recorded [æ̈v̈] (more rarely [œ̈v̈], in south D) for the reflexes of ME *ū* uniformly throughout Co, D and west So.
16. Cf. the remarks on *urge* 'retch', p. 73, above.
17. One very restricted local feature is the 'Bristol *l*'. This is an excrescent *l* added to final unstressed [ə], as in [aɪdɪəl] *idea*, [afɹɪkəl] *Africa*, in the same way that [ɹ] may be added to final unstressed [ə], and it occurs in Bristol and the surrounding area (cf. [dɪpθiːɹɪəl] *diphtheria* at So 2—Blagdon, eleven miles from Bristol; VI.12.4).
18. I have also heard it in east Co; cf. the pronunciations of YWR Keighley ([kiːθlɪ]; < OE *Cyhha's lēah*) and Barth ([baːθ]; < OE *beorg*).
19. 'The Phonology of the Living Dialect of Neston in Cheshire' (unpublished B.A. dissertation presented at Leeds University, 1958). See pp. 15, 127.
20. *EEP*, p. 834.
21. Cf. E. Kolb, 'Skandinavisches in den nordenglischen Dialekten', *Anglia*, lxxxiii (1965), 153: 'Die Humber-Lune-Linie ist die älteste und stärkste Sprachscheide in England'.
22. By F. Rohrer. See the article cited at Note 6, above, loc. cit.
23. Ibid.
24. G. L. Brook, 'The Future of English Dialect Studies', *LSE*, n.s. ii (1968), 15.
25. A glance at the maps for *boots* (p. 199) and *tooth* (p. 201) in E. Kolb's *Phonological Atlas* is also very illuminating in this respect. They show [uː] and [u:~ɔ] forms respectively penetrating right to the far north, replacing the traditional reflexes of ME *ǭ* in this area.
26. In 'Interrelation between Regional and Social Dialects', *Proceedings of the Ninth International Congress of Linguists*, ed. H. G. Lunt (The Hague, 1964), pp. 142–3. Professor Kurath further notes that it would be of interest to know whether other dialects reject 'foreign' phonemes and make adjustments within the native systems of sounds when concessions are being made to a socially superior dialect. He does not, however, consider the difficult origins of [œː] (my number 1), which, together with [øː], etc., also represents ME isolative *ǭ* in Nb and north Du today: see, e.g., VII.2.11 *both*, VI.14.6 *coat*, IV.10.2 *oak*.
27. *An Introduction to a Survey of Scottish Dialects* (Edinburgh, 1952), p. 14.

28. *English Pronunciation*, i, viii.
29. Op. cit., ii, 594.
30. *English Pronunciation*, ii, 685, and see especially Note 3.
31. Ibid., 662.

Chapter 6

1. At Du 3, there is semantic differentiation between *shoes* and *shoon*, the latter being used, according to the informant, for horses' shoes, and at some other localities in La and Y *shoon* were said to be 'boots' formerly (cf. VI.14.23).
2. In many of the Ch localities, however, it is difficult to differentiate the reflexes of ME *ū* from those of ME *ī*. Thus the forms at Ch 1 may not be *kyes*, *kye*, but *cows*, *cow*. The pl. and sg. [iː] type at Ch 4, mentioned above (p. 163, Note 9), presumably represent *kyes*, *kye*. Cf. *OED*, s.v. Cow, 1 δ.
3. Cf. *OED*, s.v. I, 'in the forms *ich*, *utch*, *ch-*, *che*, or *utchy*, the pronoun remained in s.w. dialects till the 18th or first half of the 19th c.'
4. *EEP*, pp. 84–5.
5. In a pilot survey in 1952, a field-worker, Peter Wright, recorded [ɪtʃ] two or three times on tape in conversation with a farmer only in his forties. This was at Merriott, just west of Montacute (So 13), in Ellis's 'Land of Utch'.
6. According to *EDG*, §404, the 2 sg. pronoun is used only for familiarity, contempt, in addressing children and in times of strong emotion—not used to a superior without impertinence (except in Gl, where it is due to Quaker influence). But according to *SED*, the use of this pronoun now implies no discrimination.
7. But *her* may simply be the unstressed reflex ([hə], [ə]) of OE *hēo* 'she' plus the *r* which is often attached to final unstressed [ə]. For a discussion of this, see the paper by P. Duncan, cited in the Select Bibliography. *He* 'she' is also found in Brk and K: see IX.7.2/3/9/10. This apparently represents a direct development from OE *hēo*, parallel to *hoo* in those areas of the country in which OE *ēo* > ME *ȏ* > NE [uː].
8. According to *EDG*, §405, *en* may be used of inanimate objects as well as of people, and in west So of feminine animals, though never of women.
9. Perhaps it derives from phrases such as [bɛın + əm] *bain't 'em* ('aren't they?') > [bɛı + nəm], with subsequent metathesis of [n] and [m] (cf. popular *anenome* for *anemone*, etc.), and then usage as an independent word meaning 'them'. But *EDD*, recording *mun* pron. from So, D and Co, suggests that the form arises from the dropping of *hy* from ME *hymen* 'them', a form derived from *hym* + the nominal inflexional suffix *-en*, added to differentiate *hym* 'them' (pl.) from *hym* 'him' (sg.), and found in south-western texts (cf. *MED* hemen).
10. *EDG*, §411, records the use of the personal pronoun, subjective or objective, *instead* of the possessive, especially in unemphatic contexts and to children, as follows: *we*—St, Nt, R, Lei, Nth, Wa, Sf, Ess; *us*—Y, La, Ch, St, Nt, L, Lei, Nth, Wa; *thee*—O, Brk, Wight, W, So; *ye*—So, D; *you*—So; *he*—So.
11. There appears to be some confusion in the use of *thick*, etc. *OED* (s.v. Thilk) states that *thick* generally means 'that', but in some places 'this', in which cases it is contrasted with *thuck*, *thock*, *thack*. One or two examples from *SED* IX.10.1/2 will show, however, that mainly different systems of contrasts operate at present:
    So 9 *thick* 'that'   *thicky* 'this'

	10	*that*	*thick*
	11	*thick*	*this one*
	12	*that*	*thick*
W	2	*thuck*	*thick*
Co	1	*that, thucker*	*thicky*
	2	*that*	*thicky*
D	1	*thicky there*	*thicky*

At So 5 *thick* appears to mean both 'that' and 'this', and the same is true of *thicky* at So 8. It is obvious from the mass of information given in *EDD* (s.v. Thic(k)) that there is great variation in systems from area to area. See further M. Harris, 'Demonstrative Adjectives and Pronouns in a Devonshire Dialect', *Trans. Phil. Soc.* (1968), 1–11.

12. The omission of the relative pronoun in Standard English has been ascribed to Scandinavian influence, but the evidence for this is doubtful: see M. S. Kirch, 'Scandinavian Influence on English Syntax', *PMLA*, lxxiv (1959), 503–10.

13. See V. Engblom, *On the Origin and Early Development of the Auxiliary Do* (Lund, 1938).

14. *A Modern English Grammar on Historical Principles*, Part iv (Heidelberg, 1931; reprinted, London, 1961), Chap. 12.

Chapter 7

1. For these, and a full discussion of *crew*, *cree* and *crow*, see my article, ' *Crew*, *Cree* and *Crow*: Celtic Words in English Dialect', *Anglia*, lxxxvii (1969), 273–81.

2. See my article, 'Welsh Influence in the West of England: Dialectal *Tallet* ', *Folk Life*, viii (1970), 72–80. Incidentally, few words of Welsh origin have been found in western ME texts. Two notable exceptions are the *Poem on the Names of a Hare* (see Chap. 4, above, Notes 8, 17), and 'Annot and Johon' (MS Harley 2253; see Carleton Brown's text and notes in *English Lyrics of the XIIIth Century*, Oxford, 1932, No. 76).

3. M. V. Barry, 'Yorkshire Sheep-scoring Numerals', *TYDS*, xii, Part lxvii (1967), 21–31; 'Traditional Enumeration in the North Country', *Folk Life*, vii (1969), 75–91.

4. Cf. A. J. Ellis, *EEP* (1889), p. 171, referring to his District 12 (west Co): 'Many words of Cornish origin remain'. H. Jenner, in 'Cornwall A Celtic Nation', *Celtic Review*, i (1905), 234–46, stated that a considerable number— perhaps a hundred or more, mostly names of things—were still in use among the Cornish working-classes (241).

5. In a most useful article on snail-charms, 'Bulorn and its Congeners', *Old Cornwall*, v. 7 (1956), 311–15, R. M. Nance lists other, comparable nicknames for the snail both from Co and outside—from Co *malorn*, *jinjorn*, *bull-jig* (cf. *bull-gog* from L), *snarleyorn* from west So, *snail-horn* from other counties.

6. On this phenomenon, see L. Bloomfield, *Language* (New York, 1933), pp. 468–9. Out of some 612 'provable' and 'probable' ON loans in English dialect, Thorsen (see Select Bibliography), p. 7, makes the following analysis: 56 denote natural features; 57 implements and tools; 42 animals and parts of animals; 36 persons and parts of the body; 31 woods, trees, plants; 21 natural phenomena (fire, weather, etc.); 18 agricultural items; 17 houses and

building material, furniture; 17 abstractions; 11 social obligations, taxes, etc.

7. The question of the extent of Scandinavian influence in southern English speech is raised by the word *kettle* (< ON *ketill*). The OE form *cietel* would regularly have given modern English **chettle* if it had survived (the last *OED* occurrence is 1463), but the date at which it finally disappeared in local speech is unknown. It survives in place-names, e.g. Chattlehope (Nb), Cheddleton (St), Chittlehampton (D), Chettle (Do); cf. Kettlewell (YWR).

8. But cf. MLG *vlike*.

9. The other northern words for 'stream' are also of interest: *burn* occupies the whole of Nb, occurs in two localities in Cu, and is well-attested in Du, while *brook* (< OE *brōc*) occupies south La and occurs in YWR. Beside *stream*, recorded sporadically are *sike* (< OE *sīc*, ON *sík*), *gil* (Y 5; < ON *gil*), *gote* (Y 23; < OE **gota* 'water-channel'), *stel* (Du 5; perhaps < OE *stell* 'a leap', cf. *stellan* 'to leap') and *dike* (YWR; < OE *dīc*, ON *dík*).

10. A. Mawer, *The Place-Names of Northumberland and Durham* (Cambridge, 1920), p. xix.

11. According to Wright, 1154 dialect words were collected beginning with [sk], and assumed by him to be of Scandinavian origin. Few such words have been recorded from the northern counties by *SED*.

12. 'Skandinavisches in den nordenglischen Dialekten', *Anglia*, lxxxiii (1965), 127-53.

13. I have tried to suggest some answers to the problem of *kirk*'s recession in my essay, 'Dialect and Place-Names: The Distributions of *Kirk*' in *Patterns in the Folk Speech of the British Isles*, ed. M. F. Wakelin (London, 1972).

14. Op. cit., p. xviii.

15. Cf. A. K. Hamilton Jenkin, *The Story of Cornwall* (London, 1934; reprinted, Truro, 1962), pp. 93-4: 'Life in such cottages was, of course, very primitive. Few of them had any upstairs rooms. Where the family was a large one, a stage of boards, called a 'talfat', was generally constructed beneath the rafters of the roof. This extended over half the living-room, and was reached by a ladder. Here the children would sleep, lying close together to keep themselves warm on the bare, draughty floor.' It should, however, be noted that *EDD* records *planching* 'planking, boarded floor', etc. (but not necessarily referring to an upstairs floor), not only from Co, but also from So, D and East Anglia (cf. also Planch, Plancher).

16. So far as is known to me. There may be others as yet unclassified. Two words perhaps directly from Italian are *parapet* (< It. *parapetto*), which used to mean 'pavement' in Ch and La (cf. *OED*—'The ordinary name [for a pavement] in Chester, Liverpool, and the district from Crewe to Lancaster, but disappearing eastward'), and *cupola* (< It. *cupola*), which is used as a Sheffield steel term meaning 'casting furnace', and is listed by *EDD* also from Nb, Y, St, Db and Sa. See also under Fishing Vocabulary in Chapter 8.

Chapter 8

1. Cf. Specialized Vocabularies in Chapter 3, above.

2. See P. Wright, 'Yorkshire Steel Terms To-day', *TYDS*, xii, Part lxvi (1966), 41-7.

3. *Grove* is found in Db place-names meaning 'mine-shaft, -workings', etc., in 1562, 1658 and 1671, with two possible earlier examples *c.* 1250 and 1374.

See K. Cameron, *The Place-Names of Derbyshire* (Cambridge, 1959), p. 731. This semantic development is not, however, peculiar to Db alone, being exemplified by *EDD* (s.v. Groove) also from Nb, Du, Cu, We, Y, St, L and So. It is not clear, however, whether the word is, in fact, < OE *grāf* 'grove, copse', or early modern Du *groeve* 'ditch'. Cf. *OED*, s.v. Groove.

4. See A. H. Stokes, *Lead and Lead Mining in Derbyshire* (Peak District Mines Historical Society Special Publications No. 2, 1964), p. 78; and C. T. Carr, *The German Influence on the English Vocabulary* (SPE Tract 42, 1934), pp. 44–6.

5. Ed. P. A. S. Pool (Marazion, 1963). This work was apparently almost complete in manuscript *c*. 1920, but the author continued to add notes to it until shortly before his death in 1959. Some of the material was collected direct from fishermen, but Nance also states (p. 24) that he added much from printed and other sources. Its heterogeneous nature thus puts it in the same class as *EDD*, in so far as it is not a record of material collected by a uniform method at any one time.

Chapter 9

1. 'Linguistic Class-Indicators in Present-day English', *Neuphilologische Mitteilungen*, lv (1954), 20–56, reprinted in a condensed and simplified version as 'U and Non-U: An Essay in Sociological Linguistics', in *Noblesse Oblige* by A. S. C. Ross, Nancy Mitford *et al.* (London, 1956).

2. See, e.g., D. Lawton, *Social Class, Language and Education* (London, 1968), Chap. 6. Basil Bernstein's work is some of the earliest and best-known in the field of linguistic analysis in relation to social class.

3. In a paper read in April, 1970, by Mr Howard Giles of Bristol University, it was reported that 177 pupils in comprehensive schools in Wales and Somerset, aged 12–17, and balanced in terms of sex and social class, were asked to assess tape-recorded local accents in terms of pleasantness of sound, status and the degree of comfort felt in the presence of each speaker. Out of the thirteen different types, 'BBC English' was placed top on all three counts, while a Birmingham accent was given the lowest rating for status. See *The Times*, 14 April 1970.

4. If we are to believe Professor Dobson (as I think we must), a similar situation has prevailed for some time. Commenting on Puttenham's well-known dictum (see p. 37, above), he remarks: 'What I take Puttenham to mean...is that the common people everywhere spoke dialect and the standard language was the possession only of the well-born and the well-educated; that in the Court and the Home Counties one might expect all well-born and well-educated people to use this standard language, but beyond those limits, though one might still find men who spoke pure standard English, the greater part of the gentry and scholars were influenced by the speech of the common people (i.e. they spoke 'modified Standard'), and finally that in the far West and the North the standard did not apply at all'. And as Dobson further points out, had it been normal for a man of Sir Walter Raleigh's position to use his native dialect, his well-known use of Devonshire dialect would have passed unnoticed. See 'Early Modern Standard English', *Trans. Phil. Soc.* (1955), 32–3.

5. 'The Tyneside Linguistic Survey', *Zeitschrift für Mundartforschung*, Beihefte, Neue Folge, Heft iv (1968), 791.

6. *Introduction* to *SED* (Leeds, 1962), p. 15. This fact was also noted by the earlier dialectologists. Cf. *EEP*, p. 3 (bottom), *EDG*, p. iv (4th para.).
7. 'Interrelation between Regional and Social Dialects', in *Proceedings of the Ninth International Congress of Linguists*, ed. H. G. Lunt (The Hague, 1964), p. 136.
8. Cf. G. L. Brook, 'The Future of English Dialect Studies', *LSE*, N.S. ii (1968), 17: 'Linguistic variations in towns depend on occupation or social class rather than on place of birth, and the study of town dialects is likely to develop side by side with the study of class dialect.' See also J. T. Wright, 'Urban Dialects: A Consideration of Method', *Zeitschrift für Mundartforschung*, xxxiii (1966), 235: 'The dialectologist's task in relation to towns is to show, how social complexities are reflected in the linguistic behaviour of their inhabitants'.
9. C. D. Heath, 'A Study of Speech Patterns in the Urban District of Cannock, Staffordshire' (unpublished Ph.D. dissertation of the University of Leeds, 1971).
10. 'The Social Differentiation of English in Norwich' (unpublished Ph.D. dissertation of the University of Edinburgh, 1971).

Select Bibliography

The bibliography is intended as a supplement to fill the inevitable gaps in the treatment of topics in this book. It is, in other words, a guide to 'further reading'.

1 Introduction to Dialectology

On different types of English (including Standard English and RP) and on accent, see P. Strevens, 'Varieties of English', *English Studies*, xlv (1964), 20–30; and A. C. Gimson, *An Introduction to the Pronunciation of English*, 2nd rev. edn., London, 1970.

For the study of dialect and linguistic geography in general, see: L. Bloomfield, *Language*, New York, 1933 (Chap. 19); G. Bottiglioni, 'Linguistic Geography: Achievements, Methods and Orientations', *Word*, x (1954), 375–87; A. Dauzat, *La Géographie Linguistique*, Paris, 1944; W. P. Lehmann, *Historical Linguistics: An Introduction*, New York, 1962 (Chap. 8); A. McIntosh, *An Introduction to a Survey of Scottish Dialects*, Edinburgh, 1952; B. Malmberg, *New Trends in Linguistics*, trans. E. Carney, Stockholm and Lund, 1964 (pp. 54–68); L. R. Palmer, *An Introduction to Modern Linguistics*, London, 1936 (Chap. 7); S. Pop, *La Dialectologie*, 2 vols., Louvain, 1950; S. Potter, *Our Language*, Penguin Books, London, 1950 (Chap. 11); S. Potter, *Modern Linguistics*, Penguin Books, London, 1957 (Chap. 6).

The only two general treatments of English dialects are: W. W. Skeat, *English Dialects from the Eighth Century to the Present Day*, Cambridge, 1911, and G. L. Brook, *English Dialects*, London, 1963; but the reader should certainly also see A. H. Smith, 'English Dialects', *Trans. Phil. Soc.* (1936), 76–84.

Journals dealing with English dialectal subjects are, among others: *Journal of the Lakeland Dialect Society*; *Journal of the Lancashire Dialect Society*; *Orbis: Bulletin International de Documentation Linguistique* (Louvain); *Transactions of the Yorkshire Dialect Society*.

Dictionary: J. Wright, *The English Dialect Dictionary*, 6 vols., Oxford, 1898–1905 (Vol. vi includes Wright's *English Dialect Grammar*, also published separately).

On 'Dialect study in its wider setting', see Chap. 2 of A. McIntosh, *Introduction to a Survey of Scottish Dialects*, Edinburgh, 1952. A Word and Object atlas for the British Isles was enthusiastically advocated by J. Orr, 'Linguistic Geography', *Times Literary Supplement*, 21 March 1929, 232.

2 Historical Background

For bibliography, see W. Bonser, *An Anglo-Saxon and Celtic Bibliography 450–1087*, 2 vols., Oxford, 1957.

On the Anglo-Saxon invasion and settlement, see: P. H. Blair, *An Introduction to Anglo-Saxon England*, Cambridge, 1956; R. G. Collingwood and J. N. L. Myres, *Roman Britain and the English Settlements*, 2nd edn., Oxford, 1937; R. H. Hodgkin, *A History of the Anglo-Saxons*, 2 vols., 3rd edn., Oxford, 1952; K. H. Jackson, *Language and History in Early Britain*, Edinburgh, 1953 (Chap. 6); F. M. Stenton, *Anglo-Saxon England*, 3rd rev. edn., Oxford, 1971.

The *Anglo-Saxon Chronicle* is available in numerous editions and translations (e.g. in Everyman's Library, 1953), the standard edn. being C. Plummer and J. Earle, *Two of the Saxon Chronicles Parallel*, 2 vols., Oxford, 1892–9. The standard edn. of Bede is that of C. Plummer, *Venerabilis Baedae Opera Historica*, 2 vols., Oxford, 1896; it is conveniently translated in Everyman's Library, 1954, and Penguin Classics, 1955, and there is a new, definitive edn. (with translation) by B. Colgrave and R. A. B. Mynors, Oxford, 1969. For other primary sources, see the bibliographies in the books listed above, and also D. Whitelock, *English Historical Documents*, Vol. i: *c. 500–1042*, London, 1955.

OE and its ancestry are discussed in most books on the history of the English language, and there are innumerable OE grammars. Standard reference works are: K. Brunner, *Altenglische Grammatik*, 3rd rev. edn., Tübingen, 1951; A. Campbell, *Old English Grammar*, Oxford, 1959; J. and E. M. Wright, *Old English Grammar*, 3rd rev. edn., Oxford, 1925.

On the OE dialects, see: A. Campbell (above), including the Select Bibliography, pp. 360–7; D. De Camp, 'The Genesis of the Old English Dialects', *Language*, xxxiv (1958), 232–44; H. C. Wyld, *A Short History of English*, 3rd rev. edn., London, 1927 (Chap. 4). The chief OE dialectal texts are ed. H. Sweet, *The Oldest English Texts*, EETS 83, 1885.

Celtic survival is discussed by: M. V. Barry, 'Traditional Enumeration in the North Country', *Folk Life*, vii (1969), 75–91 (gives various references); Collingwood and Myres (above, pp. 444 ff.); Jackson (above; Chap. 6, and especially pp. 234 ff.); P. H. Reaney, *The Origin of English Place-Names*, London, 1960 (pp. 83 ff.).

On the Scandinavian invasions and settlements, see: E. Björkman, *Scandinavian Loan-Words in Middle English*, Halle, 1900–2 (useful summary in Chap. 3); Blair (above; Chap. 2); E. Ekwall, 'The Scandinavian Settlement', Chap. 4 in *An Historical Geography of England before A.D. 1800*, ed. H. C. Darby, Cambridge, 1948.

On the Scandinavian languages in England, see: E. Ekwell (below), and also 'How long did the Scandinavian Languages survive in England?' in *A Grammatical Miscellany offered to Otto Jespersen on his Seventieth Birthday*, Copenhagen, 1930—reprinted in *Selected Papers*, Lund, 1963; E. V. Gordon, *An Introduction to Old Norse*, 2nd edn., rev. A. R. Taylor, Oxford, 1957 (Appendix, 'The Old Norse Tongue in England', pp. 326–9).

For place-name evidence, see: K. Cameron, *English Place-Names*, London, 1961 (Chap. 6); E. Ekwall, 'The Scandinavian Element', Chap. 4 of the *Introduction to the Survey of English Place-Names*, ed. A. Mawer and F. M. Stenton, Cambridge, 1924; Reaney (above; Chap. 7); the northern volumes of the publications of the English Place-Name Society.

Most books on the history of the English language discuss the relative positions of French and English. See also: P. V. D. Shelly, *English and French in England 1066–1100*, Philadelphia, 1921; and R. M. Wilson, 'English and French in England 1100–1300', *History*, N.S. xxviii (1943), 37–60.

On contacts with the Low Countries, see: J. F. Bense, *Anglo-Dutch Relations from the earliest Times to the Death of William the Third*, The Hague, 1925; G. N. Clark, *The Dutch Influence on the English Vocabulary*, SPE Tract xliv, 1935; E. C. Llewellyn, *The Influence of Low Dutch on the English Vocabulary*, Oxford, 1936. On German contacts, see C. T. Carr, *The German Influence on the English Vocabulary*, SPE Tract xlii, 1934.

For works on various ME dialects, see further p. 172, below. Bibliographies listing editions of ME texts are: M. S. Ogden, C. E. Palmer and R. L. McKelvey, *Bibliography of Middle English Texts*, Ann Arbor, Mich., 1954—also printed (pp. 17–105) in the *Plan and Bibliography* of *MED*; W. L. Renwick and H. Orton, *The Beginnings of English Literature*, 3rd edn., rev. M. F. Wakelin, London, 1966; J. E. Wells, *A Manual of the Writings in Middle English 1050–1400*, with nine supplements, New Haven, 1916–51—this is now being gradually rewritten and expanded in separate fascicles, under the general editorship of J. Burke Severs, as *A Manual... 1050–1500*, New Haven, 1967–.

The rise of Standard English is discussed by most books on the history of the English language. See also: E. J. Dobson, 'Early Modern Standard English', *Trans. Phil. Soc.* (1955), 25–54 (cites statements of early writers); M. L. Samuels (below). On the adoption of vulgar and regional forms in early Standard English, see Dobson, 'Early Modern Standard English', and also *English Pronunciation 1500–1700*, 2 vols., 2nd edn., Oxford, 1968; U. Jacobsson, *Phonological Dialect Constituents in the Vocabulary of Standard English*, Lund, 1962.

On the statements of writers, see under 3, below, and on the literary use of dialect, G. L. Brook, *English Dialects*, London, 1963 (Chap. 8); W. Craigie, 'Dialect in Literature', *Essays by Divers Hands*, xvii (1938), 69–91. Spellings have been frequently used by dialectologists to illustrate the development of dialectal forms, e.g. by Orton and Hedevind (p. 176, below).

On ME dialectology, see H. C. Wyld, *A History of Modern Colloquial English*, 2nd edn., London, 1921, and *A Short History of English*, 3rd rev. edn., London, 1927. The work of S. Moore, S. B. Meech and H. Whitehall is described in *Middle English Dialect Characteristics and Dialect Boundaries*, Ann Arbor, Mich., 1935; and that of McIntosh and Samuels in A. McIntosh, 'A New Approach to Middle English Dialectology', *English Studies*, xliv (1963), 1–11, M. L. Samuels, 'Some Applications of Middle English Dialectology', ibid., 81–94.

Studies of individual ME dialects: H. Bohman, *Studies in the ME Dialects of Devon and London*, Göteborg, 1944; G. Kristensson, *A Survey of Middle English Dialects 1290–1350: The Six Northern Counties and Lincolnshire*, Lund, 1967; S. Rubin, *The Phonology of the Middle English Dialect of Sussex*, Lund, 1951; B. Sundby, *Studies in the Middle English Dialect Material of Worcestershire Records*, Bergen-Oslo and New York, 1963; J. K. Wallenberg, *The Vocabulary of Dan Michel's Ayenbite of Inwyt*, Uppsala, 1923.

3 Dialect Study in England

The abbreviation 'S.P.', below, refers to a facsimile reproduction in the Scolar Press series *English Linguistics 1500–1800*.

Higden-Trevisa: *Polychronicon Ranulphi Higden Monachi Cestrensis*, ed. C. Babington and J. R. Lumby, Rolls Series, 9 vols., 1865–86 (ii, 162–3).

Caxton: *Caxton's Eneydos 1490*, ed. W. T. Culley and F. J. Furnivall, EETS, E.S. 57, 1890 (pp. 2–3 of the Prologue).

Smith: See E. J. Dobson, *English Pronunciation 1500–1700*, 2nd edn., Oxford, 1968 (i, 46 ff.).

Puttenham: G. G. Smith (ed.), *Elizabethan Critical Essays*, 2 vols., Oxford, 1904 (ii, 1–193); G. D. Willcock and A. Walker (edd.), *The Arte of English Poesie*, Cambridge, 1936, reprinted 1970; S.P., 1968.

Coote: Dobson (above; i, 33–7); for a study of the features enumerated by Coote, see W. Horn, 'Zur englischen Grammatik, II: E. Coote's Bemerkungen über englische Aussprache (1596)', *Anglia*, xxviii (1905), 479–87; S.P., 1968.

Carew: Smith (ed., above; ii, 285–94); F. E. Halliday (ed.), *Richard Carew of Antony: The Survey of Cornwall*, London, 1953.

Gil: Dobson (above; i, 142–3); O. L. Jiriczek (ed.), *Alexander Gill's Logonomia Anglica*, Strassburg, 1903 (Chap. 6); H. Kökeritz, 'Alexander Gil (1621) on the Dialects of South and East England', *Studia Neophilologica*, xi (1938–9), 277–88; S.P. (1621 edn.), 1968.

Daines: Dobson (above; i, 327–36); M. Rösler and R. Brotanek (edd.), *Simon Daines' Orthoepia Anglicana (1640)*, Halle, 1908; S.P., 1967.

Wallis: Dobson (above; i, 218–46, especially 244); S.P., 1969.

Browne: Tract VIII is usefully printed by W. F. Bolton, *The English Language: Essays by English and American Men of Letters 1490–1839*, Cambridge, 1966 (pp. 70–82).

Cooper: J. D. Jones (ed.), *Coopers Grammatica Linguae Anglicanae (1685)*, Halle, 1911; B. Sundby (ed.), *Christopher Cooper's English Teacher (1687)*, Lund, 1953; S.P. (1685 edn.), 1968, (1687 edn.), 1969.

Sheridan: S.P., 1968.

The dialect glossaries compiled up to the beginning of the twentieth century are listed under their counties in the bibliography to *EDD* (Vol. vi). For some of those published since, see *The Cambridge Bibliography of English Literature, I (600–1660)*, ed. F. W. Bateson, Cambridge, 1940

(p. 45), and the *Supplement*, ed. G. Watson, 1957 (pp. 30–2). Series of reprints of the earlier glossaries are currently being undertaken by S.R. Publishers Ltd, Wakefield, and by other publishers.

Coles's *English Dictionary* is S.P., 1971, and Kersey's *Dictionarium* S.P., 1969. Bailey's *Dictionary* has been reprinted as No. 52 in the series *Anglistica and Americana*, Hildesheim and New York, 1969. The dialect element is usefully abstracted by W. E. A. Axon, *English Dialect Words of the Eighteenth Century*, EDS, 41, 1883.

Nowell's *Vocabularium* is edited, with Introduction, by A. H. Marckwardt, *Laurence Nowell's Vocabularium Saxonicum*, Ann Arbor, Mich., 1952.

John Ray's *Collection of Words not Generally Used* was printed as EDS, Series B, No. 6, together with the letter from Thoresby. S.P., 1969.

Francis Grose is discussed by R. M. Dorson, *The British Folklorists, a History*, London, 1968 (pp. 25–8). The *Provincial Glossary* is S.P., 1968.

For the history and progress of continental dialectology, and also for a list and description of the various atlases, see S. Pop, *La Dialectologie*, 2 vols., Louvain, 1950. A useful outline is given in B. Malmberg, *New Trends in Linguistics*, trans. E. Carney, Stockholm and Lund, 1964 (pp. 54–68). For reports of the latest plans of linguistic atlases, see the periodical *Orbis*.

For biography of Joseph Wright, and history of *EDD*, see E. M. Wright, *The Life of Joseph Wright*, 2 vols., London, 1932; and on 'The English Dialect Society and its Dictionary', W. Viereck in *TYDS*, xii, Part lxx (1970), 28–33. Wright's *Grammar of the Dialect of Windhill* was published as EDS, 67, 1892. For *EDD*, *EDG*, see under 1, above.

Monographs written in the school of Wright include: A. Hargreaves, *A Grammar of the Dialect of Adlington* (*Lancashire*), Heidelberg, 1904; E. Kruisinga, *A Grammar of the Dialect of West Somerset*, Bonn, 1905; J. Kjederqvist, *The Dialect of Pewsey* (*Wiltshire*), London, 1906 (*Trans. Phil. Soc.*, 1903–6); T. O. Hirst, *A Grammar of the Dialect of Kendal* (*Westmorland*), Heidelberg, 1906; K. G. Schilling, *A Grammar of the Dialect of Oldham* (*Lancashire*), Darmstadt, 1906; B. Brilioth, *A Grammar of the Dialect of Lorton* (*Cumberland*), Oxford, 1913; W. Klein, *Der Dialekt von Stokesley in Yorkshire, North-Riding*, Berlin, 1914; G. H. Cowling, *The Dialect of Hackness* (*North East Yorkshire*), Cambridge, 1915; P. H. Reaney, *A Grammar of the Dialect of Penrith* (*Cumberland*), Manchester, 1927; H. Kökeritz, *The Phonology of the Suffolk Dialect*, Uppsala, 1932; H. Orton, *The Phonology of a South Durham Dialect*, London, 1933; J. E. Oxley, *The Lindsey Dialect*, Leeds, 1940.

More recent treatments are: B. Widén, *Studies on the Dorset Dialect*, Lund, 1949; B. Hedevind, *The Dialect of Dentdale in the West Riding of Yorkshire*, Uppsala, 1967.

The monographs of the school of Brandl are listed in E. Dieth's article mentioned in Note 8, p. 159, above.

Ellis's *On Early English Pronunciation, Part V: The Existing Phonology of English Dialects* was published by EETS, E.S. 53, 1889.

The Dieth-Orton *Questionnaire for a Linguistic Atlas of England* was published by the Leeds Philosophical and Literary Society, 1952, and reprinted, with alterations and additions, in Orton's *Introduction* to the *Survey of English Dialects*, Leeds, 1962. The *SED* Basic Material is published in four vols., ed. H. Orton *et al.*, Leeds, 1962–71.

For organization, history and description of *SED*, see: Orton, *Introduction* (above); 'An English Dialect Survey: Linguistic Atlas of England', *Orbis*, ix (1960), 331–48; 'Remarks upon Field Work for an English Linguistic Atlas of England', *English Studies*, xxxiv (1953), 274–8; H. Orton and E. Dieth, 'The New Survey of Dialectal English', in *English Studies Today*, ed. C. L. Wrenn and G. Bullough, Oxford, 1951 (pp. 63–73); S. Ellis, 'Fieldwork for a Dialect Atlas of England', *TYDS*, ix, Part liii (1953), 9–21; and 'Dialectal English and the Scholar', *TYDS*, xi, Part lxii (1962), 28–41; W. Viereck, 'Der English Dialect Survey und der Linguistic Survey of Scotland', *Zeitschrift für Mundartforschung*, xxxi (1964), 333–55.

Detailed plans for the forthcoming *LEA* were outlined by Orton in a presidential address delivered on 7 September 1970 at the Durham meeting of the British Association, and published as 'A Linguistic Atlas of England', *The Advancement of Science*, xxvii (1970), 80–96.

The classic paper on structural dialectology is U. Weinreich, 'Is a Structural Dialectology Possible?' *Word*, x (1954), 388–400, which has stimulated further discussion, especially in the journals *Word* and *Language*.

The Linguistic Survey of Scotland is treated by A. McIntosh, *An Introduction to a Survey of Scottish Dialects*, Edinburgh, 1952, and by J. C. Catford, 'The Linguistic Survey of Scotland', *Orbis*, vi (1957), 105–21. See also J. C. Catford, 'Vowel-Systems of Scots Dialects', *Trans. Phil. Soc.* (1957), 107–17.

For a useful general summing-up, see R. I. McDavid Jr, 'Structural Linguistics and Linguistic Geography', *Orbis*, x (1961), 35–46.

Urban dialect research is discussed by J. T. Wright, 'Urban Dialects: A Consideration of Method', *Zeitschrift für Mundartforschung*, xxxiii (1966), 232–46.

The Tyneside Linguistic Survey is described by B. Strang, 'The Tyneside Linguistic Survey', *Zeitschrift für Mundartforschung*, Beihefte, Neue Folge, Heft iv (1968), 788–94. In addition to the published works by Sivertsen, Viereck and Houck, mentioned on pp. 160 and 161 (Notes 20, 26, 27) above, the following short monographs on urban dialects have appeared in *Le Maître Phonétique:* J. D. O'Connor, 'The Phonetic System of a Dialect of Newcastle-upon-Tyne', lxxxvii (1947), 6–8; E. M. Higginbottom, 'A Specimen of East Lancashire Speech Modified towards RP', cxviii (1962), 24–7; C. Painter, 'Black Country Speech', cxx (1963), 30–3; K. R. Lodge, 'The Stockport Dialect', cxxvi (1966), 26–30; J. Kelly, 'On the Phonology of an English Urban Accent', cxxvii (1967), 2–5 (south-east La).

On 'The Future of English Dialect Studies', see G. L. Brook in *LSE*, N.S. ii (1968), 15–22.

174

4   English Word Geography

The indispensable adjunct to any study of English dialectal vocabulary is (with reservations) *EDD*. The lexical collections of the EDS were used in this work, but may be consulted in the separate vols. published by the Society. Other dialect glossaries have been compiled since *EDD*, for which see under 3, above. The vols. of the various linguistic journals (e.g. *Anglia, Orbis, Studia Neophilologica, Notes and Queries*) contain articles on dialect words.

On bird names, see C. Swainson, *Provincial Names and Folk Lore of British Birds*, EDS, 47, 1885. Maycock's 'Survey of Bird-Names in the Yorkshire Dialects' is described in *TYDS*, ix, Part liii (1953), 29–32, ix, Part liv (1955), 47–8, and x, Part lvi (1956), 28–38.

On plant names, see J. Britten and R. Holland, *A Dictionary of English Plant-Names*, EDS, 22, 26, 45, 1878–86; and H. Friend, *A Glossary of Devonshire Plant Names*, EDS, 38, 1882.

On local taboo words, see R. M. Nance, *A Glossary of Cornish Sea-Words*, ed. P. A. S. Pool, Marazion, 1963 (see s.v. the words cited above); also A. Macdermott, 'Some Old Beliefs and Superstitions of Seamen', *Mariners Mirror*, xlii (1956), 254–5; W. A. King-Webster, ibid., xliii (1957), 60; H. Henningsen, 'Taboo-Words among Seamen and Fishermen', ibid., 336–7.

On children's words, in addition to I. and P. Opie, *The Lore and Language of Schoolchildren*, Oxford, 1959, see S. Ellis, 'Yorkshire Expressions for "To Play Truant"', *TYDS*, x, Part lvii (1957), 48–9.

5   Local Accents

Historical phonology is dealt with in books on the history of the English language, but for present purposes, see especially K. Luick, *Historische Grammatik der englischen Sprache*, 2 vols., Leipzig, 1914–40, and E. J. Dobson, *English Pronunciation 1500–1700*, 2 vols., 2nd edn., Oxford, 1968; also J. and E. M. Wright, *An Elementary Middle English Grammar*, 2nd edn., Oxford, 1928. Early spellings for (and discussion of the development of) many of the features discussed are to be found under the appropriate headings in Dobson, ii, and in U. Jacobsson, *Phonological Dialect Constituents in the Vocabulary of Standard English*, Lund, 1962.

EEP (abridged as *English Dialects, their Sounds and Homes*, EETS, 1890) surveys the phonology of the English dialects at the end of the last century, and was used in the compilation of *EDG* (1905). The most recent overall survey is *SED*, the northern vol. of which provided the material for E. Kolb's *Phonological Atlas of the Northern Region*, Berne, 1966.

A general survey of some local features, mainly urban, is J. C. Wells's 'Local Accents in England and Wales', *Journal of Linguistics*, vi (1970), 231–52. A. C. Gimson, *An Introduction to the Pronunciation of English*, 2nd rev. edn., London, 1970, mentions dialectal variants as appropriate.

For the phonology of the various individual dialects, see the list of monographs under 3, above. For (the history of) northern dialectal developments in particular, see: H. Orton, *The Phonology of a South Durham Dialect*, London, 1933; A. H. Smith, *The Place-Names of the West Riding of Yorkshire*, 8 vols., Cambridge, 1961–3 (vii, 77–94); C. Dean, *The Dialect of George Meriton's 'A Yorkshire Dialogue' (1683): Studies in the Stressed Vowels*, YDS Reprint III, Kendal, 1962; B. Hedevind, *The Dialect of Dentdale*, Uppsala, 1967; W. Viereck, 'A Diachronic-Structural Analysis of a Northern English Urban Dialect', *LSE*, N.S. ii (1968), 65–79 (on Gateshead, Co. Durham).

On the northern/north-Midland dialect boundary, see: Smith (above) and Hedevind (above); F. Rohrer, 'The Border between the Northern and North-Midland Dialects in Yorkshire, *TYDS*, viii, Part 1 (1950), 29–37; G. Kristensson, *A Survey of Middle English Dialects 1290–1350*, Lund, 1967 (pp. 241–6).

Other individual matters:

H. Orton, 'The Isolative Treatment in Living North-Midland Dialects of OE *ĕ* Lengthened...', *LSE*, vii–viii (1952), 97–128.

M. F. Wakelin and M. V. Barry, 'The Voicing of Initial Fricative Consonants in Present-Day Dialectal English', *LSE*, N.S. ii (1968), 47–64 (see the references in this article to works on the same subject).

H. Kökeritz, *The Phonology of the Suffolk Dialect*, Uppsala, 1932 (§§188, 223, 353, 370 on the substitution of [w] for [v]).

W. Matthews, *Cockney Past and Present*, London, 1938 (pp. 180–81 on [v ~ w] interchange).

On Northumbrian [ʁ], see H. Orton, 'The Dialect of Northumberland', *TYDS*, v, Part xxxi (1930), 14–25; and references (Note 15) in Viereck (above).

RP influence on northern dialect is discussed by E. Kolb, 'Die Infiltration der Hochsprache in die nordenglischen Dialekte', *Anglia*, lxxxvi (1968), 1–13.

6 Grammatical Variation

The last general survey of regional grammatical features before *SED* was *EDG*. For grammars of various individual dialects, see the list of monographs under 3, above.

On the origin of *she*, see: A. H. Smith, 'Some Place-Names and the Etymology of "she"', *Review of English Studies*, i (1925), 437–40; E. Dieth, '*Hips:* A Geographical Contribution to the "she" Puzzle', *English Studies*, xxxvi (1955), 209–17; R. D. Stevick, 'The Morphemic Evolution of Middle English *She*', *English Studies*, xlv (1964), 381–8. On the forms of the feminine personal pronoun, see P. Duncan, 'Forms of the Feminine Pronoun in Modern English Dialects', in *Patterns in the Folk Speech of the British Isles*, ed. M. F. Wakelin, London, 1972.

On *its*, see *OED*, s.v.; and J. and E. M. Wright, *An Elementary Historical New English Grammar*, Oxford, 1924, §326.

On the regional distribution of the forms of the definite article, see: W. E. Jones, 'The Definite Article in Living Yorkshire Dialect', *LSE*, vii–viii (1952), 81–91; M. V. Barry, 'The Morphemic Distribution of the Definite Article in Contemporary Regional English', in *Patterns in the Folk Speech of the British Isles* (above).

7 The Foreign Element in English Dialect

Although the foreign element in Standard English has been frequently treated, this is not the case with the dialects, which urgently demand attention from this point of view. Studies of individual words are occasionally to be found in the periodical literature, but the whole subject awaits a book to itself.

I have discussed the Cornish loan-words (including their phonology) in my forthcoming book on the dialect of Cornwall. See also R. M. Nance, *A Glossary of Cornish Sea-Words*, ed. P. A. S. Pool, Marazion, 1963. The vols. of *Old Cornwall*, *The Journal of the Royal Institution of Cornwall*, *Devon and Cornwall Notes and Queries*, and other local journals should also be consulted.

The only full-scale English works on the Scandinavian element in English dialect appear to be: A. Wall, 'A Contribution towards the Study of the Scandinavian Element in the English Dialects', *Anglia*, xx (1898), 45–135; P. Thorson, *Anglo-Norse Studies: An Inquiry into the Scandinavian Elements in the Modern English Dialects*, Amsterdam, 1936. Neither of these works deals fully with the regional distribution of the words examined, however. E. Kolb, 'Skandinavisches in den nordenglischen Dialekten', *Anglia*, lxxxiii (1965), 127–53, deals with the distributions and implications of a number of Scandinavian words, and is illustrated with fifteen excellent maps.

For ME, E. Björkman, *Scandinavian Loan-Words in Middle English*, Halle, 1900–2, is standard, and for place-names, H. Lindkvist, *Middle English Place-Names of Scandinavian Origin*, Uppsala, 1912 (see also the works mentioned under 2, above).

8 Occupational Dialects

On mining dialect, see P. Wright, 'Coal-Mining Language: A Recent Investigation', in *Patterns in the Folk Speech of the British Isles*, ed. M. F. Wakelin, London, 1972; E. C. Llewellyn, *The Influence of Low Dutch on the English Vocabulary*, Oxford, 1936 (Chap. 11). Manlove's poem is reprinted in Stokes (see Ch. 8, Note 4, p. 167 above), pp. 61–8, and also in EDS Series B, No. 5 (1899), together with two other short glossaries of Derbyshire mining terms (1681, 1802).

On fishing dialect, see Nance's *Glossary* (under 7, above); P. Wright, 'Proposal for a Short Questionnaire for Use in Fishing Communities', *TYDS*, xi, Part lxiv (1964), 27–32; P. Wright and G. B. Smith, 'A Lancashire Fishing Survey', *Journal of the Lancashire Dialect Society*, xvi (1967),

177

2–8; P. Wright, 'Parasitic Syllabic Nasals at Marshside, Lancashire', *LSE*, vii–viii (1952), 92–6; M. S. Tindall, 'Crab and Lobster Fishing at Staithes in the North Riding', *TYDS*, viii, Part 1 (1950), 44–50; A. L. Binns, 'Humber Words', *TYDS*, x, Part lvii (1957), 10–25.

Other industries: B. R. Dyson, 'The Sheffield Cutler and his Dialect', *TYDS*, v, Part xxxiii (1932), 9–36; F. W. Moody, 'Some Textile Terms from Addingham in the West Riding', *TYDS*, viii, Part 1 (1950), 37–43; and 'The Nail and Clog-Iron Industries of Silsden in the West Riding', *TYDS*, ix, Part li (1951), 39–48; P. J. Ambler, 'The Terminology of the Beer Barrel at Queensbury in the West Riding', *TYDS*, ix, Part liv (1954), 21–6; D. R. Sykes, 'Dialect in the Quarries at Crosland Hill, near Huddersfield, in the West Riding', ibid., 26–31; W. Cowley, 'The Technique and Terminology of Stacking and Thatching in Cleveland', ibid., 35–40; G. J. Goundrill, 'Ploughing and Pressing Wheat on the Wolds Thirty Years Ago', ibid., 40–7; G. Williams, 'Dry-Stone Walling in South Westmorland: the Craft and its Terminology', *TYDS*, ix, Part lv (1955), 33–44.

Early records: R. Offor, 'Two Mining Account Books from Farnley Colliery, 1690–1720', *TYDS*, v, Part xxxiv (1933), 9–28; A. S. C. Ross, 'The Vocabulary of the Records of the Grocers' Company', *English and Germanic Studies*, i (1947–8), 91–100; J. J. Wilkinson, *Receipts and Expenses in the Building of Bodmin Church A.D. 1469 to 1472*, Camden Miscellany, vii, 1875.

9 Social Class and the Dialects

Little is published on this subject, although much research is currently being done in general sociolinguistics. For Standard English, see under 2, above, and for the town dialects, under 3, above, and p. 168, above, Notes 9 and 10.

Glossary of Linguistic Terms

This glossary is provided both for the benefit of readers who may have little existing linguistic background and for the convenience of those who may wish to have short definitions of linguistic terms at their elbow. For fuller explanations the reader is generally referred to the many books on linguistics and, for phonetic definitions in particular, to A. C. Gimson, *An Introduction to the Pronunciation of English* (2nd rev. edn., London, 1970). Page references are given below, however, when a more detailed explanation of an item is to be found in the text of the present book.

ACCENT: The phonetic or phonological aspect of dialect (p. 1).

AFFRICATE: Consonant produced by a complete closure at some point in the mouth, behind which air pressure builds up and is released relatively slowly (cf. PLOSIVE), e.g. [tʃ].

ANALOGY: The adoption of a new linguistic pattern by forms originally belonging to another, e.g. the adoption of weak p.ts. in *-ed* by verbs originally strong (pp. 122–3).

ANGLO-NORMAN (AN): Dialect of French which developed in England after the Norman Conquest (pp. 21–2).

ARTICULATE (v.): To produce a speech sound or sounds.

ARTICULATION: Production of a speech sound or sounds.

ASSIMILATION: Sound-change by which two neighbouring sounds become more similar to each other, e.g. [n] > [m] before [f] in *comfort* < OF *confort*.

BACK VOWEL: Vowel pronounced with the back of the tongue raised towards the soft palate near the back of the mouth, e.g. [ɔː, ɑː].

BILABIAL CONSONANT: Consonant articulated with both lips, e.g. [p, b, m].

BILINGUAL: Able to speak two languages or dialects (p. 5).

BLEND: Word produced from the combination of two others, e.g. *smog* < *smoke* + *fog* (p. 74).

BRITTONIC: Branch of the Celtic family of languages comprising Welsh, Breton, and Cornish.

BROAD (PHONEMIC) TRANSCRIPTION: Phonetic symbolization in terms of significant elements of the utterance, e.g. /pɔːst/ *post* (cf. NARROW TRANSCRIPTION).

BUNDLING OF ISOGLOSSES: Coincidence of several isoglosses (p. 9).

CELTIC: Branch of the Indo-European family of languages, further subdivided into Gaulish, Brittonic, and Goidelic.

CENTRALIZATION: Movement of vowels towards centre of mouth.

CLOSE VOWEL: Vowel in which the tongue is high in the mouth, e.g. [iː, uː].

COGNATE (adj.): Derived from the same sound or word in the parent language, e.g. OE *wulf* 'wolf' and ON *ulfr*, Standard English *newt* and dialectal *evet*.

COLLECTIVE NOUN: Noun singular in form but expressing a plural, e.g. (a brace of) *pheasant*.

DIACHRONIC: Relating to the study of the historical development of language (p. 3; cf. SYNCHRONIC).

DIPHTHONG: Combination of vowel and glide (q.v.), e.g. [ɛɩ] in *gate*, [aɷ] in *cow*.

DISTRIBUTION: (1) The geographical occurrences of a dialectal feature; (2) the occurrence of a phoneme in a given context.

DOUBLE PLURAL: Noun in which a new plural inflexion has been added to a pre-existent plural form, e.g. *bellowses* 'bellows'.

ELLIPTICAL: Referring to an utterance in which the part needed to complete the sense is omitted.

EXCRESCENT CONSONANT: Redundantly added consonant, e.g. [k] in [sʌm-θɩŋk] *something*.

FLAPPED *r*: An *r*-sound produced by a single tap of the tongue against the teeth ridge.

FOLK-ETYMOLOGY: Popular interpretation of unfamiliar words in terms of more familiar ones (pp. 71–3).

FRICATIVE CONSONANT: Consonant in which the air passage is narrowed so much that friction is produced, e.g. [f, s, x, ß].

FRONT VOWEL: Vowel pronounced with the front of the tongue raised towards the hard palate, e.g. [iː, eː] (see PALATAL VOWEL/CONSONANT).

FRONTING: Movement of a sound to the front of the mouth.

GEMINATE (n.): Doubled consonant.

GEMINATION: Doubling of consonants.

GERMANIC: Branch of the Indo-European family of languages, further sub-divided into North, East, and West Germanic (p. 12).

GLIDE: A sound made as the speech organs move from one position to another.

GLOSSES: Explanatory translations of words in a text, usually given between the lines (interlinear) or in the margin.

GOIDELIC: Branch of the Celtic family of languages comprising Scots, Irish and Manx Gaelic.

GRAPHEMIC: Referring to graphemes—the distinctive units of the writing system of a language or dialect.

GRAPHIC: Written.

GREAT VOWEL SHIFT: Name given to systematic development of ME long vowels to their present-day reflexes.

HYPERCORRECT PRONUNCIATION: A pronunciation which, in aiming at correctness, adopts by analogy a feature which does not properly belong to it, e.g. the use of [h] in *hisn't* 'isn't'.

IMPRESSIONISTIC TRANSCRIPTION: Phonetic transcription based on the listener's auditory impressions of the speaker.

INFLEXION: Variation in the ending of a word to express grammatical relationship.

INTERNATIONAL PHONETIC ALPHABET (IPA): Systematic method of phonetic writing authorized by the International Phonetic Association.

INTERVOCALIC: Occurring between vowels.

INVERTED SPELLING: Interchange or transposition of spellings for two or more sounds which have become identical, e.g. the use of *v* for older *w* (p. 96).

ISOGLOSS: Line drawn on a map defining an area characterized by a specified linguistic feature (pp. 7–9).

ISOLATIVE: Referring to the occurrence of a sound in a phonetic context in which it is uninfluenced by neighbouring sounds, e.g. ME isolative ǭ (as distinct from, e.g., ME ǭr).

180

LEXICAL: Relating to lexis (q.v.).

LEXICOLOGIST: Student of lexicology (i.e. the study of words, their form, history and meaning).

LEXIS: Vocabulary or word-stock of a language or dialect.

LOAN-WORD: Word adopted from another language or dialect, e.g. *village* < OF *village*, *skin* < ON *skinn*.

LONG VOWEL: Vowel given approximately twice as much length as short vowel, e.g. [ɑː] in *cart*, [uː] in *fool* (cf. *cat*, *full*).

LOWERED VOWEL: Vowel pronounced in a lower or more open position in the mouth.

MEDIAL: Situated in the middle of a word.

METANALYSIS: Mistaken division of two words, e.g. *naunt* < *mine aunt*.

METATHESIS: Transposition of neighbouring sounds or letters in a word, e.g. [wɒps] *wasp*, [ɡəᵊːt] *gurt* 'great'.

MIDDLE ENGLISH (ME): The English language between *c.* 1100 and *c.* 1450.

MINIMAL PAIRS: Pairs of words which are different in respect of only one sound segment, e.g. *pen*, *ten* (distinguished only by a change in the initial phoneme). By the discovery of such minimal pairs and the oppositions they exemplify, it is possible to establish the phonemes of a language or dialect.

MONOPHTHONG: A relatively pure or unchanging vowel, as compared with a diphthong.

MORPHOLOGY: The pattern of the inflexions of a language or dialect.

MUTATION PLURAL: Noun plural formed by a change in the stem vowel, e.g. *goose*, *geese*; *mouse*, *mice*.

NARROW (ALLOPHONIC) TRANSCRIPTION: Phonetic symbolization indicating detailed sound values, e.g. [pʰəʊ̂stʰ] *post* (cf. BROAD TRANSCRIPTION).

NEO-GRAMMARIANS: Late nineteenth-century school of German philologists who formulated the theory that all sound-changes, as mechanical processes, take place according to laws that admit no exceptions within the same dialect, and that the same sound in the same phonetic environment always develops in the same way.

NEW ENGLISH (NE): The English language from *c.* 1450 to the present day.

OLD ENGLISH (OE): The English language from the time of the first Anglo-Saxon settlements up to *c.* 1100 (p. 11).

OLD NORSE (ON): Name given to the older stages of the Scandinavian dialects collectively.

OPEN SYLLABLE: Syllable that ends in a vowel.

OPEN VOWEL: Vowel in which the tongue is low in the mouth, e.g. [a, ɑː].

OPPOSITIONS: Series of contrasts by which the phonemes of a language or dialect system are distinguished from each other.

ORTHOEPISTS: Early (mainly sixteenth- and seventeenth-century) writers on pronunciation.

ORTHOGRAPHY: System of spelling.

PALATAL VOWEL/CONSONANT: Sound in which the front of the tongue articulates with the hard palate near the front of the mouth, e.g. [yː, ç].

PARADIGM: Pattern of inflexions, e.g. of nouns or verbs.

PERIPHRASTIC: Formed analytically (of constructions, etc.), e.g. with the use of an auxiliary verb—*did go* 'went'.

PHONEME: Unit of contrastive or significant sound within the system of a language or dialect, e.g. /a/ in *bat*, *mat*, *pat*, as distinct from /ɛ/ in *bet*, *met*, *pet*.

PHONEMICIZE: Analyse speech in phonemic terms.

PHONETIC: Referring to the sounds of a language or dialect.

PHONOLOGY: Pattern or system of sounds of a language or dialect (p. 2).

PLEONASTIC: Redundant.

PLOSIVE CONSONANT: Consonant produced by a complete closure at some point (lips, teeth, etc.), behind which air pressure builds up and is released explosively, e.g. [p, b, t, d, k, g].

PORTMANTEAU WORD: See BLEND.

R-COLOURING: The effect on a preceding vowel of an *r*-sound, e.g. in [bəʳːd] *bird* (p. 99).

RECEIVED PRONUNCIATION (RP): Educated southern British English (p. 5).

RECESSION, RECESSIVE: Terms used to describe withdrawal of dialectal forms in the face of opposition from more dominant forms (pp. 6, 71).

REFLEX: Result of the historical development of an earlier sound, e.g. ME *ǭ*, the reflex of OE *ā*; present-day RP [əʊ], the reflex of ME *ǭ*.

RETRACTED: Drawn towards a back position.

RETROFLEX: Pronounced with the tip of the tongue curved backwards to articulate with the foremost part of the hard palate.

ROUNDED VOWEL: Vowel accompanied by rounding of the lips, e.g. [ɔː, œː, yː].

RUNIC INSCRIPTIONS: Inscriptions in runes, i.e. system of writing used by early Germanic peoples.

SEMANTIC: Relating to meaning.

SEMI-VOWEL: Glide sound functioning as a consonant, e.g. [j] in *yacht*, [w] in *wait*.

SOUND-LAW: A law formulated to describe a regular change in pronunciation that occurs in a language or dialect during some given period of its history, e.g. 'OE *ā* > ME *ǭ*'.

STOP CONSONANT: General term for a consonant produced by a complete closure at some point, behind which air pressure builds up, and is then released by removal of the blockage, e.g. [tʃ, d, k].

STRONG NOUNS: Nouns which belonged to one of the OE strong declensions, having inflexions which are mainly vocalic (cf. WEAK NOUNS).

STRONG VERBS: Verbs which show change of tense by a change of stem-vowel, e.g. *sit–sat* (p. 122; cf. WEAK VERBS).

SUBSTRATUM: An original language underlying another adopted by a community, who may carry over their speech habits from the older to the newer tongue.

SYNCHRONIC: Relating to the study of language as it exists at a given moment in time, as distinct from the study of its historical evolution (p. 3; cf. DIACHRONIC).

SYNTAX: The branch of grammar which relates to the ways in which words are arranged in sentences.

UNROUNDED VOWEL: Vowel unaccompanied by rounding of the lips, e.g. [a, ɑː, iː].

UVULAR *r*: An *r*-sound produced by the back of the tongue articulating with the uvula.

VELAR CONSONANT: Consonant in which the back of the tongue articulates with the soft palate or velum, e.g. [k, g, ŋ, x].

VERNACULAR (n.): Language or dialect of one's native country or region.

VOCALIZED: Given the quality of a vowel sound, e.g. 'dark' *l* pronounced [ɤ] in *field*, *full*, etc.

VOICE: A phonetic term referring to the musical tone produced by the air from the lungs passing through the vocal cords when brought close together in the windpipe and, by causing them to vibrate, giving rise to 'voiced' sounds (e.g. [v, z, b, g, l], all vowels), as distinct from voiceless sounds (e.g. [f, s, p, k, l]), produced with the vocal cords in wide open position.

VOICING: The adoption of the character of VOICE.

WEAK NOUNS: Nouns which belonged to the OE weak declension, having a base-form ending in a vowel and adding an -*n* in their inflected forms (cf. STRONG NOUNS).

WEAK VERBS: Verbs that show change of tense by addition of a suffix containing *d*, *t*, e.g. *talk*, *talked* (p. 122; cf. STRONG VERBS).

ZERO: Term used to denote absence of a sound, inflexion, etc.

General Index

In the following indexes, 'n.' following a page number refers to a note or notes on pp. 158–68. Reference is usually made to such notes only when a new subject is introduced in them, and not when a subject already introduced in the text is merely commented upon or supported by references. The occasional citation of notes pages without specific reference to a note indicates that much of the page is relevant.

a, development of ME, 95; before *f*, *s*, *th*, 9, 86, 102; before *lf*, *lm*, 86, 102; before nasals, 39, 96, 104, 106; before [ʃ], [tʃ], [ʤ], [g], 92–4
ā, development of ME, 9, 39, 52, 89, 102, 105–6, 107–8
Accent, 1, 2, 5, 37–42, 49, 84–108, 162–3, 169, 175–6
Addison, Joseph, 121
Adjectives, comparative and superlative, 52, 117–18, formation in *-en*, 117
Ælfric, 14
Æthelred the Unready, 18
Aʒenbite of Inwyt, 9, 24, 172
al + consonant, development of ME, 86
Alfred, king, 14, 17, 104
Alliterative verse, 21, 24, 65
American influence on English, 82
Analogy, operation of, 7, 92, 115, 116, 119, 122–4
Ancrene Riwle, 21
-angl-ong, development of ME, 90–1, 102
Anglian (dialect of OE), 13
Anglo-Irish, 41
Anglo-Norman, 21–2
Anglo-Saxon Chronicle, 11, 14, 16, 21, 170
Anglo-Saxon invasion and settlement, 11–12, 70; Anglo-Saxon period, 12 ff., 23, 29, 70
Animals, circumlocutions for, 79
'Annot and Johon', 165 n.2
Anstey, C., 45

Arte of English Poesie, The, 27, 37
Article, definite, 51, 125, 177; indefinite, 125
Aspiration, of [p, t, k], 128; of *r*, 98–9; of [w], 97
Assimilation, ON, 133
Athelstan, king, 17
Atkinson, J., 43
au, development of ME, 86–8, 102
'Aureate diction', 36
'Autochthonous roots', 69
Auxiliary *do*, 120–1, 125

Badger, names for, 70
Bailey, Nathan, 43, 173
Basket, names for, 140
Battle of Maldon, The, 21
BBC, 1, 5, 28, 56; 'BBC English', 153, 167 n.3
Bede, 12, 170; *Death-Song*, 13; *Historia Ecclesiastica*, 11, 13
Beer barrel, terminology of, 178
Benedictine Rule, OE, 14
Beowulf MS, 14
'Best room', names for, 139
Bible, 41; Authorized Version of, 3, 113, 115, 121
Biblical paraphrases, ME, 24
Bilingualism, 16, 22–3; in dialect speakers, 5, 30, 49, 59, 84, 154
Bindweed, names for, 77
Bird names, 69, 75–7, 128, 175
Blends, 74–5, 114
Blickling Homilies, 14; *Psalter*, 13
Bobbin, Tim, 45
Borde, Andrew, 45

185

Linguistics, historical, 36. *See also* Diachronic method
Linguistic Survey of Scotland, 58, 160 n.15, 174
Literature, *see* Dialect, use in literature; works in; and under individual ME and OE texts and authors
Loaning, *see* Borrowing, dialectal
Loan-words, 24, 36, 177. *See also* Foreign element
Lollards, 25
Lorica Glosses, 13; *Prayer*, 13
Losh, J., 43
Low Countries, 23, 141, 171
Low Dutch, 132, 177. *See also* Foreign element; Phonology
Lunch, names for, 145
Lyrics, ME, 24

Malmesbury, William of, 34
Manlove, Edward, 145–6, 177
Mannyng, Robert, 24
Marlowe, Christopher, 118
Marshall, William, 43
Martyrology, West Saxon, 14
McIntosh, A., 25, 31–3, 106, 171
Mercia, 10, 12, 17, 19, 102, 137; Mercian (dialect of OE), 13, 15
Meriton, George, 45, 176
Metanalysis, 40, 66
Metathesis, of [n] and [m], 164 n.9; of *r*, 67, 73, 98–9
Middle English (ME), 3, 5, 6, 11, 13, 22, 58, 65, 165 n.2; adjectives in, 117; development of sounds of, 59, 85–108, 137, 160 n.18; dialects of, 12, 15, 24–7, 31–3, 171–2, (London) 5, 24, 25 ff.; loan-words in, 126–41 *passim*, 177; morphological characteristics of, 31; nouns in, 109–11; phonological characteristics of, 31–2; pronouns in, 31–2, 112–14, 116, 164, 176; spellings in, 13, 31–3, 96, 100, 107; verbs in, 119–24; vocabulary of, 65. *See also* under individual ME authors and texts and individual ME sounds
Middle Low Franconian, 92
Miner's working place, names for, 144
Minimal pairs, 58, 62

Mining, 4, 23–4, 46, 52, 75, 102–4, 138, 143–6, 155. *See also* Dialect, mining
Monographs, dialect, *see* Dialect, monographs on
Monologues, *see* Dialect, works in
Moore-Meech-Whitehall, 31–2, 96, 171
Morphology, 52, 109–25. *See also* Middle English; Old English
Mud, names for, 68
Mystical writings, ME, 24

Nail and clog-iron industries, terminology of, 178
Nance, R. Morton, 76, 128, 130, 146–50
Negation, 125
Neo-Grammarians, 6–7, 46, 48
NE period: adjectives, 117; dialects, 28–30; Lancashire dialect, 44; nouns, 111; phonological developments, 39, 70, 95, 96, 100
Net-making, expressions for, 148
Newcastle-upon-Tyne, University of, 61
New York, 61, 156
ng, development of ME, 96, 104
Norden, John, 36
Norman Conquest, 21–3, 26
Normandy, 18
Northumbria, 10, 12, 17, 19, 102, 137; Northumbrian (dialect of OE), 13, 15, 119, 126
Norwegian, 1, 38
Nouns: collective (in Cornish), 129; compound, 111–12; plurals of (double), 73, 110–11, 127, ('mutation') 110–11, (triple) 110, (weak) 39, 40, 109–10, 136; possessive forms of, 111, 115
Nowell, Laurence, 36, 43–4, 65, 173

o + nasals, development of ME, *see* *a*; + [ʃ], [tʃ], [ʤ], [g], 93–4
o- lengthened, development of ME, 89, 102
ǭ, development of ME, 3, 9, 88–9, 97, 102, 104–6, 107, 108
ǫ, development of ME, 89, 102, 104–6, 107, 108, 163 n.26
Olaf Guðfriðson, 17

189

Index of Places

The items in this index are principally names of localities and counties mentioned as the sources of various dialect forms. For the sake of convenience, county abbreviations, as used in the body of the book, are given in brackets after their full forms. They are occasionally used without brackets for purposes of identification. Place-names cited for their phonological interest are included in the Index of Words and Notions. Foreign names will be found in the General Index.

193

195

Index of Words and Notions

In this index, early and dialectal spellings of words are usually subsumed under their present-day Standard English forms where possible; verb forms are usually entered under their infinitive forms; nouns are given in the singular unless they occur only in the plural, and 'weak' and double plurals are not specially cited. Place-names discussed in the book are cited only in their modern forms. The words in Browne's list (p. 40) and Manlove's poem (pp. 145–6) have not been indexed, except for those picked out for special mention. An occasional OE, ON, etc., word is cited when its Standard English equivalent does not occur in the book. 'Notions' (entries followed by 'names for', 'expressions for') are items such as 'ant', 'dumplings' expressions for which do not occur on the pages cited, but which are mentioned simply as notions (mainly on pp. 53, 64, 68, 78), as distinct from similar citations in the General Index, which refer to places in the book where such expressions are collected.

Flitter-bat, -mouse, 142
Floor, 105
Flow, 122
Fluke (of an anchor), 147
Foal, 89, 91, 162 n.6
Foal-foot 'colt's-foot', 162 n.6
Foggy, fog it, fogs (denote gaining possession, etc.), 80
Follow 'baptize', 78
Food, 65, 88, 95, 97
Fool, 88
Foot, 110
For, for to (+ infinitive), 118
Fore-and-after 'priest, minister', 79
Fork, 147
Forks 'wooden supports', 145-6
Four-legged-emmet 'newt', 74, 161 n.6
Four-legged-evet 'newt', 73-4, 161 n.6
Four-legger 'land animal', 79
Fowl-grass 'couch-grass', 77
Fowls'-house, 112
Freckles, names for, 64
Fresh, 92
Front-, 139
Fuggan 'pastry dinner-cake', 129
Fumade, see Fermade
Funnel, 140
Furrow, 6
Fussock 'donkey', 70
Fuz 'fat, idle woman', 68

Gammerstang 'hoyden', 68
Gammy 'dull', 68
Gander, 96
Gang 'go', 39
Gange, ginge, 'fasten a hook to a fishing-line', 148

Gape 'yawn', 136
Garland 'water-channel', 144
Garn 'yarn', 133
Garth, 131, 133
OE gāt, 131
Gate, 106, 154
Gawky 'stupid', 129
Gawp 'yawn, stare', 136
Ged 'pike', 147
Geeking 'gaping', 129
ON geit, 131
Get, 40, 121, 123-4
Gil 'stream', 166 n.9
Gin 'if', 38
Ginge, see Gange
Girl, 99
Girn 'gnash the teeth, distort the face', etc., 67
Girth, 37
Give, 122, 123
Glance 'bounce', 64, 141
Glass, 156
Glaur 'mud', 68
Gloves, 88
Gnat, 37
Gnaw, 37
Go, 119
Goat, 105
Go away!, expressions for, 38
Golden, 117
Good, 88, 97
Goodies 'sweets', 82
Gook 'bonnet', 129
Goose, 88, 102, 106, 110, 154
Goose-grass, names for, 78
Gote 'stream', 66, 166 n.9
Gowk 'cuckoo', 53
Grant, 86
Grass, 5, 9, 84, 102
Grave 'dig', 66
Great, 99
Greener, 117
Green-house, 88

Greeting 'crying', 66
Grey 'badger', 70
Griff 'valley, chasm', 142
Grift 'channel', 142
Griglans 'heather', 129
Grill 'snarl, snap, grin', 142
Grin, 67
Grindstone, 89
Groop 'drain in cow-house', 142
Ground, 7, 90, 102
Ground-ivy 'bind-weed', 77
Groushans 'dregs', 129
Grove 'mine', 145-6
Grow, 122
Grub 'lunch', 145
Gull, 85
Gurgoe 'warren', 129
Gweans 'periwinkles, scallops', 147
Gyte 'herring spawn', 147

Hacky 'prostitute', 68
Hag 'haw', 44, 73
Hagag 'haw', 44
Haggle 'haw', 44
Half, 37, 86
Hall 'best room', 139
Hand, 96
Hand skoon 'fishermen's fingerless gloves', 149
Hang, 54, 96
Hat, 2
Have, 39, 119-20
Haver 'oats', 136
Haw, 44, 110
He, 119, 'him', 113, 'his', 164 n.10, 'it', 113-14, 'she', 164 n.7
Hear, 95
Heave 'retch', 75
Heckmondwike (place-name), 101
Hedge, 92
Hell 'pour', 136
Hen, 111

205